the

MONTANA COWBOY

the

MONTANA

AN ANTHOLOGY OF WESTERN LIFE

COWBOY

edited by WANDA ROSSELAND

TWODOT®

GUILFORD, CONNECTICUT
HELENA, MONTANA
AN IMPRINT OF GLOBE PEQUOT PRESS

A · T W O D O T® · B O O K

Text design/layout: Maggie Peterson
Project editor: Ellen Urban
Map: Daniel Lloyd © Morris Book Publishing, LLC

Library of Congress Cataloging-in-Publication Data is available on file.

ISBN 978-0-7627-7213-1

Printed in the United States of America

10 9 8 7 6 5 4 3 2

This book is dedicated to my father and mother—

Boone Weber Whitmer
Marilee Calk Whitmer

True Montana cowboys

With heartfelt thanks to each of the contributors
for their wonderful stories and photographs

CONTENTS

Introduction . . . xii

The Outside Circle . . . xiv

Chapter 1: **Cowboys I Wish I'd Known** . . . 1

A Fine Old Timer . . . 1

Fred Spears . . . 2

Cowboy Teacher . . . 4

Doc Logan . . . 6

Leo Taylor . . . 8

Oscar Shipstead . . . 9

Harry Goyen . . . 11

Tom Frost . . . 14

Ray Pierce . . . 15

Chapter 2: **On the Trail** . . . 19

Horse Thief Ridge . . . 19

Louse Creek Bench . . . 24

Muggins Creek . . . 25

Silver Spurs and King . . . 28

Hell Creek to Miles . . . 31

The Final Drive . . . 32

Moving with the Wagon . . . 39

Chapter 3: **Living to Tell About It** . . . 44

When the Lightning Struck . . . 44

Smokey Joe! . . . 47

Andy at the Well . . . 50

81 Years of Riding . . . 50

The Dark Side of the Breaks . . . 52

The Vigilantes . . . 55

Tom Ryan . . . 56

Chapter 4: **Out of the Chute** . . . 58

"Thanks, but no thanks." . . . 58

Ride a Good Horse . . . 63

Alice Greenough . . . 68

Sheep Mountain . . . 71

Tooke's Bucking Horses . . . 73
Leo Cremer . . . 77
Fanny Sperry Steele, a Rodeo Legend . . . 79
"Queen of the Cowgirls" . . . 84
You Think the Bull Riding Is Tough! . . . 86
Could'a Watched It for Nothin'! . . . 88

Chapter 5: **Blazing the Way** . . . 90
Remember All Those Days . . . 90
On the Powder River . . . 91
A Midnight Ride . . . 96
Ben Wilson . . . 100
C. L. Askin . . . 103
My Granddad, Steve Marmon Sr. . . . 105
Dave Huston . . . 111
Herb and Othelia Cayer . . . 116
William C. "Bill" Huntington . . . 119
Susan Quinn Haughian . . . 122
Dave Willoughby . . . 123
Ord Ames . . . 125
"Are you ridin' or hangin' on?" . . . 128

Chapter 6: **Young Squirts** . . . 133
Kids and Colts . . . 133
A Good Plan . . . 135
The Hollow Tree . . . 137
Ramrodding the Buggy . . . 138
56 Below . . . 139
Wiley King . . . 140
The Will-o'-the-Wisp . . . 141
Two Boys Are Half a Boy . . . 142

Chapter 7: **Ranch Life** . . . 145
The Calving Season from Hell . . . 145
A Cow Can Be Cantankerous . . . 149
Back to the Past . . . 150
Not Quite the Holiday Inn . . . 152
Life in a Covered Wagon . . . 155
Caved In . . . 158
On the Etchart Ranch . . . 158

Henry, the Stud Horse . . . 161
Throwing the Hoolihan . . . 164
The Furstnow Saddle #700 . . . 165
I Learn to Milk a Horse . . . 167
Gathering the Blackfoot . . . 169
Roping the Cat . . . 170
A Touch of Romance . . . 171
Ranch Life in the Bear Paws . . . 173

Chapter 8: **Ranching Log** . . . 174
Badlands Terrain . . . 174
Moving In . . . 177
Swimming with a Steer . . . 182
Horse "Wrasseling" . . . 186
Snake-Bite Medicine . . . 194
Getting Our Goat . . . 199
The Bronc Riding Cat . . . 204

Chapter 9: **Around the Campfire** . . . 211
O, I Dearly *Loved* that Ford Car . . . 211
Never Forget to Check for Evidence . . . 213
Mystery Bank Robbers and One Six-Shooter . . . 215
The Shoot-Off . . . 218
The Eagle Eyes . . . 219
Mrs. Moo . . . 220
Heiser Saddles . . . 222
Some Wild Stories! . . . 223
Brim and Mitch . . . 224
Silver Engraver Jim Wolfe . . . 226

Chapter 10: **The Great Divide** . . . 228
RIP Tana and Boots . . . 228
The Big Snowstorm . . . 230
Death in the Yellowstone . . . 231
When Dreams Go Up in Flames . . . 232
Charlie Gannon . . . 236
The Brass Buttons from Fort Keogh . . . 238
Joe Holtz . . . 240
The Cowboy Preacher . . . 242
The Wagon . . . 247

About the Editor . . . 249

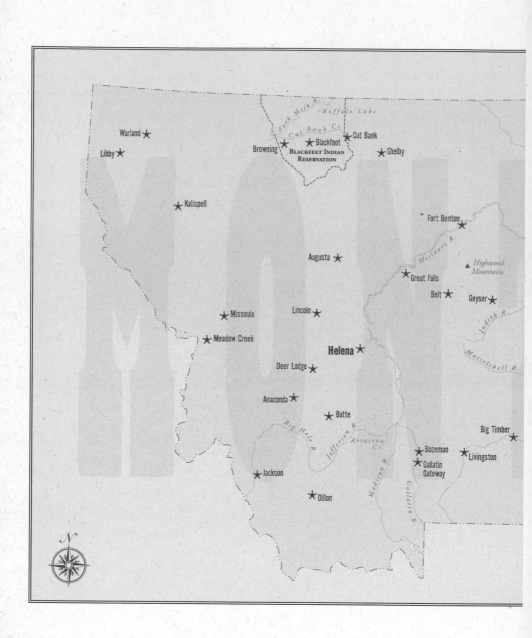

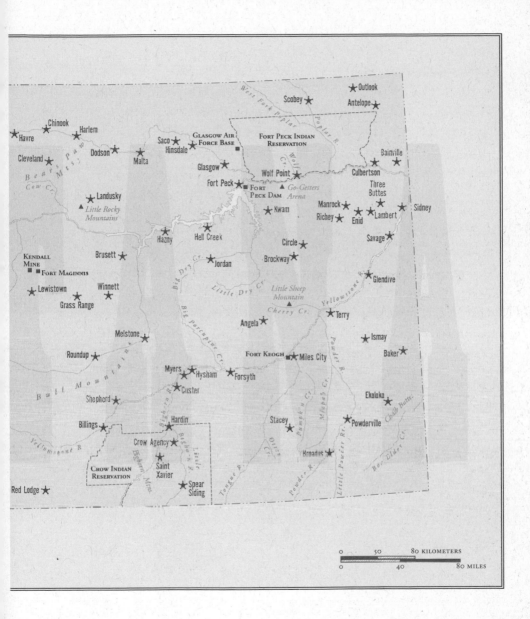

★ Outlook
★ Scobey
★ Antelope
★ Chinook Harlem
★ Havre
★ Cleveland Dodson
★ Saco GLASGOW AIR FORCE BASE FORT PECK INDIAN RESERVATION
Hinsdale
★ Malta Bainville
★ Glasgow Culbertson
★ Fort Peck Wolf Point Three Buttes
FORT PECK DAM Go-Getters Arena
★ Landusky Kwam Manrock Lambert Sidney
Little Rocky Mountains Richey Enid
★ Hazny Hell Creek Savage
★ Brusett Circle
KENDALL MINE Jordan Brockway
FORT MAGINNIS Glendive
★ Lewistown Winnett Little Sheep Mountain
Grass Range Cherry Cr. Terry
★ Angela Ismay
★ Melstone Baker
★ Roundup FORT KEOGH Miles City
Myers Hysham Forsyth Ekalaka
★ Shepherd Custer
★ Billings Hardin Stacey Powderville
Crow Agency
CROW INDIAN RESERVATION Saint Xavier Broadus
★ Red Lodge Spear Siding

West Fork Poplar
Poplar R.
Wolf Cr.
Bears Paw Mts.
Cow Cr.
Big Dry Cr.
Little Dry Cr.
Big Porcupine Cr.
Yellowstone R.
Powder R.
Mizpah Cr.
Pumpkin Cr.
Chalk Buttes
Bull Mountains
Yellowstone R.
Big Horn R.
Little Big Horn R.
Tongue R.
Powder R.
Little Powder R.
Box Elder Cr.

0 ... 50 ... 80 KILOMETERS
0 ... 40 ... 80 MILES

INTRODUCTION

To the cowman forever searching for good grass, the long reaches of plains sweeping down from the mountains of Montana held more wealth than all the peaks to the west. On them they found a gold that did not have to be pried out of creek or rock. It waved across the hills with new growth every year, tall stems brushing the stirrups of a rider's saddle; short, curly buffalo grass bunched close to the ground, filled with the perfect mix of nutrients and strength needed to raise cattle. And all of it free.

As soon as cowmen learned about this bonanza, they started pushing cattle north, navigating herds of longhorns, three thousand and more strong, up from Texas, setting their course by the light of the North Star, shining with a brilliance easily traced in the midnight sky.

A few Texas longhorns still dot the Montana prairie. Mike Karrels of Terry, Montana, owns this exceptional steer. PHOTO BY WANDA ROSSELAND

To the Powder they came, then across the Yellowstone to graze between it and the dirty Missouri, spreading out to the Canadian border and into the mountain valleys. Acres and miles the cattle covered, grazing the lush grass in summer and feeding on the cured-out stalks during the winter cold. And with them, the cowboy.

Open range, land with no fences, allowed cattle to roam at will, held only by water and graze, which required cowboys to oversee them. Spring brought the roundup to sort by owner, brand calves, and move strays onto their own range. Fall work consisted of sorting off beeves to be sold, then trailing to the railhead to be shipped out. Men and horses. The Montana cowboy.

This book brings together stories of those cowboys: ones who have chased wild horses in the Missouri badlands, ridden through freezing blizzards and followed the roundup wagons through spring and fall. These stories show the fortitude and toughness needed to survive when Montana was nothing more than a land of wolf tracks and unfenced grass. Others relate more modern experiences, some dangerous, others unpredictable, as so often happens when working with livestock from

Early day Montana cowboys. Will James is in the center looking left; Sarpy Sam McDowell, father of Corrina Smith, is on horseback. COURTESY OF RAY KRONE

birth to death, and include stories of women as well, who worked and rode alongside the men, and were given no quarter, expected to do the same work, and did.

Through them all, a thread of humor and respect runs like an invisible strand, a mark of the cowboy that lasts yet on our modern-day ranches, showing the cowboy's heart is never far from a jest or a practical joke. Horses, cows, grass. As long as there is grass, there will be cowboys.

THE OUTSIDE CIRCLE

If you are out workin' on the Wagon, gatherin' cattle in the fall,
Sleepin' in a bed tent, and wakin' up to cookie's call,
And every morning after breakfast, when the wagon
boss tells off the crew,
You are mounted on your best horse, cause there's lots of work to do.

You have drawn the Outside Circle, and there's lots of miles to ride,
But you don't complain or grumble, in fact it's a point of pride,
The extra effort is worth it, and you'll sleep real good tonight,
And you'll make that outside circle, again at morning's light.

Joe Charter
Billings, Montana

 CHAPTER 1

COWBOYS I WISH I'D KNOWN

A FINE OLD TIMER

Brig Yost told me one time that he came out of Utah (maybe Brig is short for Brigham) trailing seven hundred horses to Montana. Brig never ever claimed to be a bronc rider, but he said when your horse got tired, you jerked your rope down and rode into the bunch and roped

The roundup crew with the Bird Head wagon. Brig Yost is driving the bed wagon in the middle. The chuckwagon is on the left. COURTESY OF RAY KRONE

the first horse you got close to. Brig said he never lost his hackamore all the way to Montana—not bad for anyone.

Brig nighthawked the horses for the Bird Head till they went broke and of course drove the bed wagon when they moved. He was an expert teamster and ended up in Hardin, where he had a dray service. He always had a team of broncs and drove the back alleys making deliveries to the saloons and stores.

He had a big police dog, and when he stopped he'd give the reins to that big dog, and the dog would hold the team till Brig got back. Hardin had a two-bit deputy at the time, and he shot Brig's dog for not having a dog collar on.

Brig went to his shack, rummaged around in his war bag, came out with his old .45, and hunted up the deputy. Brig said, "Just go for your gun, you son of a bitch, and there will be a stranger in Hell for breakfast." Luckily, some onlookers jumped in and saved any bloodshed. The deputy quit his job and left the country; I think he showed good judgment.

To my knowledge, Brig saw every young fellow in Big Horn County that left for the Armed Forces in World War II and gave them a send-off.

There was a long wooden platform at the Hardin depot. Brig would shake hands with the boys and visit with them till the train pulled out. Then that fine old gentleman would run the length of the platform waving his hat and giving the cowboy yell—a cowboy send-off for a bunch of fighting men.

Ray Krone
Augusta, Montana

FRED SPEARS

A good many years ago, probably in the 1930s, when I was an aspiring cowboy of eleven or twelve years old, I knew a cowboy named Fred Spears. He rode for the Cattleman's Association on Swamp Creek and Lake on the west side of the Big Hole Valley.

Fred was quite a small man, probably not five and a half feet tall, and, like a lot of cowboys, was real quiet. What impressed me the most was his large handlebar mustache and that, in a pocket sewn into his chaps, he always carried a very large .45-caliber revolver. That got my attention.

Fred lived by himself in a log cabin just outside the forest boundary along the bank of Swamp Creek. Besides his riding job, he helped out whenever someone was in the need of cowboy help.

A good friend of his ran a saloon in Jackson. His name was Jim Johnson, and through conversations I heard at times, they both came from Wyoming. It seems they were there during a disagreement between the cattlemen and the sheep men in Johnson County. From what I gathered, they had worn out their welcome there and weren't likely to be welcomed back anytime soon.

One day while Fred was checking cattle up one of the canyons, his horse fell, throwing Fred off. When he tried to get up, one leg wouldn't work. He quickly figured out it was broken and all the help he was going to get was already there.

His horse wasn't hurt and hadn't run off, so Fred crawled over to him and managed to pull himself up enough to get a piggin' string, a short rope to tie up calves when you're working alone, from his saddle. The next problem was getting back on his horse.

Leading his horse, he crawled to a nearby large rock and convinced the horse to stand by it until he crawled onto the rock and onto the horse.

It was several miles back to his cabin, and he knew he would have to go to a doctor. With typical cowboy reasoning, he wouldn't consider going in his work clothes, so he found a couple of sticks for crutches. He then built a fire in his stove, made several trips to the creek for buckets of water, heated it, and took a bath in a galvanized round tub.

He put on clean clothes and managed to get back on his horse and head for Jackson—a mere twelve miles across the valley. He said he had to go through seventeen gates that he had to open and close, which he could do from his horse.

Upon arriving in Jackson, he tied up his horse to the hitch rail in front of Jim's Saloon, hobbled into the bar, and climbed onto the bar stool. There were no other customers in there, and Jim was in the back room. He soon returned to the bar and was sort of surprised to see his old friend there at that time of day, but he didn't mention it.

Fred had a couple of shots of his favorite firewater while visiting. Finally, he asked Jim if he knew of anyone driving to Dillon that afternoon. Jim replied that most anyone going would already be gone, since it took several hours to navigate the fifty miles of rough gravel road, and why did he want to know?

Fred replied that he had a broken leg and probably should see about getting it fixed. After Jim cussed him out for not saying anything sooner and asked why he hadn't stopped at any of the four or five ranches he had passed, Fred replied that he was already on his horse and didn't want to bother them.

Jim got his car ready and loaded up Fred, but not before Fred insisted his horse be taken care of. Only then did they start for Dillon to get the tough old cowboy patched up.

Jay Nelson
Jackson, Montana

COWBOY TEACHER

Back in the late 1930s, John Taylor, a well-known Wolf Point rancher, had just finished a semester of college (it may have been two semesters) and returned home to the ranch to live.

Times were tough. Many young men started college and couldn't finish because they ran out of money. Whether this was true in John's case, I don't remember him saying. I do know he said money was hard to come by and was made worse by the lack of rain. The ranchers had a little advantage over the farmers, as there was some grass in the coulees and along the creeks for cattle to graze on.

Winter was coming when John received a letter from the Roosevelt County Superintendent of schools, asking him to come to Wolf Point; he wanted to see him on some business. As things were slacking up, John rode to town, right curious as to what the letter was all about.

"John," said the County Superintendent, "would you like to make some money this winter?"

"Depending on what you want me to do," replied John.

"I need a teacher at the Warmbrod School, up Wolf Creek. Would you like the job?"

"What's wrong with the teacher? Did she come down sick?"

"No, she quit."

"There must be teachers in Wolf Point you can hire?"

"Yes, there is, but I want you."

"Why me?"

"We're having troubles keeping teachers at the Warmbrod School, and I think you can do the job. We need someone the students will respect. Do you want the job?"

"I can't take the job. I smoke."

"I didn't ask you if you smoked. Do you want the job?"

"I swear."

"I did not ask you what language you use. Do you want the job?"

"Well, I drink."

"I did not ask you if you take a drink or two. Do you want the job?"

"Okay, as long as you know what you bargained for."

After he arrived at the school, John learned the rest of the story from the younger students. Several older students that lived north of the school sat the two previous teachers on the piano and made them stay there all day.

Back in those days homesteaders kept their boys home until freeze-up, then took them out of school when spring seeding began. Many would get only four or five months of school each year. It was not uncommon to have several students in school that were over twenty years old. Such was the case when John arrived to teach.

John said that after teaching for a few hours, he had identified the problem students and decided to correct their behavior. He went to the school door and dismissed all the students to recess, except three older boys.

"Now you three are going out this door one at a time, and when you come back in, you will do what I say. Before each of you go out the door, we are going to fight. And after I whoop you, I will throw you out the door," said John.

After John took care of the behavior problem students, he resumed school. John said he did not have any discipline problems the rest of the year.

Jim Marmon
Wolf Point, Montana

DOC LOGAN

Broady Saddler was one of the best cowboys I ever had the pleasure of working with, and I worked with a lot of them. He must have had one hell of a pump for a heart. I've been out with him when it was 20 below zero. I'd have my mittens on, and my hands would be so cold I could hardly hold my bridle reins. Broady would just have yellow canvas gloves on, and he'd take them off and stick them under his arm, take his Bull Durham out and roll a cigarette like it was 80° above. I could have killed him.

He was an expert with rawhide, and as a kid with the roundup wagon, I've seen him set in the shade of a tree and make the whole hide of a butchered critter into hobbles. All the hands on the Crow had Broady's hobbles hanging on their saddles. I have a grandson named after him.

This story is about an early-day veterinarian on the Crow Reservation; his name was Doc Logan. Today's vets come to your ranch in a fancy four-wheel-drive pickup with nearly a mobile clinic in the back, a telephone, and the whole nine yards. I guess that's progress. Doc Logan came to your ranch riding a good horse, with his bed packed on another horse. He'd throw his bed in your bunkhouse and stay till he had you cleaned up and then go on to the next ranch.

The Crow Res at this time was suffering an epidemic of the scab in the cattle, and because of this there were four dipping vats constructed that I knew about; maybe there were more. Doc Logan was a government vet sent to clean this disease up, and single-handed he rid the Crow Res of the scab. This was in the days of the big cow outfits, so think of the thousands upon thousands of cattle that this man caused to be run through dipping vats. Doc mixed the dope that went into the water in the vats and made sure you got everything dipped. Whoever owned the land where the dipping vats were located would let everyone in the area use his vats. Doc would finish at one vat and then go on to the next until he'd covered the whole Res. Some job, right?

I was maybe five years old when he came to our ranch, and I remember him and my Dad going down to the horse corral to doctor a

Running cattle through the dipping vat. FRANK GREENOUGH, EAGLE SPRINGS RANCH

horse. They had a bucket of water, a sharp axe, some rags and a butcher knife. I wanted to go with them, but my Dad wouldn't let me. They said the horse got all right.

In later days Bill Greenough invited Doc back to the Crow when they (Matt Tshargi's outfit; Bill was wagon boss) had their roundup wagon out dehorning Mexican steers. They would throw a bunch of steers together and two men would head and heel the steers and drag them out to the ground crew to dehorn them. The boys said they all liked to see Doc rope, as I guess he was a little wild and broke quite a few legs, so they always had lots of beef to eat.

Ray Krone
Augusta, Montana

LEO TAYLOR

I went back to Montana and started working for the CBC horse outfit. Some of the outfit rounded up horses while I broke some horses. They called them the "ruff string." Kincade stayed with me. One horse, a big black, was temperamental—if something touched him he'd really buck. So when Slim Boyce started working there, they had him ride him. They had to ear him down before he could get on him—that triggered him off! Slim got thrown so hard and high!

We were camped on Maguire Creek by the Kwam place night herding the horses when an electrical storm came up. There was Shirley and Paul Bridges, Murrey Long, Dink Hines, Lorn Gross, McCulloch, Slim Boyce, and Jim and Walter Thomas there. The horses stampeded, but we all got back to camp except Murrey Long. Shirley Bridges said, "If Murrey has the horses in a corner of the fence, I'll give him a bonus." Next morning they found him on a hill, and the horses were in the corner of the fence.

One time Shirley Bridges, who was the foreman, sent me to Itchart to get a horse. I was to ride the horse about one hundred miles home. I didn't have any food, so Shirley gave me a big roll of baloney, and I tied it to my saddle and started riding him home. He began bucking, and he bucked until he couldn't buck any more, but when he got his wind back, he would buck again. I rode him about seventy-five miles the first day and was so tired of him bucking I sat down on the highway and waited for someone to come along. I was going to turn him loose. No one came along, so I rode him on in.

When Beglow hired out for the outfit, they gave him a horse from my string to ride named Pluto. He didn't tighten up the back cinch, and I asked him if he wasn't going to tighten it up. He said, "I ride this way." When we started down the hill, the back cinch flew up and hit the horse, and he bucked him off.

Another time we were trailing horses to Miles City, and I picked up a box and threw it at the horses to get them going. One horse ran into the fence and got a roll of wire around his neck. He strung wire for a long ways. Jeff Nix said, "What has Taylor done now?" Although he knew what happened, Kincade was a pretty good guy and said nothing.

We trailed our saddle horses 186 miles back. Kincade and I had forty head to bring back with just two saddle horses. My horse got lame, so Kincade roped one of the horses, and I rode him on in.

Daisy Taylor
Wife of Leo Taylor
Our Times on Prairie Elk

Contributed by Onie Taylor
Daughter-in-law of Leo Taylor
Dannebrog, Nebraska

OSCAR SHIPSTEAD

Boys, as well as grown men, were drawn to the western prairies in search of adventure and excitement during the late 1880s and early

1900s. One of these was Oscar Shipstead, who recalled with fondness the days of his teenage cowboy adventures.

"I was always after adventure and finding something new. I left Minnesota in February 1895 with my brother, Ole. I was a month short of sixteen, and Ole was eighteen. We got off the train at what is now Havre; it was then called Bull Hook. We went to Fort Benton, and I drifted on down to Judith Basin. I got to breaking horses and I loved it.

"There wasn't much for a cowboy to do when he wasn't working except to go to a saloon. One time when I was eighteen years old, I was sitting in a bar at Kendall, and this old lady came and sat on my lap and started admiring my hair. She kept saying it was just like Wild Bill's. I was so embarrassed I didn't know what to do. Finally, I got away from her and later learned that she was Calamity Jane."

Oscar's brothers, Ole and Henry, started sheep ranching on the Middle Fork of the Poplar River in eastern Montana, and in 1903 Oscar decided to join them. The following year, homesick for his old range, he sold his horses to his brothers and returned to the Judith Basin. There he bought horses from a sheep rancher who needed the money and brought them back to his brothers. This time he decided to stay.

On one occasion he was fixing dinner for himself when a rider mounted on a beautiful white horse appeared. The man was Andy Duffy, an outlaw who had just acquired a bullet hole through the upper part of his leg in a brush with the Canadian Mounted Police.

"Make yourself at home," Oscar told the outlaw. "I have to make a trip to town and won't get back until tomorrow."

Oscar returned the next day, and the outlaw was gone. But Oscar's few valuables were still there, untouched, including a gold watch that hung plainly on the wall.

In 1911 Oscar married Rose Sibbits, a sixteen-year-old girl of Sioux and Assiniboine parentage, who was born in Wolf Point. Rose's mother died four days after her birth, and she had been raised by Kitty and William Sibbits. Kitty was Rose's mother's sister, and Sibbits was an Indian agent under Major Scobey, for whom the town of Scobey was named.

Like many other cowboys Oscar settled down to farming and ranching and to raising a family. He and Rose had ten children, two of whom died in infancy. Another son was killed in a horse accident. The Shipsteads continued to live in their home in the Silver Star community south of Scobey until Oscar's death in 1968. Rose died in 1971.

Dorothy Rustebakke
Area Historian
Scobey, Montana

HARRY GOYEN

My father, Harry Goyen, packed for the Forest Service from the late 1920s to the early 1940s out of the Libby and Warland Districts of northwestern Montana's Kootenai Forest.

Dad was 41 years old and recently married when he came to Libby in 1928. He had left behind some 20 years of cowboy life and, needing permanence in which to raise a family, hired on as a packer for the Forest Service in the spring of 1929. Dad's work was seasonal, usually running from early spring through late fall. My memories of those years Dad packed for the Forest Service are fragmented and not altogether accurate, as I was still very young when he died. I remember the sawbuck pack saddles he always used, and it seems I remember watching him tie the packs down securely with a diamond hitch and then the horses, standing in a line packed and waiting.

It was said that he made a record-breaking pack trip into a fire, although this cannot now be substantiated, and if I recall correctly, a postcard once carried a picture of his pack string. But mixed in with those memories is one that stands out foremost in my mind. I call it "the shooting of Red."

Red was a packhorse, undoubtedly a sorrel or bay that fell off the side of a mountain and broke his leg. A bullet in the head ended his life. Dad owned his own stock, all named and all, at least to him, as individual and perhaps even as well loved as any member of the human herd (with, I should hope, the exception of his family). At any rate Red was one of those horses. He should have been known to me, this Red, but evidently, he wasn't, for when I heard of his broken body and seeing my father's obvious despair, I, being very young, assumed Red was a man and my father's dearest friend. In my mind's eye I could see that red-headed man lying, screaming, in twisted agony on the canyon floor, and knew without recrimination that my father, unable to help his friend, had saved him hours of needless pain.

As a youngster, my brother Earl rode with Dad on many of those packing trips. His memories are much more lucid.

"The packer working alone," Earl says, "usually handles about six horses because in leading them the back ones will start pulling back and causing a lot of problems. But with someone riding behind to keep them from hanging back, the packer can handle eight, ten, even twelve to fourteen head. And so that's what I did. I rode along behind because I was too small to lead them.

"Dad was packing out of Warland the years I rode with him. Earlier, he'd packed out of Libby, generally off Blue Mountain and that vicinity where the ski resort is now. I believe he had five or six lookouts he went to about once every other week, and early in the season there were a number of trail crews. When a new lookout was to be built, the lumber . . . well, just about everything, including the kitchen stove, had to be packed in to the site.

"Most of his regular packing trips were fourteen-hour days to and from, but some were four-day trips. Eventually, the Forest Service went almost entirely to using mules for packing. The last year or so Dad packed those Forest Service mules, but he had no love for them."

I was surprised to hear of Dad's dislike for mules, but I had always known of his love for horses. I remember a big gray gelding, bad tempered and feisty with all but Dad, and Mother used to tell of an incident he told of his cowboy days that perhaps best expresses man and horse's mutual regard.

Saturday nights on the town have long been known for exuberant celebration, and the cowboy has been known at times to be the most exuberant of all. Dad might not have been much of a drinking man, but he was all cowboy, and so it seems that after a time, being in need of a place to "sleep it off," he went out and crawled under his horse. Eventually, noting his absence, the others went looking for him and, upon finding him asleep under his horse, intended to reach under and shake him awake. But the horse had different ideas. He stood firm, muscles tensed, ears laid back, and teeth bared, guarding Dad much as a dog might have done.

Other incidents in Dad's life lead me to believe that he was an accomplished teller of tales as well as something of an actor, so that may have been a staged performance. But if it was true, one has to admit that he knew his horse. This deep affection for horses was evident very early in life. As a boy in Oklahoma, he accidentally shot and killed a neighbor's horse while on a coyote hunt. The incident filled him with such grief and remorse that his parents feared he would take his own life.

Dad's passion for horses was equaled only by his love of the out-of-doors. Buildings suffocated him and even the curtains Mother hung at the windows seemed to add to his feeling of confinement. In the last days of his life, on a cold winter day and unheeding of Mother's protests, he went out once more into the open air. I think to the day she died Mother believed that outing contributed to his death.

Three of his children, Earl and Dan Goyen and Mabel Beebe, stayed in the Libby area. We other four scattered into other states. I'm in Kansas; Margaret Neu is in Copeland, Idaho; Larry Goyen is in Torrington, Wyoming; and June Garetson is in Jacksonville, Florida. Our brother Dan died in Libby in 2006. Dad died of a respiratory ailment in 1943, and our mother, Hazel Cline Goyen, died in 1957. All three are buried in the Libby cemetery.

Although my father, along with many of the old-time packers, is gone now, if a place called heaven exists, you can bet he has not opted for the use of a harp or a trip on the golden stairs, but a good saddle horse, long stretches of uninhabited land, and yes, sure, a short string of pack ponies would be just fine. And if it's all the same, he'd just as soon throw his own diamond hitch.

Eunice Boeve
Phillipsburg, Kansas

TOM FROST

Tom was a professor at a high-toned girls' college in Vermont, and he got to drinking real bad and was about to lose his job. One day Tom went on a full-blood drunk, so a bunch of his friends took him down to the depot and shook him down and bought him a ticket west, as far as his money went. Tom said when he got off the train he was in Hardin, Montana.

He went to work for the Bird Head as a flunky and finally got to wrangling the cavvy. The cowboys all liked Tom; whenever he drew his pay, he'd buy the guy who was his favorite of the moment a pair of spurs or a nice bit.

This all took place in the '30s, and soon the Bird Head went broke and the Antler was out of business, so there was no work for a cowboy. Tom was staying with Phil Spear when they heard there was work in Nevada. Tom had a horse of his own, and Phil Spear gave him a horse to pack his bed, and Tom followed the Rocky Mountains to Nevada— not bad for a dude from Vermont.

Vic Pepion—the   Blackfeet Indian cowboy—who also had worked for the Bird Head, went to Nevada, too, but Vic went on the bus or train. He said this cow outfit picked him up at some whistle-stop and they bounced out across the desert for fifty miles till they got to where the wagon was camped, and Tom Frost was wrangling the horses for this outfit.

Vic said Tom never even looked at him till supper, and when Vic filled his plate, he set a little ways away from the rest of the crew, and

Tom sidled over and set down beside him and whispered, "What name you using down here, Vic? I'll introduce you to these boys."

I knew Tom when I was going to high school in Hardin and would go out to our ranch on the weekends. Tom was staying in a shack above our ranch on Soap Creek, caking some steers for John Kern, and he'd come down on Sundays and have dinner with us.

All we had in those days was a radio, and when there was a big ski meet in the East, Tom would know most of the contestants. To my knowledge he never went back to Vermont.

Ray Krone
Augusta, Montana

RAY PIERCE

My grandfather was one of the many sixteen-year-old kids gathered up by the British and brought to Miles City in 1908 to break horses for the Boer War in South Africa.

In 1902, preparing for this, the British remount people had gone out with American and English thoroughblood studs, all over eastern Montana. Every time they came onto a bunch of wild horses, they would shoot the stud that was with them, then turn out one of their studs. That way in 1908 there would be good-quality remount type four- to five-year-old horses to break.

In 1908, usually about twice a month, a bunch of riders would go out as far as Big Dry, Mizpah, or further and points east and west to gather these horses and run them to Miles City to be worked.

My grandfather always talked real bad about it. He said the first thing to happen was that all the foals were orphaned. Then when they got there, they sorted off all the old or weak stock, what had got crippled, etc., and shipped them to the meat factories in New Jersey.

While they were bringing the horses to Miles City, it was my grandfather's job to ride one of them to give his horse a rest, in case one of the horses they were riding played out or got lame.

What they would do, to do this, was to spot a big young stout one, rope it, and throw it down. Then they'd put his saddle on it and a rope halter to help steer a little. My grandfather would straddle it, they would untie the horse, take off the blindfold, then on to Miles City at a dead run. By the time they got to the yards at Miles City, he said it was darn near a broke horse.

Then when things would calm down to what we would today call an out-of-control rodeo, they would break and train for the next couple of weeks. Horses under twelve hundred pounds were broke to ride, and the ones over twelve hundred pounds were broke to drive for the artillery.

When they had a trainload, forty head to a car, they shipped the horses to Long Island, New York, where they were put on a ship for two to six weeks to South Africa. On one ship, my grandfather said, half the horses died. He also said that the life span for a horse in South Africa was at best three months. One reason was that the native people developed a really keen taste for horsemeat. My grandfather never had a good word to say about the whole process, from start to finish.

After the British were done, Ray Pierce started breaking horses for the U.S. Cavalry at Fort Keogh near Miles City. His claim to fame was that he broke six horses for Captain Pershing, later famously known as General (Black Jack) Pershing. General Pershing told him that they were the best six horses he ever rode. When General Pershing died in 1949, my mother was working for the FBI at the time in Washington, D.C. She asked to be allowed to attend the funeral. She was allowed to sit with the U.S. senators, while the rest of Congress had to stand in the back. Mrs. Pershing hadn't forgotten my grandfather, still remembered him after all those years.

The next big event in Ray Pierce's life was the rodeo put on at the future town site of Olanda, approximately 20 miles northeast of Terry in Prairie County.

The rodeo was part of a big promotion to auction off building lots. They had a big free picnic, horse races and so on. Before the auction was the saddle bronc contest, which my grandfather was talked into by his neighbors on Cherry Creek. The judges were from out of the area, and they picked an out-of-area bronc rider as the winner. This was before the Cowboy Turtle Association standardized rules. The local people thought that Ray Pierce had won; they got mad and started a riot, and a bunch of people got hurt.

Then the promoters tried to have the auction. Only four lots sold, and everybody left. The town of Olanda never really got built. My grandfather never went to another rodeo the rest of his life. No matter how hard I tried to talk him into it, he'd just say, "If I want to see a rodeo, I'll just open the tent flap."

The next cowboy mishap my grandfather was involved in was when he was the cook for the Mizpah–Pumpkin Creek workings. They had a young man hired to wrangle and ride the broncs that the cowboys couldn't fork. As the story goes, and I got this story from a Mr. Thex from Otter Creek, not my grandfather, one morning the kid kept getting bucked off, right where my grandfather was cooking breakfast, getting dirt on everything. My grandfather finally, with utter disgust, caught the horse and rode it out. It so embarrassed the kid that he grabbed his riggin' and quit. From then on, according to Mr. Thex, everybody had to ride his own brone. From then on Ray Pierce was no longer just famous for his apricot pie, but after feeding you, he could also stomp your brone, too.

Another interesting episode in Ray Pierce's life wasn't riding horses but driving a Buick Touring car where he had ridden chasing horses for the British.

During Prohibition he was the reason the city of Sheridan, Wyoming, never went totally dry. What he did was haul good Canadian whiskey from Canada down to Wyoming, but he was never stopped, arrested, or even suspected. How he was able to do it was this:

He had an older brother, Joe, living with the Assiniboine who brought the illegal whiskey from Canada to the Missouri River. They got the whiskey across the river by using a long thick rope and a board raft.

Then my grandfather would drive all night using only carbide lights, so nobody would see him. Then he slept all day at Sid Johnson's dugout northwest of Terry on the edge of the Terry Badlands. Mr. Johnson, whom my grandfather partnered with on some horses, would have food and fuel for him and never once failed him.

The next night he crossed the railroad bridge on the Yellowstone River west of Terry, next to the ferry. He couldn't use the ferry, because the ferryman was required to keep a daily log of everybody's coming and going for the federal marshals and treasury agents.

He then drove the rest of the night to a brother-in-law's homestead south of Powderville. There Bob Anderson also had fuel and food for him and a place to sleep.

The next night he drove to the U-Cross Ranch northeast of Sheridan, where another brother-in-law, by the name of Billy Anderson, lived. Then he took the whiskey into the city of Sheridan for distribution.

As you can see Ray Pierce never passed through a town, bought fuel, etc. As far as I know, I'm the first person in the family to relate this bit of history; nobody outside the family ever knew, that we know of. Because he had ran horses and cowboyed the whole area, he was able to pull it off, once a month for nine years, scaring my poor grandmother Cora to death. She always knew that some night the train would get him.

Ward Jackson
Glendive, Montana

CHAPTER 2

ON THE TRAIL

HORSE THIEF RIDGE

The Indian Health Service dentist shows me the two molars he had just pulled, one from each side of my mouth.

"There," he utters. "They were quite infected. These should give you a few pain-free days." He hands me an envelope of pills. "Take these until they're gone. Two every four hours. And keep the gauze in the holes until tomorrow. You'll have to drink only liquids to keep food out of them." I nod as I get out of the chair.

I walk the mile to my great-uncle Joe's place on the edge of town. He has a four-year-old bay mare he will loan me to help drive a herd of cattle north to Milk River near the badlands, at the northeast corner of the Blackfeet Reservation. Keeping my mouth shut so I won't get cold air hitting the gums, I saddle her and head east for Cut Bank Creek near the Meriwether Road, about twelve miles away. A slight drizzle starts, so I don my yellow slicker. Low gray clouds hang over the fenceless prairie, this late-June day of 1949. I tie my neckerchief over the top of my head, making sure I cover my ears, and knot it under my chin, then replace my sweat-stained one-gallon hat. I once heard Dad say that "95 percent of our body heat goes out through the top of our head."

I arrive at sundown at Slobberin' Ron's ranch, where I will meet up with the other two teenage cowhands and the boss. That "Slobberin'" is Ron's nickname, due to the huge cheek full of chewing tobacco he keeps going. When he spits, some of the saliva drips off his chin. The one hundred and some head of Hereford cows we will drive north are grazing in his forty-acre pasture.

I feed, water, and unsaddle Nancy; put her in with the other horses; then go into the house. My gums are quite swollen, pushing my cheeks out and making my face look like a pocket gopher. Clint, nineteen; Leo, eighteen; and Hugh, the fortysome-year-old bowlegged boss, are drinking coffee and smoking roll-your-own cigarettes. "Why is your face so fat?" Hugh asks me.

"Tooth pulled," I mumble, as I point to my cheeks.

He nods. "You better go to the bunkhouse and lay down," he tells me. I do. I'm hungry but don't dare eat anything for fear of the pain I may incur on my raw gums. I lie down on the cot fully clothed. I don't take off my boots because I'm afflicted with very stinky feet, and the cow crew will kick me out of the shack rather than torture their nostrils.

Hugh wakes us at dawn. We splash water on our eyelids, make a toilet call, then go into the house for breakfast. I manage to get three hotcakes with plenty of Karo syrup down, without causing me too much pain, chewing only with my front teeth.

We saddle our horses and push the cattle out through the pasture gate. Ron's wife Ruby hands me a widemouthed tin canteen and a cloth sack full of dry meat that white people call jerky. "You can make some broth later today," she says. "It's nourishing, and you won't have to chew. You must have caught cold in your gums." I tie the sack and canteen to the saddle horn.

It's still drizzling. A gray, cloudy, cold morning. Clint takes point, with Leo and Hugh on each side. I am assigned to drag. We cross Cut Bank Creek on the newly constructed bridge. The herd spreads out, grazing the fresh springtime grass. The line shack at Horse Thief

Ridge, where Hugh says we will spend the night, is only about fifteen miles away. Keeping a herd of cattle moving over this delicious green grass is slow going, so we know it will be late when we arrive. My gums hurt, and I'm freezing, shivering like an aspen leaf in the wind, even with the heavy wool coat Uncle Joe loaned me under the slicker. My leather gloves and cowboy boots are soaked. We arrive at the shack in late afternoon. Hugh says his rheumatism is bothering him and he needs to "get some heat into my carcass." We drive the herd into the forty-acre pasture, and Hugh starts a fire in the woodstove while Leo and I take care of the horses. At the same time Clint chops more firewood and takes it into the house.

We warm up and dry off while coffee is brewing, and I put a couple of chunks of dry meat in the can. Water comes from a rain barrel next to the woodshed. After my soup boils and cools off somewhat, I slowly drink the concoction. I immediately feel strength filling my emaciated almost-sixteen-year-old body.

"How you feel?" Hugh asks me. "You look like you have a fever."

"Well . . ." I answer. I do feel hot.

"You better hit the sack," he says. I walk to the door and spit out the gauze. I don't taste any salt, so the bleeding must have stopped. I lie on the floor near the stove, covered with the coat and slicker, fully clothed, and don't even awaken to drain my bladder.

We arise at dawn. Hugh has a fire going. I smell coffee brewing. The other two boys and I water the horses, saddle them, then head back to the shack for food. Hugh has a stack of hotcakes on the back of the stove with a bottle of Karo syrup and a small can of lard for butter. I heat up my leftover dry-meat broth. Suddenly, I remember the pills the dentist gave me! I take two and promise myself I won't forget to take more later in the day. The sky is still overcast with the continuing drizzle, without any of us having a timepiece, I'll have to guess when four hours pass.

Hugh lets the fire go out. We swing aboard our horses, drive the cattle out of the pasture, and head north. The boss puts me on point.

I don't feel as cold this morning but I'm still shivering by the time we reach Twin Buttes, about five miles away. I know the area. I've taken horses to the Blackfoot stockyards a number of times from upper Milk River. It's about four miles farther from where we are to Buffalo Lake.

On the west side of the lake the boss calls a halt for the noon meal. I still have a couple of pieces of dry meat, so I brew a cup of broth over the cedar-post bonfire Clint has lit to warm us up. I take my pills with the soup. We stand around, hands toward the heat, steam rising into the air from our wet clothes, while they get somewhat dry. I'm so tired every place I look at is a coveted bed. It is a relief to get back into the saddle, to sit and, as my mother would say, "rest my weary bones." Hugh puts me on the west side of the herd with Leo on point and Clint riding drag.

We arrive at Milk River at sunset. It is quite high but not deep enough that the cattle have to swim across. Leo ropes a long-horned cow and leads her through the rushing water. The rest of the herd reluctantly follow, bawling loudly. It's fortunate that we don't have any small calves to contend with. We are now on Hugh's land, so we leave the herd grazing and ride the quarter of a mile to the ranch, take care of our horses, and wearily walk into the house where the boss's wife should have supper waiting.

Selma stares at me and exclaims. "What's wrong with your face?"

"Well . . ." I start to utter.

"He had two teeth pulled day before yesterday," Hugh answers for me.

"And you made him ride thirty-five miles in the cold and rain? He should be in bed! I'll bet he has a fever! It's a wonder he doesn't have pneumonia!"

"I didn't make him come with us. But I'm glad he did. We would have had a hard time getting that herd here without him." That makes me feel good even though all I want to do is lie down and sleep. I sure as hell am not hungry! But I force myself to drink a cup of soup Selma hands me.

I walk to the bunkhouse and flop onto a bed. I don't even want a cigarette. I must have immediately gone to sleep and slumbered through the night because I don't wake up until I hear the dinner bell clanging a call for breakfast. Gray dawn under a dark blue sky promises a nice day.

At the horse trough I splash water on my eyelids. My reflection shows my cheeks are not as swollen as yesterday. I run my fingers over them and confirm that they are indeed going down. I don't feel hot. I walk to the house for food. I'm ravenously hungry this morning.

Selma has cooked scrambled eggs, bacon, and hotcakes. I leave the bacon alone. After I eat and smoke a Golden Grain roll-your-own cigarette, I walk to the toilet, empty my bowels and bladder, then return to the house.

Hugh asks me if I want to stay on. I tell him no. I have to get Uncle Joe's horse back to him. He gives me a five-dollar bill in pay. Selma gives me a flour sack of grease bread and some dry meat.

I saddle Nancy and head for the river, riding south back to town. The river is a lot higher than yesterday, so I have to ride west to find a wide, shallow place to cross. Late morning is beautiful! No wind and warm sunshine. I ground-hitch Nancy, sit, and take off my boots. Whew! I can hardly stand the smell of my feet myself! I remove my "religious" socks (they're holey) and plunge both my feet and them into the cold water. The feeling of the cleansing fresh water is great! I remove my feet from the freezing river and lean back, enjoying the warm sunshine, and fall asleep. When I awaken Nancy is nowhere in sight. I hastily put on my now-dry socks and boots and walk up the slope north of me. She is cropping grass about five hundred yards away. What a relief! She didn't cross the river and head back home to town. I don't know how I would get across afoot.

I catch her, cross over, and start home at a walk. My gums will pain me if I make her dogtrot, her natural mile-eating gait. Finally, I decide to bear the agony and alternate between a slow lope and a trot. If I don't make time, it will be way after dark when I get to my parents' place at Blackfoot. I intend to stay there and take Nancy back to Uncle Joe's in Browning tomorrow. I slowly chew some grease bread with my front teeth only. At Cut Bank I dismount and bear the agony of drinking the cold water while Nancy fills her stomach.

I get home about midnight, according to the position of the Big Dipper. I unsaddle Nancy and turn her into the pasture with the other horses, then silently go into the house. My younger brother is in my bed. I carry him to our sisters' bed and place him under the covers next to them. I'm so tired I stagger and fall onto the cot exhausted. A few seconds later I'm asleep.

That was my first long-distance cattle drive and the most miserable because of my aching gums and the weather. The second one was farther, but it was in warm summer. I enjoyed each hour of that one. I was much older as well, seventeen point two. The year after next ended my days as a cowhand: I joined the navy and stayed for a career.

Henry Boyle
Great Falls, Montana

(*Editor's note:* Dawn at the end of June in northern Montana is around 4:00 a.m. Sunset takes place after 9:00 p.m.)

LOUSE CREEK BENCH

I was repping for the 79 at the Big State wagon in the Judith Basin when Charlie Russell was a nighthawk. He had held this same job for eleven years. Pete Vann, Bill Skelton, and Teddy Blue Abbott were also there. In later years Vann and Skelton became well-to-do cattlemen in the Geyser country, and Abbott ran cattle below Fort Maginnis.

We had camped on a high divide west of Judith River, about fifteen miles from the river, where there were a number of big springs.

Charlie Russell was as lousy as a pet coon. Pete Vann and Bill Skelton told him to pull off all his clothes and lay them on some anthills nearby.

"Will that take care of the situation?" asked Charlie.

"Yes, the ants will eat all the lice," Bill Skelton answered.

Charlie pondered over this a second or two, then began undressing, putting his clothes on the anthills. The first thing he pulled off was his hat, then his coat and shirt; then off went his pants and, lastly, his boots. The ants sure had a feast and devoured all the lice. Skelton and Vann walked down to the roundup wagon, bringing back some cottonwood sticks and boards. They drove the stakes into the ground, tied the boards to the sticks with some rawhide strings, took a piece of charcoal from the fire, and printed this sign:

Louse Creek Bench

This bench is known by that name to this day.

Bob Kennon
From the Pecos to the Powder
University of Oklahoma Press

MUGGINS CREEK

On a recent blustery day, Beau and I trotted up to the Spring Pasture to gather our six loose saddle horses and move them to the Three Sections pasture. We had been meaning to move the horses for some time but had been delayed by the spring runoff. [Reader, let me familiarize you with the territory. Hold your right hand in front of you, palm up, fingers spread and pointing away from your body. Lift your thumb to point toward the sky and hold that position. Okay, the tip of your middle finger is Horse Camp, where we live. The tip of your thumb is the Spring Pasture, positioned atop Eastern Montana's version of a mountain. The tip of your pinkie is Three Sections, our destination. The lines in your palm represent the meandering Muggins Creek, which was still swollen with runoff, and serves as an obstacle between the Spring Pasture and Three Sections. Finally, the bottom of your palm is the location of the ranch headquarters, about eight miles down the creek in the Yellowstone Valley.]

Anyhow, on this particularly windy day, Beau and I decided that the creek was down low enough that we could safely move the horses across. Brave soul that he is, Beau saddled up a three-year-old colt, reasoning that it would be a good opportunity to teach the colt to move out. I threw my wood on my idea of a more reliable mount, eight-year-old Ranger. I've had Ranger since he was a weanling, I've been riding him for six years, and I've trusted him to carry me through many miles of wild and hostile country.

The trot out to the Spring Pasture was fairly uneventful. Our dog, Angel, ran along with us. (It's not that we encourage her to herd horses; in fact, she has been spanked several times for doing just that. But we can't stand to see her pouting when we leave her behind.)

By the time our ascent to the Spring Pasture was complete, the wind was sucking my breath away before I could breathe it. We located the loose horses and started them back down the hill to a gate leading to the pasture where we would cross Muggins Creek. The loose horses were feeling very frisky and raced away, leaving us in the dust (not by Ranger's choice, but mine). We caught up to them at the gate and let them through. Before we could remount (closing the gate was a team effort), the loose horses were out of sight, headed down to the creek bottom.

As we followed behind at a slower pace, Ranger thought we could relive a few scenes from the film *The Man from Snowy River.* I kept him checked to a restrained lope, and Beau hooked his little colt on right behind.

The loose horses were waiting for us down in the creek bottom, pondering the water, which was higher than we expected. The snowmelt had flooded out of the deep, narrow channel and onto old hay meadows. About two hundred yards of water knee-high to our horses glistened between us and the opposite bank.

We live in eastern Montana, so our horses rarely see water and thus are scared of it. The loose horses raised their tails to the wind and headed south along the flooded creek at an all-out run. Because we were no longer on a ninety-degree slope, we were better able to keep up. But we were going a little too fast for my taste.

"I'm scared!" I shouted back to Beau as we raced along. I was beginning to question my faith in Ranger, who was remembering his feral ways.

"How do you think I feel?" Beau replied from the back of the colt.

"A horse with a rider can't outrun loose horses!" I shouted to him. I find this a very worthy piece of advice and share it often with Beau when we are in a tight spot with loose horses. "We're going to be at the ranch in about twenty minutes!" (Review the location of the ranch.)

Luckily, before we got too far, the wild steeds cut to the right into a soggy meadow below a dike in the creek. We loped several circles in the meadow's deep mud before the loose horses finally followed Beau and his colt across the dike. There was a small meadow to cross, this one about a foot deep with water, but at least we didn't have to cross the channel.

As we plunged into the shallow runoff, one of the loose horses decided to confront his fear of water. He collapsed on his side in the icy overflow and rolled like a pig in mud. Evidently, Ranger thought it was a group therapy session, because one second we were upright and the next I was bailing off into the water as Ranger first knelt and then flopped on his side. My furious screaming triggered Angel's natural instinct, and she charged into the loose horses, herding them very quickly across the meadow.

As the water flooded over the top of my boots and submerged my saddle, my screaming also brought Ranger to his senses. He jumped to his feet, I jumped into the saddle, and we over-and-undered it through the water and up the opposite bank.

The swim was a humbling experience for everyone, as not long afterward the overall pace of our herd slowed. Two gates later we had the horses well under control. As we trotted the last mile to Three Sections, the loose horses strung out between Beau in front and me behind. Angel brought up the rear, and we put our herd through the final gate as the sun slipped behind the western hills.

Tami Arvik Blake
Hysham, Montana

SILVER SPURS AND KING

I saw a poster that read "Endurance Ride, 50 Miles." The prize to the winning rider was a pair of silver inlaid spurs, and the prize to the best-conditioned horse was a silver cup for its efforts. I thought to myself, *I can do this; I have a great horse for an endurance ride.*

The silver spurs and "Best Conditioned" cup Dan Hanks won in the Silver Spur Endurance Ride, 1969. COURTESY OF DAN HANKS

I'd bought old King from my neighbor, Les Reed, about five years before. He wasn't a real big horse, but he was built for endurance. He was a papered Arabian, and his lineage went back to some horses that were bred by an Arabian prince.

I went home and mapped out a plan for training. I only had six weeks to get King in shape for that long ride. He was already in good shape, but he needed to be in tip-top condition, as I wanted to win both prizes! I put him on a six-day-a-week schedule, resting him the seventh day. We rode in the summer fallow in the mornings for two hours, and in the evenings we did a pleasure ride around the farm.

I fell ill with a bad case of the flu the week before the race and was unable to ride. My mother saddled up her mare, Ginger, and took King on his daily route. I finally felt good enough to finish up his training with only two more days to prepare.

I wanted King to be fresh for the race, so the day before I rode him over to Bud Balder's place, as he lived just down the road from the starting line, at the Go-Getters' Rodeo Arena.

The morning of the race I fed King a big feed of oats, then saddled him about an hour before the race started. I wanted him to be relaxed, because he had a habit of bucking me off before each ride. Today I would be prepared for it! I got on him, and to no surprise I had my hands full, but this time I came out on top.

At 8:00 a.m. a vet gave every horse the once-over to make sure it was fit for the run. Then we lined up, and the race was on! We all started out at a slow pace. It was a cool September morning, and I thought I would speed things up a bit, so I gave King a little nudge and he started into a slow gallop. Everyone in turn did the same.

We rode to the halfway mark. We had to unsaddle the horses for a rest and another vet check. We had a thirty-minute wait before the race resumed. King was in great shape; he hadn't even worked up a sweat.

Bob Jensen was my closest rival. He had a big Thoroughbred mare in great shape. I knew I would have to stay close to him, not to give him too much of a lead. We stayed neck and neck.

Along the marked path we somehow lost the flags marking the route. So we had to double back to find our bearings. We made it back to Prairie Elk, found our way back to the route, and crossed the creek. It was shallow and had a good gravel bottom.

We hit the next marker and crossed Sand Creek. This wasn't as easy. We found a spot to cross and fell in above our stirrups, but this helped cool off the horse. The next turn was through the old Cusker place, south of our place. Bob and I are still sticking to each other like glue. We had to climb the Bad Lands that King knew well. He recognized where he was and thought it was time to stop; we had a small battle, I finally won, and away we went up the side.

About ten miles from the finish line, Bob and I were both trying to figure out the other's strategy. I decided it was time to let King go. And go he did! We started to lope and stayed at that pace until about a mile from the finish at Bud Cahill's place on the river bottom. South of Cahill's place was a fifty-foot bank that dropped into the river bottom. I got there first, let King have his head, and away we went. We slid off the bank, and I kicked him into overdrive. He was at a full gallop; I looked over my right shoulder to see where Bob was, and to my surprise he and that big Thoroughbred were right on my tail.

I told King, "This is it. This is what all the work has been about."

He gave me all he had—that tough Arabian never faltered. We covered that last quarter mile in a blur. He and I had done it! We won!

The vet was there to check the horses. He told me that horse could run another fifty-mile race today! King and I had both won. That horse knew what he had done; he pranced around like a youngster. We were presented the spurs and the cup. What a great day we had, and what an experience for a nineteen-year-old!

I got back on King to put him away, and low and behold, he got the last word: He bucked me off!

Dan Hanks
Wolf Point, Montana

HELL CREEK TO MILES

The entrance fee for the endurance ride from Hell Creek to Miles City was $125.00. There were a few rules and regulations, which I've sort of forgotten now. There were two rest stops between the starting point and the ending point, one in Jordan and the other one at Angela. There were a lot of entrants, and again I can't remember just exactly how many, maybe fifty or sixty even.

When we were getting ready for the big race, we lived on Snow Creek. We had a big rain, and the creek got so big that we couldn't get across with a pickup to haul my horse, Skip, so I led him over to Archie McDonald's on the head of Hell Creek the day before the race. The mud was about six inches deep and it was eight miles over there, so that was tough on Skip, too. He was a tough horse, though, half Thoroughbred and half Morgan.

The day of the race I went to Archie's place, and we led my horse twelve miles down Hell Creek to where the race was to start. Archie took the extra horse and went back home. So I had twelve miles into my horse in deep mud before we even started the race.

As we were gathering to begin, I heard Bud Pfeifer ask one of the other fellows if he could have a feed of oats for his horse, and the guy said, "Let me look at your horse first." Bud was riding a little white horse that belonged to Tot Robertson, and while he was a tough little horse, he wasn't much to look at. When the fellow looked at the horse, he said, "My God! Yes, you can have fifty pounds!" The little white horse couldn't outrun a three-legged pig at the start of the race but could still run as fast at the finish, and Bud won second on him. There were horses dropping out all the way, and damn few made it past the hundred-mile mark. When you ride over a hundred miles, you'd better be horseback!

I pulled my horse out at the Fort Keogh bridge because someone came back in a car and said that Tim Irions's horse was in and Bud Pfeifer was going in and two others were only out about a mile fighting it out for third. I was next, and my horse was not played out, but I didn't see any use in making him go another couple of miles when the money was already gone. I would have pushed Skip faster if I hadn't had that extra twelve miles in him before we started.

Warner Burchett and another fellow were sitting in the barrow pit beside the road down on the Rock Springs divide, watching the race and drinking. A cop pinched Warner and took his driver's license away. Warner is 93 now (in 1992), and he never has asked for it back. He said if they wanted it that bad they could keep it. He didn't want it back.

There were lots of cars along the way with people giving their support and advice on how to win and so on. It was a once-in-a-lifetime experience for me, and I've always been glad that I made the run.

Dave Huston
Brusett, Montana

THE FINAL DRIVE

Now I want to tell you about the most memorable summer of my life, when we made the final drive of horses off the east shores of Fort Peck from Rock Creek to the Haxby Country.

Bill Twitchell, or "Windy" as we called him, because he never talked much at home, but he'd get in a bar having fun and you couldn't shut him up. If I ever had a second father, it was Windy. He was a very kind man and treated me like a son. Sometimes when we were in town having fun, he'd call to me, "Come here, son." That made me feel good because I really liked him and had a lot of respect for him. We spent a lot of time together now and again. As I was growing up, I would ride over to the Dutch Y and work for him.

Windy was getting together a few men to help gather the horses up in those parts and take them to Brockway to the railroad yards to be sold as canners. Everyone was fencing up the range, and the Fish and Game didn't want wild horses there, I was told. Windy lost a lot of the lease on government land, and most of the horses belonged to the Twitchells, brothers Windy, John, and Walter. Others running there belonged to people from the Bear Paws to the CBC.

Steve Twitchell, John's son; Jack Vallan; and I rode the summer before roughing out a remuda. They weren't broke. We just got them going until they kind of knew what to expect. I remember we thought it was like heaven that summer because we all loved horses and the prairie.

We would get up at horse camp when the sun was just coming up. The prairie dogs were barking, the sage hens dancing. You'd see a doe and her fawn moving off into the coulee from where a mourning dove would call and an occasional owl would hoot. You would hear the gentle splash of the lake water and an old mare nicker to her foal and usually hear the howl from a coyote. You'd smell the fresh morning

Artist Will James on Smokey, the horse he wrote about in *Smokey, the Cowhorse*, ran and broke wild horses, before becoming a bestselling author.
COURTESY OF RAY KRONE

dew and the sagebrush fire we had going for breakfast. Many people say there is nothing out there in those badlands, but they are alive with more life than I tell about here, and I could write a small book on it alone.

I remember the first day like it was yesterday. Jack and Steve pulled a trick on me. After breakfast, Jack went out and wrangled the horses we had fenced into the area we call horse camp. He roped one, Steve eared him down, and I put my saddle on him. They opened the gate, and out we went, down through the sagebrush to a creek full of water, where he balked.

All of a sudden, Jack and Steve came riding up behind me yelling and whooping. That big old bay I was on lunged straight into the air and started bucking right into the water, fell down, and soaked the both of us. When I got him under control, they were laughing about it. It turned out that horse was that way: No one could ride up behind him real quick or he would buck. They set me up and said I passed the test. Every newcomer that got hired was given that horse, and I got to set them up myself after that.

The next day it got a lot worse. I got one that no one had ever been on before, but it was fun. The horses were wild, big, and tough. One bit me one day and rolled up some skin on my arm. We did a lot of moaning and groaning with sore muscles after all day in the saddle or the next morning after sleeping on the ground, but we enjoyed every minute.

We'd also slip into Jordan for some fun sometimes on a Saturday night. Jack had a new Ford pickup so we even went into Wolf Point and Miles City a couple of times. I know of one time we went to Glasgow for a whole weekend and just got back to camp before Windy rode in on Rufus, his favorite big black horse, to see how we were doing. Boy, a close call, as we were supposed to stay in camp.

Johnny would come, too, and bring us some grub once a week and check on us; he also brought Bull Durham, as Windy wouldn't let us smoke "uptown cigarettes," as we called the factory-made ones.

Windy said Bull Durham won't start a prairie fire; it would go out if you didn't keep puffing on it. You could give your horse a sack of Bull Durham, and it would kill a worm, so they said, and I think so, too. (*Editor's note:* I also heard from my father that tobacco was given to horses to kill the worms.)

I had bought and trained a lot of horses for a lot of different people all over the country, but this was different from anything I'd ever done before.

Jack, Steve, and I became very close that summer, like brothers, maybe even closer. We would stick together even if we didn't agree. Steve was the boss, and Jack and I stuck to whatever Steve wanted; it worked better that way. Some cowboys came and went on the horse roundup, but it was Steve, Jack, and I that was there from start to finish working for Windy. When it came time to drive them to Brockway, there were a bunch of new faces besides Steve, Jack, Windy, and me, plus the cooks—Ivan Collins and sometimes John Twitchell. They were both good cooks.

One time Ivan went out to drag up some firewood when his horse got spooked and started bucking. He had it tied hard and fast. Steve saw this and had his horse already saddled, so he took in after him and caught him. The rest of us just sat around the campfire laughing our heads off. It could have turned out to be a disaster. Ivan did get bucked off. He was falling all over the horse but didn't get tangled up in his rope that was tied to the log, as it was hitting the sage and flying up in the air with his horse running and bucking and kicking at it. You just had to be there.

One morning Jack went out to wrangle the remuda. He got up, put his slippers on, jumped on a gentle horse, and off he went. Jack was like that. It was just a joke or something to laugh about, and we did. But a while later when Jack didn't come back with the horses, Steve and I got concerned and went looking for him. His little sorrel horse had slipped on a slick gumbo spot, because it had been raining the day before, and fell on him. His leg was underneath the horse and was broken. Afterward that horse was called Slippers.

Sometimes we would get company at night when we were gathering horses. I remember one night in particular Sid Vallan and Shirley Bridges came. Both these men were foremen for CBC Horse Ranch. Shirley was on the south of Wolf Point unit and Sid the Miles City unit. Boy, did we get some storytelling going on.

Sid said one time Shirley was rounding up horses with some of the boys to cut studs and brand them. A big stud kept quitting the bunch. Shirley yelled out, "Run that bunch quitter by me." Shirley shook out his fifty-foot rawhide rope as the stud came by on a dead run. He dropped a loop on him. Shirley's little horse knew what was coming, so he turned straight away and squatted close to the ground. Shirley leaned forward for the jerk to dump the big stud, but when the stud hit the end of his rope, the cinch broke. Sid said old Shirley and his saddle went flying through the air. Somehow Shirley flipped over in midair, landing on the ground, and the stud fell. The boys were quick to rope him, so Shirley jumped right up and said, "See, boys? That's what you do when your cinch breaks. I still got me a horse." Just as though he had done it on purpose. Back in those days the saddles had taller horns, and Shirley's had stuck in the ground. That's what stopped the horse.

That just about topped them all that night.

Shirley told one on Sid. I didn't get it all, but as best I recall, here it is. Sid got into it with a young feller one night about night watch at the herd. It seems there was a dance in the area somewhere that the young cowboy would rather attend. The argument ended with the young cowboy shooting Sid. But Shirley said Sid was too damned ornery to die.

But something told me that either one of them would stick up for the other in a tight spot. No doubt about it, if you see two old cowboys telling on each other or into it, just go your own way. Don't get into the middle, or they will turn on you. It's just being proud and their way of having fun. Nowadays, if those old timers were here, you wouldn't understand them at all.

Windy told about being out riding with his dad when he was just a kid. Off in the distance they saw a rider with a pinto horse. When he got closer they saw he had a silver-mounted saddle. At first his dad said, "It is the sheriff." But when he got closer he saw it wasn't the sheriff, but it was his horse. The guy came up and sat and talked a while. Then Windy's dad asked, "How did you come by that fancy saddle and horse?" The cowboy said, "I shot the sheriff." Windy's dad didn't believe it but later learned it was so: He shot the sheriff to get the horse and saddle.

I remember we got brown as a berry from the sun all day long. Also my legs got really chapped and red after the first hard day. Jack showed up and told me how to put my pant legs in my boots to prevent that. You put the fold behind your ankle to the outside. You get tough as nails when you work with horses every day. You learn to think faster than normal. If you don't you're in a lot of trouble. You always have to be one jump ahead. You have to know what the horses might or might not do when they get to the top of the ridge or to the bottom of a canyon and be there all ready or you will lose them. That will cost you another day and make some cowboys mad as heck.

After you live on the prairie for a while, you learn how to tell what the weather will do. You watch for signs, like different moods of the horses. They will get restless before a storm. Some say when the dipper stands on its tail, it means a change in weather. If the whirlwinds are changing directions, it can be wet or dry. When there is moisture in the air, it will howl through the trees; you can feel it in the air. Just when the sun is coming up, it's the coldest part of the day—that's when the snakes usually try to crawl in with you. Some say put your lariat around your bedroll and they won't crawl in. I did, and they never. But I knew of a couple of times they did with others, and one got bit, too.

One day Windy said, "I think we got most of them. Tomorrow we'll take them to Brockway." So the next morning we started out. It was a pretty big herd of them, and we had to make it to a trail section near Brockway that night. They ran over some sheep on the way, and we got company from the sheriff the next day. We had a stud that kept breaking away, so we roped him, tied his tail to his head, and went back later to get him. We had a colt that broke his leg, so the cook cut his throat. We couldn't shoot him, as it would spook the herd. But all in all we kept them together and made it to the trail section late that night. We didn't have time to change horses all day, and it was a long ways, so they were tired, to say nothing of how the cowboys felt. But we didn't have any trouble that night, and no one had to herd them. Johnny Twitchell was there and cooked us a good supper. It was a welcome change from Ivan's cooking, not that he wasn't a good cook also.

That night Jack, Steve, and I got our money together to send Ivan into Brockway for a bottle of whiskey. We snuck him out of camp, told him to hurry and be quiet about it. While waiting we all talked a lot and planned our strategy for corralling the next day at the railroad yards—who would ride point and so on. Well, Ivan didn't come back with our whiskey (that we weren't supposed to have) until just a short while before sunup. I woke up hearing somebody singing off in the distance. I woke Steve and Jack, and we snuck out to find Ivan. He was about a half mile away in a coulee lying with his feet sticking up on a bank, flat on his back, drunk as heck and singing a song. We got him back to camp as the sun came up. Johnny said, "Pass that whiskey around so no cowboy gets drunk. We need you all today. Then eat up; we got to corral those horses today."

Corralling went good that day, except there were too many for the size of the corral gate, and it took a while to get them through the gate into the pens. Some we could not hold at the gate long enough. They spilled past and started back towards Timber Creek, but we thought that might happen, so we were ready for them. We got them headed off and back across a creek and into the corral. But I didn't make it across that creek at the same time as the rest. My horse tried to jump it too soon and fell into the water. When I got to the corral, the crew laughed at me, as my horse and I were muddy and wet. I took my boots off, dumped the water out, and wrung my socks out. Then I couldn't get my boots back on wet. They were all laughing and taunting me while I barefooted it to the chuck wagon to get dry socks. Jack said, "Old Gale just couldn't wait to take a bath."

The horses were then sorted off into different sizes, weighed, and loaded into railcars bound for the canner somewhere. The smaller ones, under a thousand pounds, sold for three to four cents a pound.

It was so sad for me to see them go, but you can't stop the progress of man. They eat too much grass, and there was no use for them anymore, they said.

That's why I wrote the song "An Old Dying Breed"—as a tribute to the old cowboys and the mustangs that are gone forever except in my mind, and I can still see them running for their lives.

Gale Drewry
Savage, Montana
An Old Dying Breed

MOVING WITH THE WAGON

After Jr. and I were married in 1944, he started putting a roundup wagon together. He made the plans for a mess box and asked Derby Bond, who was a carpenter, if he would make it for us. He made it to fit into a wagon that he had cut down to fit a small trailer chassis. He had a ball hitch made to fit on a pickup and then went to Sheridan, Wyoming, to the Sheridan Tent and Awning Company to have a tent and fly made. He had it roped like the big wagons. He found a stove that was just right, too.

In the middle of April 1948, Jr. made plans with Jack Willey to run our cows on his ranch that was on the south side of the Bear Paw mountains, about fifty miles from Big Sandy.

At that time Jr. and I were living at the N Bar ranch on Rotten Grass Creek, working for Jack Smith Jr.'s dad. Mr. Smith was running the N Bar ranch for the Faddis-Kennedy Cattle Company, based in Sheridan, Wyoming.

By that time we had a Jeep station wagon, so we had room for men to ride. We loaded up the wagon with groceries, tent, fly, and beds for the men. There were four men besides Jr. They were Floyd Gossney (who agreed to cook), Morgan Deneen, Roger Staps, and Jr.'s nephew, Wells Mayer, who was called Bub. They drove our cows to Spear Siding yards. The cows and horses were loaded on the train, and Bub went on the train with the cattle.

I wanted to go along, so I packed a suitcase and one for our son Aubry. Grandma Smith took care of our second son, Tim, who had been born in February. Mr. Smith took Aubry and me to Billings to catch the train to Big Sandy. It was morning when we got to Big Sandy, and Floyd met the train to get Aubry and me. He took us to the wagon and gave us some breakfast. I helped him do dishes and load up the wagon. Jr. told us where to camp for dinner. It took about five days to get to Jack Willey's place; they averaged about ten miles a day.

When they rode in to the ranch, a man by the name of Philip, I can't remember his last name, went out to meet them. We camped the wagon down by the creek away from the ranch house. The cattle got there around five that evening, and Jr. helped Philip put the cattle where he wanted them.

Jr. and I had a teepee that I set up every night, so after supper I put Aubry to bed. He was just a little past two years old.

After breakfast the next morning, Jr. took Aubry and me to Malta to catch the train to Billings. I got our tickets and got on the train. Another passenger got on, too. His name was Casey Tibbs—the famous bronc rider. It was sure interesting listening to him talk all the way to Billings.

From the train station we walked to the James Hotel. When I got in the door, Aubry laid down screaming and wouldn't get up. I took our suitcases up the stairs, then I went back down to get him. I picked him up, and we went upstairs. I got a room, and we went to bed.

The next morning after we had breakfast, we walked down to the bus stop and got a ticket to Lodge Grass. We went back to the hotel, got our suitcases, and went back to the bus depot. We got there in time to get on the bus to L. G. We got to Lodge Grass around noon. A lot of passengers got off to eat dinner at the bus stop. About two in the afternoon the door opened and in walked Jr.'s dad. Aubry was sure glad to see him, as was I. He took us back to the N Bar, and it was sure good to be home again.

In the meantime Jr. and his crew crossed the Missouri River on a barge and headed for the N Bar. They led Bub's horse a while, then they turned him loose to follow. Jr. rode his horse on the back side of Pompey's Pillar when he rode by. They would average about twenty miles a day, and it took them about eight days to get to the N Bar ranch.

In December of 1949 we got word that we had to move our cows from Jack Willey's place. So we had Dick Blakeley take our horses up to the ranch in his truck. We had Bub and Morgan Deneen with us, and we had our Jeep station wagon to pull the wagon. We got to the ranch about four in the afternoon and set up our wagon, and I got supper ready. After supper Dick went outside to see how the weather was. He came back in and said that he guessed he would go as he saw a few snowflakes fall. So he left.

We stayed camped at that place for three weeks while Jr. and the boys helped Philip gather our cows and put them in a holding pasture. We only had two hundred cows; I think they found them all but one, which was real good. Early the next morning we started for the yards at Big Sandy. Philip helped the boys get started. They would make around ten miles per day.

Whenever it snowed we would have to scrape the snow away to set the tent up. One place where we camped, Morgan helped me put the tent up. Then he said that he had to go back to the herd. It started to snow, and I didn't want any snow in the wagon so I put the fly up. It was sure hard pounding the stakes in the frozen ground, but I got it done. Jr. and the boys were sure surprised to see the fly up. It is sure nice to have a warm fire to cook supper on.

The next morning there were only three horses in camp. They were Morgan's, Bub's, and the wrangle horse. Bub and Morgan caught their horses and started the cattle on. Jr. took the wrangle horse and rode back down the road, back to the ranch where he found them. He caught them and led them back to the wagon. He got to camp about two in the afternoon. I fed him some dinner, and then we loaded up the wagon and I took off down the road. Jr. led the horses and caught up with the cattle.

I had a down coat with a hood on it. It was sure warm. I even wore it to bed. Bub and Morgan had a teepee they put up, but it was no motel.

Philip gave us a gunnysack full of big chunks of coal when we left the ranch, and it was sure a lifesaver. I'd put the eggs in the oven at night and even the clock. Everything in the wagon froze. The potatoes were like little rocks; it took them a long time to cook.

One morning as we were eating breakfast, a pickup stopped by going to Big Sandy. He asked if we knew how cold it was last night. We said we didn't know, but it was real cold. He said that at his place it was 36° below. That's cold!!

When we got to Big Sandy, we camped over by the stockyards. Jr. and I went to town to get some boxes. We got quite a few. We took them to the train cars, tore up the boxes, and nailed them to the inside of the cars to make it a little warmer in there. The engine was there, and he spotted the cars so we could load the cows and horses. And Bub went with the train to Spear Siding.

While Jr. and I were in the grocery store, an old bachelor was talking. He said that he had the Butane sisters at his house. All the men laughed and said that he couldn't have. He said that he had a stove and refrigerator. So he had the last laugh.

When the cattle were all loaded and left, Morgan, Jr., and I went to the wagon, loaded up, and pulled out for home. We got as far as Belt,

Montana, found a restaurant, and had some supper. It was sure nice to sit at a table to eat. One little girl that was sitting at another table looked at me and asked her mother, "Mom, is that a man or a woman?" Her mother said that she didn't know. I laughed and took my hood down so my hair would fall down, and I said, "I'm a woman."

After we ate supper we headed for Lewistown. We got there around eight and drove around trying to find a garage that we could park our car and wagon in. We finally found one, then found a motel and went to bed. It was Christmas Eve.

The next morning after breakfast, we headed for Spear Siding. Spear Siding was a stockyard that was used and was between Lodge Grass and Wyola. Jr.'s dad had brought hay for the cows. They were sure eating when we got there. Jr. and the boys saddled their horses and took the cows down to the Little Horn River to water. And that's all I can remember. Bub, Morgan, and Jr. are all gone, and I'm the only one left that would know. And I don't remember what we did with our cows.

Our son Tim has our wagon. He uses it for his branding.

Corrina Smith
Hardin, Montana

 **CHAPTER 3**

LIVING TO TELL ABOUT IT

WHEN THE LIGHTNING STRUCK

In the spring of 1940, I was working for the Antler outfit owned by Matt Tschirgi. We made up a herd of other people's cattle, mainly small ranchers and farmers, known as the "Pumpkin Rollers." The Antler outfit would summer six hundred head for these folks on the top of the Big Horn Mountains on the Bull Elk Divide, in what was known as the Buffalo Pasture.

Frank Greenough, wagon boss, decided to take just the bed wagon, the bed tent, and a "greasy sack" (cooking utensils and grub). Lee Wells, the designated cook, was to stay up there for the summer and scatter salt.

As best I can remember, the crew consisted of Frank Greenough, Alvy Bomar, Bob Smith (no relation to me), Slim Barton, Philip Newton, Charlie Long, Barry Roberts Jr., and me. We gathered the cattle from Buffalo Creek south of Spear Siding all the way up the Little Horn to the Tschirgi Ranch.

After a few days of gathering, we headed up Sport Creek and went over the divide and camped below Jay Owen's place. I was asked to wrangle the horses, as I had wrangled them all the summer before when the wagon was out. The next day we nooned at Red Springs on the face of the Big Horn Mountain. Then we went on up the mountain to the top and stayed all night at some sheep corrals not far from the Look Out Tower at Windy Point.

As we were moving along the top of the mountain, someone noticed a bedroll as it rolled off the bed wagon and down off a small rimrock of eight to ten feet. Two of the cowboys got off their horses and picked their way down the rimrock to retrieve the bed and drag it back up. Good thing it was noticed or somebody would have had sorry sleeping that night!

After dinner I was holding the gate rope of the rope corral while the cowboys caught the horses they was going to ride and brought them out through the gate. Alvy Bomar had a hard time getting his horse out and said to me as he passed through the gate, "I wish lightning would strike this son of a bitch!"

After loading up camp I took the horses and piloted the wagon to Hunters Cabin, which was the headquarters camp for the Buffalo Pasture. Everyone noticed some dark-looking clouds coming in from the north, so they were pushing the cattle hard, as they didn't want to get wet.

By the time they were almost to their destination, the cattle were getting pretty tired. The boys were trying to get them down over a small rimrock close to the gate of the pasture. The cattle was in a tight bunch when the storm hit. The lightning was flashing, and the thunder was cracking.

All of a sudden a flash of lightning struck Alvy Bomar on the back of his head, making two gashes! It went down his spine to his tailbone and into his saddle, followed up his saddle to the tree and into his horse, killing the horse instantly. The lightning bolt knocked four other horses down and killed twenty-four head of cattle.

Alvy's spur was bent when they were trying to get him out from under his horse, and it was quite a job freeing him.

Frank Greenough sent Philip Newton back to Lookout Tower, as there was a phone the Indian Agency had installed there in case of fire on the mountain. Philip was riding a horse that was always wanting to buck, so he didn't spare him much as he galloped him the good ten miles to the tower. He called the Indian Agency at Crow, and they called the Tschirgi Ranch and told them what had happened.

There was no four-wheel-drives in those days, and the Indian Department had the best car to climb the mountain in the mud. Philip stayed at Lookout Tower until the car came, which was about eight that evening. He then turned his horse loose and rode to camp with them.

In the meantime Frank sent Barry Roberts to camp to get some water and towels, while they pushed the cattle on through the gate.

Barry and I started back up to where the mishap happened, and we met them coming to camp. Alvy was riding behind Slim Barton on his horse. We gave Alvy a drink of water, and he drank about half the can. We wet the towels and tried to wipe some of the black off his face.

We got him to camp, undressed him, and got him into his bed. His watch was melted and the fleece was burned off the inside of his brand-new underwear and was all black. Also there were two holes burned into each knee of his underwear and into Alvy's knees, where the lightning went through both knees and into his horse.

The help got there around 10:00 p.m., and they loaded him—bed and all—and left with a can of water, as Alvy couldn't get enough water to drink. All the cowboys were pretty shook up, especially the four whose horses were knocked down with them. Slim Barton was the worst; he couldn't talk for two or three days.

Alvy finally recuperated, but it was over a year before he was his own self again and able to do anything.

Bill Bomar, Alvy's grandson, has his saddle. There is a neat little hole about the size of a .22 bullet where Alvy's tailbone was and two little holes where his knees touched his saddle.

It is said that all that saved his life was the fact that he wasn't grounded.

Junior Smith
Lodge Grass, Montana

SMOKEY JOE!

Wednesday, April 2, 2003

After several days of warm weather, a cold, windy, little slushy storm has blown in. A person can always count on these weather shifts when you're calving.

This morning before Smokey Joe and I jump in the feed truck to start rolling out hay to the cows, I decided to make a quick tour through the corrals and calving shed to check the heifers before turning them out for the day. We're getting to the tail end of the prettiest little bunch of heifers I've ever calved.

A mini cyclone packed in a fur coat, Smokey Joe knew when to disobey orders and saved Susan Stone's life. COURTESY OF SUSAN STONE

They're gentle and have had virtually no problems calving—except yesterday when we had one that just kept fiddlin' around, not making any real effort to calve. And the feet showing had some size to 'em. So after a reasonable amount of time and no further progress, the boss and I ran the heifer into the shed to pull her calf.

She seemed as cooperative as the rest of her pretty black sisters . . . until we got her in the pen with the head catch. Then she wasn't having any part of our midwifery assistance and *really* got on the fight, putting the boss up on the fence, where she succeeded in knocking him back off and banging up his leg pretty bad.

We wound up having to rope her and snub her to a post to pull the ungrateful sow's calf out. That, amazingly enough, did not improve her disposition one iota, but at least she now had a nice big bull calf to dote on. Thank God she liked him!

This morning, as I approached the gate into the corral where the heifers are, I (unnecessarily) told Smokey Joe to "stay put." After four years of being around expectant bovines, he knows I don't want him following me through the corrals or sheds unless I invite him along. He's got a long list of rules he must obey, and he does so with a willing and cooperative attitude. He's truly a top cowdog hand and my devoted companion.

As I walk through the heifers, Smokey Joe makes a big circuit on the outside of the corrals, so he can keep an eye on my activities. These heifers aren't particularly bothered by his presence. We turn them out during the day, and Smokey Joe follows along when I trot through them, making checks. And it's his job to bring them in every evening. But rules are rules! Now he has to stay out.

Halfway through the corrals, I spot a brand-new calf, on his feet and being mothered, but he's sure shivering. I decide maybe a few hours in the shed would do him some good. But the heifer-from-hell has to be moved before I can bring another pair in. She has access to the shed and a small pen out back.

With a little creative heifer handling, I succeed in running her and her calf into the shed without entering the pen. This morning she didn't seem as hostile so I felt fairly safe slipping through the pen to slide the shed door shut on her. Big mistake.

She came out of the shed like a runaway freight train, blowing snot and bellering, knocking me down before I could formulate a plan for retreat. She was really taking her grudge out on me, and she had murder in her eye. I knew she was inflicting some pretty serious injuries, and it was all happening in fast-forward. I wasn't real sure how I was going to get out of this predicament, as that ol' heifer wasn't showing any signs of weakening.

It was exactly at that moment that something that looked and sounded like a cross between a buzz saw and a porcupine streaked into the pen and built to that heifer with a ferocity that would have scared Lucifer himself! Smokey Joe had made one of those rare independent cowdog decisions that, rules be damned, the lady was in dire need of his canine capabilities, so he entered the corral to do battle with the heifer-from-hell. The fight to save my life was on.

The heifer quit me in a heartbeat and took on her new adversary. Only this one had sharp teeth, and he was making good and fast use of them. It was certainly my window of opportunity to get the hell out of the corral, and I took it. Smokey Joe didn't back down or quit the fray until the heifer beat a hasty retreat back to her calf in the shed, and by that time I was out of harm's way . . . although not out of the woods.

In spite of the serious mauling, I was able to walk to the house to use the phone to track down my boss and call 911. I was sure glad to see the local ambulance and crew of volunteer EMTs show up, since I was in dire need of some medical attention and a quick trip to town.

Final assessment: fractured ribs and vertebrae, punctured lung, several bruised organs, a ruptured spleen, and some serious internal bleeding. After some emergency surgery and a week of excellent care at Central Montana Medical Center in Lewistown, I spent another week being nursed by two loving daughters.

Smokey Joe and I are back together at home, and I'm recuperating rapidly. We're both looking forward to getting back to work. There's green grass growing, calves to be branded, cows to be trailed to summer pasture, new bulls to turn out, and, hopefully, hay to cut. Life is good!

Susan Stone
Winnett, Montana

ANDY AT THE WELL

My son Cotton and I were riding one day, and we had split up to gather. I stopped at a windmill to get off and get a drink. I was riding a large Binion horse that was pretty broncy. As I was dismounting, my off-spur caught in my hobbles, which were hanging on the back saddle string. I was in trouble, with one foot on the ground and one up in the hobbles. My first thought: *Get a good short hold of the rein and pull his head around.*

The Lord was helping me that day, as my son rode up, and I said, "Just stay back and see if I can't get loose. Be ready to get ahold of the horse's head."

I finally worked around and got my boot off, thus letting my foot down—Pretty Scary Situation.

Ann Secrest Hanson
Bowman, North Dakota
I Did It My Way

81 YEARS OF RIDING

Dave said he's been riding and breaking horses since almost before the flies and has escaped serious injury most of the time. In 1947 a big seven-year-old Thoroughbred gelding bucked him off and kicked him in midair with both hind feet. It hit him in the chest and broke a few ribs and punctured one lung. After a couple of weeks, he recuperated and was back in the saddle again.

In 1960 a fighting cow hit him on the left foot and flipped him over the right side of the horse, and he lost the reins and was hung up in the stirrup. The horse dragged him for several hundred feet before his boot slipped off. He had cactus working out of his shoulders for six months but was lucky to get off that easy.

A Shetland pony he was breaking in the '70s ran sideways and fell over, and when he put his arm out to break the fall, it dislocated his shoulder. In about 1984 a four-year-old Appaloosa bucked him off and twisted one hip, which took several months of treatments to heal. That's the extent of his horse injuries in all those years, except the one

Dave and Kathryn Huston ranched and outfitted northwest of Jordan in the Brusett area. COURTESY OF KATHRYN HUSTON

in 1997. He fell on the hard ground from the side of a little two-year-old paint stallion and broke a hip. That required pins to repair. He has about four good, gentle saddle horses, and he'll probably stick with them. He says four good saddle horses should be enough now for an eighty-one-year-old cowboy.

Kathryn Huston
Brusett, Montana
Wife of Dave Huston

THE DARK SIDE OF THE BREAKS

It was early October and the weather had snapped from nice to nippy when Jill and I took a notion to ride Cow Creek, southwest of the Little Rocky Mountains, in the Missouri River Breaks. Many different ranchers ran cattle in common on this huge summer range that made up the grazing district. We wanted to see how far-flung the cow/calf pairs were and what their condition was for the trail out of there. That could save miles of long riding during the cold Fall gather, barely a month away. There were few cross fences, no corrals, and no usable buildings in this pasture that extended for miles in all directions.

I saddled Bridger before daylight. He was a big sixteen hands, long-legged red roan with a spade brand on his right hip. I had become attached to him the last couple of years as we'd covered miles of rough country in the Breaks. He'd overcome a really bad habit of shying at anything and everything and jumping high and to the side. Then he'd stand and shake, he'd scare himself so bad. After lots of wet saddle blankets, he gradually came to trust me, and the scares were farther between all the time. He was good-natured and seemed to know I'd try to keep him out of jackpots. There were plenty of those in the Breaks. The major concern of riders in this vast, inhospitable country was the probability of being left afoot. Or hurt and afoot.

I met up with Jill at a jumping-off place inside the north fence line. I was sure glad to see Moon back out of her horse trailer, for Moon was a solid bay mare, tough in a tight spot and no spook in her. We stuffed extra vests and lunches in our saddlebags and swung into our saddles. We knew what we were in for when we planned this all-day ride but didn't know we would have an experience we would never forget. We had a lot of ground to cover, and we didn't expect to be back before dark.

Noon found us on the southern end, miles from where we started at daylight. Dinner was a handful of dried fruit and jerky to chase.

"For all the cattle and brands we've checked today, we're sure not seeing many of our cattle," Jill remarked, pulling a boot out of a stirrup to stretch a leg.

"They could have drifted into some tighter drainages, found water and good grass, and decided they didn't want to see us again," I threw in. All the possibilities of what could have happened to our cows and calves in the past five months were all too clear to both of us. When you turn out in the spring, you hope for the best, where little rainfall combined with intense heat discourages abundant life or growth of either plants or animals. The Breaks are home to every predator, save grizzlies, known to Montana, including man himself, so we were rightly concerned.

We worked our way back north, easing up to more cattle to check brands and the general condition of the cows and calves. We rode down coulees choked with six-foot-tall sagebrush, cedars, and spruce trees. We rode up and over cut banks, jumped washouts, and wound our way up dry creek beds. There were places where we had to backtrack when a trail led to sheer drop-offs or narrow ravines. At times the cuts we plunged down were so deep the top banks were level with our faces. How we dreaded the thought of meeting a rattler, eye level, waiting under a brush pile.

We rode up to the grand old Spencer Camp, a set of falling-down log buildings with well-used outbuildings, all lying in the bottom of Cow Creek. The once-stout pole corrals were set deep and close to the buildings. The sweep of the peaceful huge cottonwoods lent shelter and shade to this once-splendid river ranch.

The Cow Creek crossing leveled out at the Spencer Camp, and a barely usable jeep trail took off from it and wound several miles to the top, where our horse trailers waited. At the crossing Jill suggested, "Instead of riding up the trail, let's ride on through the holding pasture. Might find a cow or two." Knowing this route would add a couple of extra hours of riding time and that night would overtake us very soon but it might show us a few of our cows, I readily agreed. "It's worth a try."

We turned our backs to the jeep trail and hit a fast trot through the tangle of sagebrush and deer trails. A few cows turned up. Wrong brands. Farther on we strained our eyes to catch a glimpse of a cow in the fading light of evening, lifting our eyes to the rim of the basin where an orangish-reddish tinge of a Montana sunset breathed the last warmth of the day. Only the soft thud of our horses' hooves and scraping of brush against our saddles and legs gave notice of our passing through this silent no-man's-land.

Bridger picked his way through the drainages in the eerie faded light of past sundown, dodging the dense thick undergrowth. He lunged out on top of a flat and, in midstride, stopped dead in his tracks.

"Bridger!" I said. He didn't move. He stood frozen.

It was so dark now I could barely make out the outline of his head and ears. "Bridger. Come on, boy," I urged. "We've a ways to go here."

He didn't move a muscle, not a hair. A jiggle of the rein, a touch of the boot. Nothing. His head was practically in my lap as his rigid body made no move. No breath came from him. His ears seemed chiseled from stone as he strained to hear. Hear what?

Then I heard them. First one muffled unmistaken rattle of a rattlesnake near us. Under Bridger's feet. Now another. And another. Then each individual snake rattled, and I realized we were surrounded by them. In front of us, on both sides, and they were moving, westerly. Not stopping for us.

My skin crawled. How many were there? Twenty? Forty? For each one that rattled, were there three or four more?

"Jill!" I gasped, trying to keep my voice even, so as not to scare Bridger. "Don't come up here! We're in the middle of a rattlesnake migration! Don't come near!"

"My God," she answered. "Can you get out of there? I hear them!"

My hands were slack on the reins, my legs tight against Bridger's sides as I waited, wondering if he would shy and jump high to the right or left, either way into the path of a rattler. Wherever he went, I was going with him. I answered Jill with no confidence, "I'm going to let Bridger make the call."

I scarcely breathed. An eternity passed. The sounds of the rattlesnakes began to grow fainter, farther away. Always to the west. Then all the rattling came from our left side as they slithered on by us toward their den. Bridger still held rock solid. Then they were gone. Their warnings ceased. As suddenly as he had stopped, Bridger shifted his weight and moved off. He had not been struck.

We gave our horses their heads and they headed out of the Breaks at a long trot as though they were on a clearly marked trail. Jill and I were too shook up to speak, from our narrow escape from the deadly rattlesnakes. As for me, I had just put Bridger at the top of my list of "Best Horses."

We'd had a very close encounter with the dark side of the Breaks, but we would be back to find our cows during the Fall gather with Bridger and Moon and, most importantly, with a fresh and renewed respect for this raw land, the Missouri River Breaks.

Mary Ann Parks
Grass Range, Montana

THE VIGILANTES

Back in the 1890s, my granddad, Steve Marmon, had bought a herd of horses and was trailing them east to North Dakota to sell them.

It so happens that about that time horse stealing was more common than most ranchers would like, and they were on the lookout for rustlers.

Somewhere between Culbertson and the North Dakota line, Steve was apprehended by a Vigilante Committee and held at gunpoint. He showed them the Bill of Sale, but they were not too overly convinced. Finally, he talked them into sending a rider back to the previous owner. They did, not wanting to hang an innocent man. Sure enough, Steve was cleared.

Jim Marmon
Wolf Point, Montana

TOM RYAN

Tom Ryan's name has been associated with the Dutch Henry gang, but old-timers who knew him say that he found horse rustling too much work and preferred robbing banks and stealing the mail.

"Tom always said he hated petty larceny," commented Ellis Hurst, a neighbor of Ryan's in the Outlook vicinity of northeastern Montana. "He was only interested in robbing banks and trains. I saw empty mail pouches in his cabin. He didn't try to conceal them."

Hurst also recalled that Ryan made no attempt to hide. If strangers approached his cabin, he would meet them with guns on.

"They're not going to find me hiding behind a bed or in the cellar," he boasted.

Mildred Bantz, daughter of Alonzo and Celina Desonia, who settled on the Whitetail Creek in 1902, recalled that her mother claimed Tom Ryan was the most gentleman-like man she ever knew. Ryan, like other travelers in the area, often stopped at the Desonia place for food and shelter.

"He talked about everything in general, and he always left money under his plate," she said. "Once he lost his watch on a nearby hill. He said he would give $20 to anyone who found it. Mother looked for it and found it, and he gave her the $20 immediately.

"One time Ryan came by when Mother was chasing some chickens. She was flustered, and he offered to get the chickens for her. She protested but finally pointed out the chickens she wanted. He drew pistols with both hands and shot the heads off both of them."

According to the Desonias, Ryan took money from the rich and gave it to the poor.

"One time he robbed a bank in Crosby, North Dakota, and told my father to give the money to some poor people," Mildred said. "Before I was born Ryan came through with a herd of horses. He had a motherless colt. Noting that my mother was pregnant, he said he would leave the colt for the baby (which he somehow expected would be a girl). That colt lived to be twenty-nine years old. Everyone called it 'Tootsie's mare.' 'Tootsie' was my nickname. I had many offspring from her."

Ellis Hurst stated that Ryan stopped at his place one time to receive treatment for a wound he said he suffered when his horse fell on him and his gun discharged. Another account says that he also stopped at the Ator ranch near Antelope, Montana, for the same purpose. Later they learned that Ryan received the wound while making his getaway after robbing the Crosby bank.

That was the last time Tom Ryan was seen in northeastern Montana. He disappeared and left no forwarding address.

Dorothy Rustebakke
Area Historian
Scobey, Montana

CHAPTER 4

OUT OF THE CHUTE

"THANKS, BUT NO THANKS"

I was born at Lane, Montana, the year of the Big Crash (1929), so I started out in the "Dirty Thirties." I came from a large family; I had six brothers and eight sisters. Dad milked a bunch of cows to put groceries on the table during the years of the big drought and the grasshoppers, so we had a lot of bucket-fed calves. When I was three years old or so, when going out to feed the calves, I'd jump on them and ride them as far as I could go. It wasn't long I was getting pretty good balance. In a year or so I was riding the milk cows. Dad was wondering why the cows didn't give much milk once in a while. We were still working a lot of horses back then for haying and dragging and cultivating corn. I would ride the workhorses both bareback and with an old "A fork saddle." I was about twelve years old then, and I was looking for something that could buck me off. My brother Bill had a little black workhorse that he didn't want me to ride. One day when he came in for dinner, I was hiding in the barn. As soon as he started to the house, I jerked the harness off the little black horse and put the old "A fork" on him. I got outside and got on him just as Bill was going in the house. I hollered, "Watch this, Bill." I reached up and grabbed him in the shoulders. I found what I was looking for—I could buck off.

We had remount studs, and when mares were brought in, I would saddle them up for practice. When I was fourteen years old, there was a little jackpot rodeo down by Sidney, Montana. I bummed a ride with the priest after Mass from Lambert. I got in the saddle bronc and bareback riding. I won second in bareback riding and fourth in the saddle bronc. The cowboy that won the saddle bronc riding said, "Meet me out at the Triangle (a night club), the drinks are on me." I thought, *Gosh, do you have to drink to be a cowboy?* My mother wanted me to be a teetotaler.

I was at a rodeo at Hettinger, North Dakota, one time. I drew a palomino horse of Tooke's from Ekalaka, Montana. In the saddle bronc riding, I was about third from the last of the bronc riders, and I knew if I was going to win it I was going to have to come a-spurring. I got pretty wild and spurred over the buck rein. I couldn't get back off of it. So that ended my lick on that ride. I found out if I was going to fit in with the cowboys, I was going to have to drink a little booze. It went pretty good for a few years. I was making enough money for entrance fees, travel money, and booze. It wasn't long and I would start out to some of the bigger rodeos and make it to the first bar and that would be as far as I'd get. I had a brother that lived in Washington State. He told me if I would come out to Ellensburg he would pay my entrance fee. I started out for Washington, but I didn't make it out of Montana. He said the same thing about Pendleton if I would come out there. I couldn't control my drinking; it controlled me.

Some of the better stock contractors at that time were Willis Wilson from Savage; Tooke's from Ekalaka; Leo Cremer from Big Timber; Greenough and Orr from Red Lodge or Arizona; Fettig's from Killdeer, North Dakota; and Marvin Brookman from Wolf Point.

Fettig's had that Whiz Bang horse leased from Jim Barnhart from Dickinson, North Dakota. I drew him in Sidney back in 1956; that was when you rode for ten seconds. We got out there about eight seconds, and he lost his footing. One of the judges said I missed him coming out, so I didn't get a reride. Benny Reynolds won it the next day on him. He was a real fast horse. Whiz Bang got inducted into the Hall of Fame. I believe the best horse I ever was on was that "Grand Prize" horse of Marvin Brookman's. I won the bronc riding on him at Glasgow, Montana, in 1960. That was about the end of my rodeoing.

I want to add that I won the all-around in Terry, Montana, in 1958. I drew a reride in the bareback riding. They didn't have another horse. Buss Vowel said he thought his saddle horse would buck if you spurred him a little bit. He said, "I chased horses on him all morning, but I still think he would buck a little." He was tied outside the arena. They led him in and unsaddled him, opened the chute gate, and crowded him in. I put my bareback rigging on him and won second on him.

My eldest grandson, Joe Blankenship, won the all-around in Terry forty years later, in 1998. Then I want to say that twenty years after my favorite cowboy artist and author spent some time at Warm Springs (insane asylum) getting dried out, I spent three months there getting dried out. I haven't got anything against drinking, but some people just can't drink and function, and I am one of them. I wish there was some way we could get through to some of the young boys that have a lot of talent but booze is interfering. I have seen it happen, and I'm sure you have, too. I found that it is a lot easier to stay sober than it is to get sober.

I have to throw my two bits in on a couple of things: I think the judges are marking the first ones out on the rough stock too high, and then when they get a good ride, they get the scores way too high and they haven't got no place to go. That's how it looks to me. In the high school rodeos, I think they should cut back two or three of the double-rank horses and bulls that the professional cowboys don't ride very often. I don't think a cowboy is riding as good at sixteen or seventeen as he would be at eighteen on up. I know at the National High School Rodeo Finals in Gillette, Wyoming, two of the best saddle bronc riders were there by far. One was from South Dakota, and the other one was from Montana. They each drew one of the double-rank saddle broncs, and they both got bucked off. The next year one of them went to the National Finals in Las Vegas and done real good.

It didn't take very long for me to find out I couldn't handle the booze. When I started drinking, it seems like I couldn't get enough and

I couldn't stop drinking. I will never forget there was a string of rodeos starting out with the county fairs from Forsyth, Montana; Miles City; Terry; Baker; Glendive; and Sidney. Sidney was getting close to my old stomping grounds. That's where I really wanted to shine, but Glendive is as far as I got. I was so bent out of shape I didn't know where I was or how I got there. But when I woke up I was right under somebody's saddle horse lying in powdered fresh shit, wet warm shit looking up at that old horse's belly. I don't know how I kept from getting stepped on. I was one hell of a mess. The boys razzed me for a long time about sleeping at the horseshit hotel. I don't know how many times I would start out to a big rodeo and never get there.

I kind of think what really got me hitting the booze, I was at one of the Greenough and Orr rodeos. There were about ten of the cowboys there that made the big time. I can't remember what horse I had, but I put up a pretty good ride. And when I got back to the chutes, Joe Orr said to me, "If I've ever seen a natural, you are it." So like I said, if I was going to fit in with the rest of the cowboys, I was going to have to do a little drinking, and I couldn't drink just a little.

I don't like to mention names, for I might leave someone out or mention one that I shouldn't. But some of the bronc riders back in the 1920s and 1930s that I knew from around Lambert, Richey, Savage, Sidney, and Glendive were Carl Bates, Don Holt, Yank Mann, Ray Bell, Ray Mavity, Herbie Cayer, and Harold Adkins, as well as Bob Askin and Paddy Ryan. Harold was the cowboy's cowboy. He was riding broncs in the 1930s and probably up into the 1940s. He bulldogged and calf-roped, and he judged a lot of rodeos and pickup bucking horses. He team-roped about up to the time he died. He trained a lot of good bulldogging and calf-roping horses. He was always ready to help the new guy, and he spent a lot of time helping kids. I was proud to call him my friend. Herbie Cayer was a neighbor and a very good friend. We spent a lot of time together.

Back in the 1920s they rode that freak saddle, the kind you crawled in and shut the door. They had swells that went way out over your legs.

They rode the barebacks with a loose rope and two hand holds. I will never forget Yank Mann. He was at least twenty years or more older than I was, and every time I was in Sidney drinking, I would always run into him. We would ride a few broncs from the bar stool (there are still a lot of them rode from there). Yank was a good bronc rider in his day, and I would get to telling him about a few of the tough horses, and he would say, "Damn it, kid, bicycle them, scratch one side, and then the other, the judges can't see both sides." I can see where that bicycling would work with them freak saddles, but I couldn't get it to work very good with the association saddle. Paddy Ryan and Bob Askin traveled together, and Slick Stevenson was a good friend of mine and a good bronc rider. He was the cowboy that won the jackpot at my first rodeo.

I want to say a few words about a good friend of mine, Johnny Hagen. He was from Malta, Montana. He rode broncs and done it all in his younger years. Then he put a rodeo string together and put on some good rodeos. I can't remember for sure, but somewhere around 1948 or 1949, he had a rodeo at the State Line between Williston, North Dakota, and Bainville, Montana. I had an Aunt Daisy that lived north of Bainville, so my mother went with me to visit her sister. They went to the rodeo with me. I'm sure it was one of the few rodeos they ever went to. I was glad that they got to see me ride. I won a little money in the bull riding. There was a guy there from Cody, Wyoming, by the name of Cap Day. I will never forget him. He was the first cowboy I ever saw that worked all five events. He was good in all of them. I have not seen or heard of him since. I don't know what happened to him, but he was a good cowboy.

In August 1960, I'll never forget it, I was in Glasgow, Montana, drunker than $700. I ran into Johnny Hagen. He said to me, "Fritz, if you don't get off that sauce, you are going to die." It wasn't long after that, I did put the cork in the jug. I stopped and saw Johnny in Great Falls, Montana, in the 1980s; we were both off the sauce. I was proud of him, and he was proud of me. He was a great friend. December 1, 1962, I woke up, and I was sick and tired of being sick and tired. I found that it is a lot easier to say, "Good Morning, God," instead of "GOOD GOD, MORNING!" If I ever meet any of you good people, I would like you to ask me to have a drink. I like saying, "Thanks, but no thanks." My worst day sober is better than my best day drunk.

Fritz Rehbein
Rozet, Wyoming

RIDE A GOOD HORSE

Ryan Mapston, Gary Pimperton, and Jim Croff have much in common. All three were born and raised on Montana cattle ranches. All three are still owners and operators of Montana cattle ranches, and all three are actively involved in the Professional Rodeo Cowboys Association, or the PRCA. These cowboys are all living in the Judith Basin country where Charlie Russell often rode, roped, and reminisced. It's apparent these cowboys have continued Russell's love for the western way of life, and it's no secret that it was cowboys like this that inspired Russell to paint.

Pimperton and Croff have been neighbors and friends since childhood. Jim is part of the reason why Gary started riding broncs in the PRCA in 1986. Like all rookies, Pimperton's PRCA permit required him to win at least $2,500 his first year, which would qualify him as a PRCA cardholder. He has ridden in the Montana PRCA circuit finals ever since.

Ryan, on the other hand, was well on his way to becoming one of the top bronc riders in the nation when he met Geyser, Montana, Women's Professional Rodeo Association (WPRA) barrel racer Darcy Nevala in Texas. They were married May 23, 1998, and later purchased land in the foothills of the Highwood Mountains north of Belt. They are hoping their son, Ryley, will be lucky enough to ride a good horse, trail some good cattle, and make a living in what they consider "God's Country."

All three cowboys have ridden some of the toughest saddle broncs in PRCA history. All three hoped they would draw the best horses, some of which were Continental, Papa Smurf, Skitso, Painted Smile, and Cool Alley. All three cowboys are husbands, fathers, and ranchers, and like Charlie Russell all have a love affair with Montana and the cowboy world. Their western life style is something they've known since birth, and they can't imagine doing it any other way.

"Our rodeo careers could never have been without the support of our families," said Mapston. "Our dads had a real passion for bronc riding, too, but weren't in a position to go down the road." All three cowboys consider themselves lucky to have the support of family and friends.

Most PRCA cowboys begin their year at the Denver Stock Show in January, all hoping to start out with a good ride and a healthy check. In Montana the first PRCA rodeo kicks off at Belt, twenty miles east of Great Falls, sponsored by the Little Belt Cowboy Association. The PRCA rules are simple: The cowboys who draw the best, ride the best, and win the most will compete for the "big bucks" in Las Vegas in December. Ryan Mapston has done just that and qualified eight times to the National Finals Rodeo (NFR) during his rodeo career.

Gary, on the other hand, found it difficult to go down the road full time because the cattle ranch that has been in the family since 1882 was depending on him to keep things going. His wife Polly and their four children, Jeff, Alyssa, Kerstyn, and Kolby, also needed Dad around, which limited his entries in pro rodeo. However, his weekends were often on the road with rodeo partners Tom Kuka, Australian cowboy Glen Peacock, Jack Nystrom, and more recently J. T. Robbins and Jake Costello. The rodeo trips qualified him in the Montana Finals for nineteen years, with minimum mishaps. "The younger guys are starting to call me 'Dad,'" Pimperton chuckled.

One of the more serious wrecks Pimperton had on a bronc was in Canada in 2003 that kept him out of saddle bronc competition for several months. After the dust settled he was carried out on a stretcher, and the sports medicine doctors patched him up as best they could and sent him back to the States with his traveling companions for further care. Like most cowboys do when things get too serious, Jake Costello lightened up the moment from behind the wheel on the way home with, "Gosh, Gary, I thought you were dead. The other guys got mad at me 'cause I was goin' through your gear to get the best stuff."

"Humor is a major portion of our lives," says Mapston. "We put on a lot of miles, and it really breaks up the trip to laugh as we're goin' down the road."

Gary healed up and returned to saddle bronc competition the following rodeo season and enjoyed winning second in the Montana state rodeo finals in January 2005. He claims he'd like to ride his twentieth year, but "I'll have to wait and see how things go."

Rodeo has become much more organized since Charlie Russell's time. Jim Croff has been a part of organizing the Montana PRCA Rodeo Finals ever since he retired from bronc riding in 1993. He has been Montana's PRCA president since 1994.

While there are other rodeos in the state throughout the summer, such as those sponsored by the Northern Rodeo Association, only cardholders of the PRCA can advance to the NFR in Las Vegas, which is usually held the first part of December each year at the Thomas and Mack Stadium at the University of Nevada, Las Vegas.

Jim and his wife Holly ranch south of Geyser and have raised two children on their Treasure State acreage. Today both children, Jimi Rae and Dustin, are competing in rodeo. Jim spends most of his time in January taking care of details for the PRCA Montana Finals. During his bronc riding days, he's enjoyed winning three Montana circuit final titles.

Croff's organizational skills are only excelled by his cowboy poetry:

"GETTIN' OLD"
I was puttin' a rein on some colts, one day,
When I noticed a cloud a' dust headin' my way.
When an old truck and trailer pulled up to the shed,
And a weathered ole cowboy stepped out, and he said,

"I've got two nice ponys that just need one ride,
Been broke by the *hutes. . . in their work, they take pride.
They broke them both . . . nearly this year,
Didn't cost me nothin' — just a buck and a beer.

"Top 'em off myself," he spoke out so bold,
"But ma told me no! . . . she thinks I'm gettin' old.
Just give them one ride and warm 'em up a bit,
They'll be alright son" . . . (as he puffed his cigarette).

"Hell, when I was young . . . ten rides 'n my colts were sold.
Ya, I used to ride 'em . . . but now I'm gettin' old."
Then out of the trailer came a raging black steed.
His eyes stared at mine and he wasn't hard to read.

I figured the good news was . . . he's probably the worst.
Since he came a snortin' out of the trailer head first.
My thinkin' was wrong as you might of guessed.
Then I swallowed hard . . . Let me tell ya the rest.

As the old boy released him and untied the rope,
I was slowly turnin' Christian and a lookin' for the Pope.
With hate on his breath and the devil in his eye.
I knew this ol' Ap . . . would test all my try.

I rubbed down the black with an old gunny sack.
Then slipped my old Hamley on top of his back.
When I pulled the cinch tight he got a hump in his back.
You'd think he was camel . . . if he wouldn't of been black.

Well, I put him in the round pen . . . tied his nose to the right.
Thought I'd leave him a spell and see if he'd fight.
Went back to the alley to start on the Ap.
That's when he tried to put a foot in my lap.

It came so damn close . . . I felt a little sick.
But the old cowboy said, "Ah, that Appy won't kick!"
So I told him (with the pony's safety in mind),
"I think it'd be best if we tied up a hind."

A half hour later (and two pair of gloves),
His hind foot was snubbed up . . . 'n we're no longer in love.
I eased on the saddle and snugged it up tight,
When he flipped over backwards with all of his might.

I said, "if the 'hutes' rode this horse, then they're 'tougher' than I."
"They might of stretched the truth!" was the cowboy's reply.
I told the old timer, "Canner horses are up."
"It'd be a nice home for this 'Appy pup.'"

I sure was pleased—when we both agreed . . .
That it wasn't worth foolin' with . . . this Appy steed.
So we went to the round pen to check on the black.
(Guess I had no choice but to crawl on his back.)

I was half way in the saddle when we left the ground.
And my off side stirrup was nowhere to be found.
He jumped and kicked and spun like a top.
From one side to the other I was startin' to flop.

I was grabbin' leather . . . wherever it could be found.
This pony seemed determined to put me on the ground.
After all the dust settled and he came to a stop,
God only knows . . . how I was still there on top.

The cowboy just smiled and said, "Wasn't that fun?"
"Boy . . . you're a bronc ridin' son of a gun!"
"I admire a man with no lack of fear."
"Here son's — your 'buck' . . . and I owe you a beer."

The moral of this story, I truly declare,
Is all of you horse breakers . . . better beware,
Of an old weathered cowboy . . . that speaks out so bold,
That he used to ride 'em . . . but he's gettin' old.

These kind of cowboys have had a passion for breakin' horses and riding the best, both in ranching and rodeo, for over a hundred years. Sadly, their numbers are dwindling because of expanding urban population, four-wheelers, and a call for Government Monuments for wilderness land. But for a lucky few, the cowboy world is much the same as it was. Riding a good horse, trailing good cattle, taking care of the land, while living in God's country to most cowboys is better than a million dollars. They paint life with wit and wisdom, and like Charlie Russell, quitting is not a part of the picture.

Retiring from bronc riding? Maybe . . . but never from the cowboy lifestyle.

Marilyn Pimperton
Belt, Montana

ALICE GREENOUGH

In rodeo's beginning there were contests for women as well as men. Ladies paid entry fees and competed for prizes in bronc riding, relay races, trick riding, and roping. Several ladies of that era were top hands in a rodeo arena.

Ladies' contests were gradually phased out during the late 1930s. Relay races were seldom scheduled, paid contract performers trick rode and trick roped to fill in between cowboys' contest events, and lady bronc riders were only hired to ride exhibition.

Alice Greenough of Red Lodge, Montana, was one of the best lady bronc riders in rodeo history. She won money in ladies' bronc riding competition at rodeos from New York to California. When women's bronc riding competition faded away, Alice continued to ride saddle broncs as a featured added attraction.

Miles City, Montana, used to hold a rodeo and celebration called the Range Riders Roundup. Tooke Brothers furnished the rodeo stock for several years, from 1935 to 1941. To give you a little history of the Tooke Brothers, there were six of them. My dad, Feek, was ramrod of the rodeo outfit, and the rest helped wherever they were needed. They all were notorious pranksters, but I would rate Uncle Red at the top of the list. Red served with the Seabees in the Philippines during World War II. The Tooke family never worried about Red's fate when he was overseas; they assumed if Red was captured by the enemy, he would be the first prisoner sent back to the Allied lines.

Alice Greenough was one of the best women bronc riders in the world. COURTESY OF E. TOOKE

Alice Greenough was at the Miles City rodeo in the 1930s. She was scheduled to ride an exhibition saddle bronc at each of the three performances. Her first horse didn't do a very good job of bucking, and her second horse ran off.

After the second performance ended, as was the custom, cowboys, fans, hired help, etc. all headed for the nearest watering hole. The evening progressed nicely, and talk finally got around to the rodeo. One man leaned back against the bar and remarked that he didn't think Alice Greenough was much of a bronc rider.

"Her horses didn't buck," he said. "I could have ridden either one of them without any trouble. I figure they didn't think she could ride, or they would have picked horses that could buck."

Uncle Red was an Alice Greenough fan, and he didn't agree with the fellow who made the remark.

"She's a champion bronc rider," Red said. "She doesn't have to prove anything!"

One thing led to another, and it looked like the place was about to erupt in a brawl. Finally, the discussion led to a different subject, and the atmosphere quieted down, much to the relief of the innkeeper.

The next morning Red, assisted by Barb and Jane McVicker, sorted bucking horses for the last performance. Dad walked over to where they were standing and told Red, "Cut out the bald-faced sorrel that we talked about for Alice."

Red, Barb, and Jane continued working broncs. Finally, they had the horses in the right pens. Red said, "We've got to get that horse for Alice."

The pen they were looking in had three bald-faced sorrels. Barb asked Red, "Which one?"

Red looked at the horses a minute or two, then said, "That horse standing over there in the corner, that's the one we want." They cut the sorrel out and put him in a pen.

Along about the middle of the rodeo performance, they brought the horse in for Alice's exhibition ride. Alice got set, and they opened the chute gate. The horse exploded out of the chute as if he had been sitting on a keg of blasting powder. This was no ordinary run-of-the-mill bucking horse. Alice was mounted on a "real bucking horse"!

The horse sucked back, sunfished, turned back, and tried to kick the stars out of the sky. He threw everything he had at Alice, but when the whistle blew, she was still sitting in the saddle. Alice had put up a sensational ride on a terrible bucking horse.

The pickup men lifted Alice off the horse, and as she walked back to the chute, one cowboy remarked, "That was quite a ride!"

"Yes," Alice replied, "he was one of the toughest bucking horses I've ever ridden."

Red was hopping around, giggling and slapping people on their backs. Dad came running over to Red, and Dad's face was white as a sheet.

"Red!" he said. "How could you make such a mistake? That was one of the final horses!"

Red replied that he thought he had the right horse.

An indication of how tough the horse must have been was the fact that there were twenty-eight of the best bronc riders going up the road entered in the rodeo. They got two head. At the end of the second go-round, every bronc rider had bucked off one horse, and several were bucked off both broncs. Dad had saved his five best saddle broncs for the final ride, so the bald-faced sorrel was probably capable of throwing the horn off the saddle. On that day in Miles City, the people saw why Alice Greenough was considered to be the World Champion Lady Bronc rider.

Ernest Tooke
Ekalaka, Montana

SHEEP MOUNTAIN

In 1967 a four-year-old bucking horse put his name in the National Finals Rodeo record book. The name of the red roan bronc was Sheep Mountain, and he was selected as the Best Saddle Bronc at the conclusion of the rodeo. This horse was one of a kind, unique because of his ancestry. He had been bred and raised to be a bucking horse, and he was the very first bronc with this type of breeding background to win such an impressive award. Here was proof to the skeptics that bucking horses could be raised with the highest degree of success.

Sheep Mountain was born on the Tooke Ranch near Ekalaka, Montana. He was a product of Feek Tooke's bucking horse breeding program, which was put together in the early 1940s. Several hundred broncs were foaled on the Tooke Ranch, and there were a large number of outstanding bucking horses among them, broncs that consistently bucked down the best of the world champions. Sheep Mountain showed the rodeo world what Feek Tooke had known all along: Find the right combination to breed to, and champion bucking horses can be produced.

Sheep Mountain's first trip out of a bucking chute was at a high school rodeo when he was a three-year-old. He was sensational, bucking off a young rider the second jump. His next rodeo appearance was at Crawford, Nebraska, the following year. Bud Cooper was sorting bucking horses, and the roan horse was standing in the alleyway. Bud heard a whistle and a snort. He looked around just in time to see Sheep Mountain, from a flat-footed start, vault completely over a six-foot corral gate and land in the next pen. Doug Olson drew the horse in the bronc riding and was bucked off the third jump.

From there the horse went to Des Moines, Iowa, and he carried Shawn Davis to a first-place win in the bronc riding. Later that fall Shawn drew him again at the Chicago rodeo, and this time he was bucked off. Sheep Mountain went to the 1967 NFR and had two outstanding efforts in bucking off Kenny McLean and John Ivory. This super arena performance earned Sheep Mountain the Best Saddle Bronc award.

Sheep Mountain had every reason to be a top bucking horse. His sire, General Custer, was a remarkable animal. He was enormous in size, standing almost eighteen hands tall and weighed eighteen hundred pounds. The sight of this huge horse coming into a chute was enough to make a bronc rider's knees start shaking. He completely filled an average-sized bronc chute, and his back was level with the top plank. He had a short fuse in his disposition—anything could touch him off, and when he started fighting in a chute, there was nothing to do but wait until he settled down. He had unbelievable action for his size, and his power was awesome. When Custer bucked, he jumped very high, kicked almost straight over his head, and pumped his shoulders like a couple of piston rods. He would usually turn back the second jump.

When the big horse was in peak condition, physically and mentally, he appeared to be impossible to ride. We had him at a matched bronc riding in Miles City in 1962, and Alvin Nelson, a world champion, drew him. From the way the horse was acting, I could see that Alvin was going to have his hands full. Custer was in a really foul mood. It was the spring of the year, we had cut him away from his band of mares, and he was mad at the world. It wasn't safe to walk in a corral with the big stallion. He was ready to take his frustration out on anything or anybody. Alvin got him geared up without too much trouble, but the ride was a short one. Custer blasted Alvin out of the saddle the third jump.

In 1982 we were fortunate to have six stallions and eighty mares in our bronc herd that were descendants of General Custer.

Ernest Tooke
Ekalaka, Montana

TOOKE'S BUCKING HORSES

Back in the 1920s, the area of eastern Montana was heavily populated with homesteaders. There was little to do for entertainment, but a popular kind of fun was bronc riding. When word was passed that there would be bucking horses ridden on a certain day, people for miles around would saddle up, hitch a wagon, or fire the Model T and converge on the site. All of the early day cowboys were wild-horse hands, and they enjoyed getting together and topping out broncs. The homesteaders that didn't ride bucking horses themselves enjoyed watching the bronc riders and horses. The activity at these gatherings would last all day, and no one was ever in a hurry to go home. The spectators would loll around eating picnic lunches, some of the men would sample each others' home-brewed moonshine, and the bronc riders would ride bucking horses until it got too dark to see.

The horses were held in a rope corral; they didn't have bucking chutes, so a snubbing horse was used. The broncs were bucked on the open prairie. Occasionally, some of the more daring hands would ride a bronc with nothing but a mane hold.

My grandparents, Earl and Bessie Tooke, along with their family of six boys, were always in attendance whenever a rodeo took place. When the Tooke boys grew older, they became interested in the rough stock riding, so the brothers (Frank, Fay, Feek, Dick, Red, and Bill) decided to put on a rodeo of their own (Feek was my dad). They built an arena and a couple of bronc chutes, and the first rodeo was held on May 30, 1931. They had quite a number of wild horses of their own, and every farmer or rancher had extra horses. There were plenty of horses available. Some of the wildest bucking and riding ever seen took place at this time.

The bronc riders in those days were used to riding broncs out in the pasture. To get bucked off meant a long walk to get back home, so most of the cowboys could ride a pretty tough bucking horse. The horses gathered were fresh, wild, or spoiled saddle and workhorses. Some of the broncs were terrible bucking horses, and they were capable of throwing anyone off. At one Tooke ranch rodeo, twenty-nine broncs were bucked out and twenty-eight riders were bucked off. This was a rough way to have fun, but the bronc riders were young and used to hard knocks, so there were few injuries.

After staging a few successful rodeos at their ranch, the Tooke brothers decided to branch out. They furnished the broncs for several local rodeos, as well as at Miles City, Baker, and Billings, Montana; Deadwood and Belle Fourche, South Dakota; and Hettinger, North Dakota. They leased broncs to Leo Cremer, and in 1938 they furnished bucking horses for the rodeo in Chicago.

Dad was the ramrod of the rodeo outfit, and the rest of the boys helped wherever they were needed. Uncle Fay seemed to be the most accident-prone of the family. If anything happened to anyone, it was always Fay. They were putting on a rodeo in Ekalaka one year. One of the saddle broncs made a turn around the arena, bucking and running with the saddle. The horse was stirring up quite a dust storm, and when he made the turn in front of the chutes, the men all scattered like a flock of wild turkeys. One of the men got run over by the horse and turned a couple of somersaults before disappearing in the cloud of dust. All the men converged at the scene of the crash to render assistance. Grandmother Tooke had been sitting in the grandstand watching the rodeo. Since she was a nurse, she decided to go over to the arena and see what she could do. Just as she got to the edge of the crowd, one of the men happened to see her. He came running and said, "Don't worry, Mrs. Tooke, we don't think Fay's hurt too bad!"

Sometime during the mid-1930s, the Tookes were going to furnish bucking horses for a rodeo in Miles City. They trailed the herd of broncs across the Powder River and were going to load at a neighbor's corrals. The truckers had trucks with open-top stock racks. The first load of horses was going up the loading chute when one of the truckers screamed and threw a rock. The horses stampeded into the truck and kept going over the front of the rack, smashing the cab and hood. The trucker took one look at his truck, crammed himself inside of what remained of the cab and left as fast as he could. The rest of the truckers didn't like to think of what might happen to their trucks, so they left the country. Dad had to round up a different crew of truck drivers with closed-top stock racks, and they finally got the horses hauled to Miles City.

They had trouble after the first performance of the rodeo, which was held at night. They had to trail the bucking horses from the rodeo grounds, across the highway to the stockyards. It was dark, there were cars going by, and a thunderstorm was in progress. Just as the trail drive got to the highway, a close bolt of thunder and lightning stampeded the horses. They took off on a dead run through the middle of town. They turned down a side street and headed for a bridge across the Tongue River. The bridge was only wide enough for one vehicle. There was a Model A Ford car crossing the bridge; the lightning flashed and the driver of the car could be briefly seen—he appeared to be as white as a ghost, and his eyes were as big as silver dollars. The horses hit the bridge, but there wasn't room to go around the car, so they went over the top of it. There was a lot of banging and crashing, and finally, the last of the horses was gone.

The riders went over to what was left of the car. It looked like a couple of locomotives had used it for a punching bag. They got the door pried open, the driver scrambled out, and before anyone could say anything, he took off as fast as he could run, plowing through the brush along the river. Dad said they never did find out who the driver was. As far as he knew, the man might still be running through the Tongue River brush.

In the early 1940s Dad took over the rodeo production business and furnished rodeo stock at rodeos in a four-state area. He raised workhorses and saddle horses, and he was always trading for, or buying, bucking horse prospects. He decided to raise horses that would have the right disposition to be rodeo broncs. He bought a white Arabian stud from Mark Barrows. Mark was one of the best bronc riders that ever came from his part of the country; he had tried to break the horse to ride, but he was impossible to gentle down. He would bite, strike, and kick and was always watching for a chance to buck.

Dad shipped in a registered Shire stud called King Larego from a stud farm in Iowa. His plan was to raise workhorses from King, but he got just one colt from the big Shire stallion. He called the colt Prince. Prince's disposition wasn't suitable to use in a workhorse breeding program, so Dad crossed the colts out of Snowflake to Prince. He couldn't have found a better combination. Descendants from Prince and Snowflake have won six NFR top saddle bronc awards, as well as one third place award. Bucking horses with that bloodline are scattered from Florida to Canada. I think at least fifteen hundred bucking horses owe their origin to Prince and Snowflake.

Ernest Tooke
Ekalaka, Montana

LEO CREMER

Rodeo had many pioneers who contributed to the growth and development of the sport. Perhaps the most prominent leaders were the first rodeo producers. They promoted and worked to develop rodeo from a haphazard gathering of cowboys and animals frolicking for the fun of it to a smooth-running production that would appeal to the paying public.

Such a person was Leo Cremer. Born in Wisconsin, he attended law school at the University of Notre Dame. While there he played football on the same team with a man who as a coach at the same school in later years would take the Fighting Irish to the very top of the college gridiron ranks. The man was Knute Rockne.

Leo drifted to Montana in 1910 and filed on a homestead near Big Timber. From such a modest beginning, the Cremer ranch grew to be an eighty-thousand-acre spread. Leo saw his first rodeo in 1919 and a few years later started producing rodeos. His interest in the great western sport grew, and he spent time and money putting together the best string of bucking horses and bulls that he could find. His rodeo outfit eventually consisted of 350 bucking horses and 150 bucking bulls.

The majority of saddle broncs in rodeo's early years weighed between a thousand and twelve hundred pounds. Always an innovator, Leo gathered a herd of big draft horses for the saddle bronc event at Livingston, Montana, in 1925. When the saddle bronc riders got their first glimpse of the huge horses cut into the saddle bronc pens, they laughed and carried on as if it would be a big joke. It was—only the joke was on the bronc riders. When the riding got underway, the laughing came to an abrupt halt. Every bronc rider was bucked off. Leo returned all the entry fees to the thoroughly deflated bronc riders, and from that time on, Cremer saddle broncs were big, powerful horses, weighing from thirteen hundred to eighteen hundred pounds.

Leo Cremer was one of the first producers to introduce high-horned, big-humped, nasty-dispositioned Brahma bulls to the rodeo arena. Leo's bulls all were capable of throwing the best bull riders off, and they would eat the bull rider, a couple of clowns, a pickup man, and anyone else they could corner.

Leo didn't like to be bothered with the annual chore of replacing 'dogging steers, so he held them over two or three years. Leo was a strong believer in providing the best of feed for his animals, so naturally, the 'dogging steers grew quite large. Some would weigh eleven hundred to twelve hundred pounds. A 'dogger didn't jump down on a Cremer steer; he reached over and up. When a 'dogger got a hold on a Cremer steer, he usually went to the other end of the arena digging two furrows in the arena with his feet. The steer would finally shake the 'dogger loose and trot into the catch pen. The PRCA finally adopted a rule restricting the size of cattle and imposed a time limit of one season.

Leo booked the very best contract acts available: trick riders and ropers, clowns, horse acts, etc. His rodeos were strictly first-class productions all the way.

Rodeoing was a sideline to Leo; his primary occupation was his herd of Angus cattle, one of the biggest in the United States. He would usually produce eight to ten rodeos a year, and they were spread out over several months. His animals were always fresh and ready to give their best effort in rodeo arenas in such cities as Livingston, Billings, and Miles City, Montana; Mandan, North Dakota; Nampa, Idaho; Pueblo, Colorado; Omaha, Nebraska; St. Paul, Minnesota; Chicago, Illinois; and Casper, Wyoming.

I was fortunate that as a youngster I saw several Cremer rodeos. I will always feel a Cremer rodeo represented rodeo at its finest: the best of stock, classy and colorful contract acts, and each performance run like a well-oiled machine.

Leo Cremer was killed in a truck wreck, November 28, 1953. At the time of his death, he was one of the top three rodeo producers in the United States. His rodeo outfit was sold to Harry Knight.

Ernest Tooke
Ekalaka, Montana

FANNIE SPERRY STEELE, A RODEO LEGEND

An admirer once observed that Fannie Sperry Steele must have been born with glue on the seat of her pants. Horses were her life, and she loved equally the ones that bucked her off and the ones that served her faithfully. This champion Montana horsewoman is easy to spot in the women's mural that colors the south side of Helena's Livestock Building. Fannie sits astride a spirited pinto, an endearing detail that says a great deal about this top-notch cowgirl. When Fannie neared the end of her eventful life, she insisted, "If there are no horses in heaven, I do not want to go there."

Fannie Sperry was a first-generation Montanan. Her father, Datus Sperry, came west with his brother Myles and established a ranch along Seven Mile Creek in 1872. Seven years later her mother Rachel followed, accepting Datus's marriage proposal. Bringing little with her from Detroit but her sewing machine and some yellow-rose cuttings, Rachel arrived at Fort Benton via the steamship *Montana* on June 29, 1879. The couple married the following day.

The Sperrys moved to the Hilger Ranch in 1884, caring for the Hilger stock in exchange for the use of land. But Datus and Rachel wanted their own place and soon found a homestead at the base of the Sleeping Giant where Fannie, fourth of five children, was born in 1887. They ran a dairy, and Datus, an expert teamster, broke and trained draft horses and teams that were much in demand. An old injury prevented his riding, however, so it was Rachel who taught her five young children to sit a horse almost before they could walk. She would put the youngster on a gentle horse with stern instructions not to fall. When the child inevitably tumbled off, she would administer a swat, and right back up he or she would go. Consequently, all the Sperry children became exceptional riders and broke and shod their own horses by the time they were teenagers. Fannie and her friend Christine Synness were jubilant when they were old enough to ride their own horses to school at Mitchell (now the Sieben Ranch). They always raced the last half of the way.

Of the five Sperry children, it was Fannie who had Rachel's fierce love for horses, especially pintos, and a special way with them. On weekends she and her brother Walter would round up wild horses that roamed the hills and drive them into the corral, where Fannie rode the wildest ones. Her reputation for courage, skill, grit, and sticking power on the back of a bronc spread among the locals. The summer of 1903 at Mitchell, sixteen-year-old Fannie awed spectators with such a ride on a bucking white stallion that they passed the hat.

Soon after, Fannie was demonstrating her riding skills in Helena horse shows. Rodeo was in its infancy in 1904 when the Capital Stock Food Company of Helena sponsored her in a new kind of event inspired by Buffalo Bill Cody's "Pony Express Race." In the Montana version of this relay, racers rode only Thoroughbreds and distances varied, with riders changing horses and sometimes their own saddles, at top speed. Fannie and Christine rode such relays at Helena, Butte, and Anaconda. Butte promoter Walter R. Wilmot signed Fannie, Christine, and several others to ride relays across the Midwest in 1905. The "Montana Girls" did well, and Fannie won her first medal for meritorious riding in a twenty-four-mile relay at the Minnesota State Fair. In 1907 the "Montana Girls" scandalized crowds in their daring black riding bloomers, and Fannie began to branch out into bucking horse competitions. She earned a gold medal in Helena as women's bucking horse champion.

Wilmot gave up promoting, and Fannie competed in Montana for the next few years, but even though rodeo was such a young sport and women competitors were very few, her name was still widely known. In 1912 Guy Weadick organized the first Calgary Stampede rodeo and wrote to Fannie, inviting her to ride against five other top women competitors and enticing her with the possibility of winning big money. Despite an inauspicious beginning, the Stampede was a historic milestone and a hugely attended success.

Fannie, with her mother as chaperone, arrived at Calgary's Victoria Park on September 1, 1912, to a steady drizzle. As they toured the exhibition grounds, a commotion drew them to the horse barn, where a wild bronc named Red Wing had just thrown and stomped cowboy Joe LaMar to death. A depressed group of riders gathered for rehearsal an hour later. Weadick announced that the day's proceeds would be given to LaMar's wife and children, inspiring competitors to do their best.

Bad weather and sluggish broncs forced Weadick to extend the Stampede for two more days. The weather improved, and by the end nearly sixty thousand spectators had attended the performances. On the last day the sun shone as contestants gathered to draw the slip of paper that would influence their chances. Championship depended heavily upon the luck of the draw because the wilder the horse, the better the chances to show off one's skills. Fannie chose her slip of paper. Luck was with her: She would ride the killer outlaw, Red Wing.

Fannie's ride on Red Wing went down in rodeo history as one of the best rides ever made by a man or a woman. Fannie's success was partly because of her style of riding slick. This meant that she rode without tying her stirrups under the horse's belly. Tying the stirrups was called hobbling, a concession judges allowed women contestants. Most women rode their broncs with the stirrups tied together for greater stability in the saddle; it was almost like being tied onto the horse. But hobbling was very dangerous because in the event of a tumble, it was impossible for the rider to kick free.

Fannie viewed hobbling as unfair to the horse since it did not give the animal a fifty-fifty chance of bucking off its rider. Slick riding, however, demanded precision, balance, courage, and unusual strength. Fannie was the only woman rider among her contemporaries to ride her entire career slick, just like her male counterparts. That day at Calgary it was part skill, part style, and part luck that gained her the title of "Lady Bucking Horse Champion of the World." She won $1,000 cash, a $300 gold belt buckle, and a beautiful saddle with hand-tooled roses. Many decades later a reporter asked her if she was scared when she came out of the chute. Fannie replied matter-of-factly, "You just forget about being scared when you ride horses."

Fannie was a lovely slip of a young woman, ladylike and well brought up despite her bronc-riding prowess. Young men stood in line to be her dance partner, but Fannie cared more for horses than cowboys until she met bronc rider and rodeo clown Bill Steele. The couple was married in a ceremony at the Diamond Block in Helena in 1913. More than sixty years later, Fannie recalled the day with nostalgia. Although she favored saddle-worn divided leather riding skirts, on her wedding day she wore a very feminine gown of deep-blue gabardine with a high lace collar and a flounce that concealed its plunging neckline. Bill gave her a corsage of red roses that she pinned over her heart. The newlyweds spent their honeymoon rodeoing, and Fannie won the title "Woman's Champion Bronco Buster" at Winnipeg that summer. But the exciting year had a tragic end. Fannie's girlhood chum and riding partner, Christine Synness Craig, died in November following a difficult surgery. The event was one that Fannie never quite got over.

Fannie and Bill traveled the rodeo circuit and even performed with Buffalo Bill Cody in 1916 at the Chicago Shan-Kive, one of Cody's last headlining appearances. Both Fannie and Bill were crack shots and put on shooting exhibitions across the country. Among other tricks, Fannie would shoot the ashes off Bill's cigar. She rode bucking Brahma bulls bareback and some of the meanest, most famous broncs. One was a horse named Midnight that could arch his back into an inverted "V," tossing his rider into the air, then sidestepping so that when the rider came down, it wouldn't be on the saddle. She was one of few who successfully rode that bronc in New York City, riding slick and sticking in the saddle like a cocklebur.

The Steeles ranched north of Helena and supplied bucking stock to rodeos across the country. Fannie competed until 1925, when she rode her last bronc in competition at Bozeman. (She was still riding exhibition broncs, however, at fifty.) The couple bought a dude ranch at Arrastra Creek near Lincoln in 1927, and their lives changed. Horses, of course, remained central. They kept a string of pintos that were Bill's favorites, too.

Bill died in 1940, and Fannie then ran the ranch by herself for another twenty-five years. She was one of the first women to receive a packer's license, and well into her sixties spent long days in the saddle guiding hunters into rough country. She stocked Meadow Creek before environmental concerns were fashionable, packing six horses with cans of fish over treacherous terrain, stopping at every stream to keep the water cool. Until her retirement Fannie shod and broke her own horses to pack, did her own packing, and at the end of the season trailed her twenty-five head of pintos seventy miles across the Continental Divide to winter in the pastures where she used to ride as a child.

In 1974 at eighty-seven, Fannie could no longer live alone. She had long fretted about it. "My greatest worry will be the well being of my pintos. I can leave the range, since I have had a full share of life on it. I can quit the ranch and ranch house and my souvenirs, but I hate like hell to leave my pintos behind." She spent nearly another decade at the Cooney Convalescent Home in Helena and in 1975 was one of the first of three women inducted into the Rodeo Hall of Fame. A few years later, at ninety, Fannie summed up her life. "To the yesterdays that are gone, to the cowboys I used to know, to the bronc busters that rode beside me, to the horses beneath me (sometimes), I take off my hat. I wouldn't have missed one minute of it." Fannie died in 1983. She was the quintessential Montana woman, homegrown, determined, gritty, and, most of all, independent of spirit.

Ellen Baumler
Helena, Montana

"QUEEN OF THE COWGIRLS"

For many years Red Lodge, Montana, has held a big rodeo on July 4 called the Home of Champions Rodeo. The name of the rodeo was well chosen: Red Lodge was the home of Bill Dygert; Bill, Bud, and Doug Linderman; and Turk, Bill, Marge, and Alice Greenough. No town will ever produce a greater group of rodeo champions. Each was a real hand, either in a rodeo or in a pasture.

Packsaddle Ben Greenough saw to it that his children learned to ride and handle horses as soon as they could walk. His family learned fast. Three of them would go on to become celebrated in rodeo arenas throughout the United States, as well as in several foreign countries.

Alice Greenough got the urge to rodeo from her brother Turk, a real tough in the saddle bronc event. She rode in her first rodeo when she was fourteen, marking the beginning of a long and colorful career in forty-six states, Canada, Mexico, Spain, France, and England.

Alice rode saddle broncs, bareback horses, and steers, and during the late 1920s she trick rode. She was seriously injured by a bucking horse in 1930, and it was two years before she was able to compete in a rodeo arena again. In 1932 Alice traveled to Spain and took a job riding the fierce bulls into the bullfighting rings. She would ride a bull until the matador distracted him with his cape, then she would jump off and run for the fence. After several hazardous months of bull riding, Alice went on tour riding broncs in England and France.

When she returned to the United States, the tough training in Spain and Europe paid off. She won her first big bronc riding contest at the Boston Garden in 1933. The '32 tour in the foreign countries had whetted Alice's desire to travel, so she made the long trip to Australia in 1934. It was there she won the International Championship in ladies' bronc riding and steer riding. She again won the ladies' bronc riding in Boston in 1935 and '36. She returned to Australia in '39 and won her second International Championship. Finally, after several years of finishing second, she won the ladies' bronc riding in New York in '40.

The ladies' contest events were dropped from rodeo programs in the early '40's, so Alice and her sister Marge continued to ride exhibition bucking horses. Alice rode her last bucking horse at Greybull, Wyoming, in 1959.

In 1943 Alice and Joe Orr, a former bull rider, founded the Greenough-Orr Rodeo Company. They went into rodeo production with a determination to represent the best shows possible. Alice served as rodeo secretary and chute boss. Joe took care of the stock and flanked the horses and bulls. Their rodeos were well run, the kind the paying public likes to see.

They put together an outstanding set of bucking stock, a good herd to draw into as there were no "canners" in the string. The cowboys knew that any animal they drew was capable of bucking them off, and if a rider did any job at all, he was going to go to the pay window. It was not unusual for a Greenough-Orr rodeo to pay ground money in all three riding events.

Some of their best broncs were Ryan Special, Blue Heaven, Bear Paw, Double Trouble, Calico Pete, Lame Deer, Mexico Joe, Buckskin Joe, and Kid Farnum. The bull I remember the best was #25, Rusty. I got crippled up every time I got on that bull. I couldn't ride him, and he always gave me a good hooking with his horns.

Some of the Montana towns and their rodeos played were Red Lodge, Havre, Forsyth, Miles City, Baker, Sidney, Terry, Glendive, Lewistown, Shelby, Dodson, and Wolf Point. They produced rodeos in other states as well. North Dakota sites were Killdeer, Sanish, Newtown, Medora, and Dickinson. They were at Idaho Falls and

Salmon, Idaho; Milwaukee, Wisconsin; Calgary, Medicine Hat, and Red Deer in Canada; and Greybull and Cody, Wyoming.

The Greenough-Orr rodeos were sold to the Fettig Brothers of Killdeer in 1958. Alice continued to serve as a rodeo secretary and was chute boss for the Miles City Bucking Horse Sale for several years. She made her home in Tucson, Arizona, but each time July 4 rolled around, she returned to her home country, the Home of Champions Rodeo in Red Lodge.

I doubt if we will ever have another lady as versatile around a rodeo as Alice Greenough. I think those of us who had the privilege of knowing this fine lady will feel that she was the "Queen of the Cowgirls."

Ernest Tooke
Ekalaka, Montana

YOU THINK THE BULL RIDING IS TOUGH!

The following incidents took place in the early 1930s, and the setting was at the Tooke Ranch.

Granddad Tooke purchased a milk cow from Homer Pulse. We Tookes called the cow "Pulse." An excellent milk cow, Pulse was gentle; anyone could milk her, and she produced two big pails of milk every day. One thing Pulse wouldn't tolerate, however, was anyone sitting on her back. Someone (I don't know who) jumped on one day and almost got tossed through the roof of the milking shed. From that day on, every cow rider had to try Pulse, and she had a perfect record of buck-offs.

Frog Roberts was at the ranch, and he decided to show the other hands how to ride. They mounted Frog on Pulse, and he took his best wrap with an old rope. The hands pointed the cow downhill, and all hell broke loose. The third jump, Pulse really threw a "dark one" at Frog, and he flew through the air as if he had been fired out of a giant slingshot. He landed on his belly and drove his head under a corral gate. There was only about six inches of clearance between the gate and the ground, so they almost had to take the gate off the hinges to get Frog's head out.

Then Uncle Red decided to test Pulse. Red got ready; then his helpers let Pulse loose in a corral made of ash poles. After two wicked jumps Pulse pitched Red through the air, and he crashed into the side of the corral, head first. He hit the fence with enough force to drive his head through the space between two poles. Red was left hanging from the top part of the corral with his head wedged through the fence. Everyone watching was in hysterics from laughing, until finally, someone noticed that Red was probably getting short on air, as he started turning purple. It took a considerable amount of twisting and pulling to get Red out of the fence.

FROG'S FLIGHT

E. Tooke

Pulse was an exemplary milk cow, until the boys tried to ride her! COURTESY OF E. TOOKE

Uncle Dick had quite a crush on a gal, but she didn't seem to be paying as much attention to him as he felt she should. No doubt about it—Dick would have to do something fantastic to get her interested. It happened that the ranch was holding one of the annual rodeos. A cowboy planned to ride a wild Hereford cow, but she was really on the fight, and the cowboy lost his nerve. This presented Dick a chance to impress the gal, so he jumped down off the arena fence and said, "I'll take her!"

Helpers finally got Dick set on the cow and opened the chute gate. The cow threw Dick over her head, and when he hit the ground, she was on top of him. She mauled him around until Dick finally got loose and jumped up and started to run. Half his clothes were torn off, and he was skinned up and bleeding. The cow chased Dick completely across the arena; every other step she would hook him, and Dick would scream and holler as loud as he could. Dick's plan to impress the gal backfired—she laughed so hard she almost fell off the arena fence.

Bull riding at today's rodeos is an exciting event to watch, but it is doubtful anything can match cow riding at the Tooke ranch in the early days of rodeo.

Ernest Tooke
Ekalaka, Montana

COULD'A WATCHED IT FOR NOTHIN'!

We had a friend come by, and he'd been to the Hardin rodeo and been doing a little drinking. Charles decided they'd go ride out in the pasture and look at some cows, so they went out there. Charles was telling him this big windy as they rode along, waving his arms, and he lost his rein, and it wrapped around the front foot of his horse.

So he got bucked off in the cactus, and in the process I don't know where he lost his spur, but he never did find it. This guy that was with him laughed and laughed. And he said, "Here I went and paid good money to watch the bronc ridin' and I could'a watched it for nothin'!"

(If he hadn't a-been BS'ing so fast, waving his arms around and lost his rein, it would have never happened.)

Ginger May
Wife of Charles May
Hysham, Montana

CHAPTER 5

BLAZING THE WAY

REMEMBER ALL THOSE DAYS

Remember all those days when we had to ride,
Lovely horses, warm clothes,
Silk stocking pulled on like a stocking hat,

Marliee Calk and her brother James "Spike" Calk on horseback, Jim Calk, Emma Calk (parents), Rebecca Calk and Joe John Calk (boy in hat) at the ranch on Steve's Fork, west of Jordan. COURTESY OF WANDA ROSSELAND

Beneath our rain breaker,
And we wore two pair of Levi pants,
Mittens that didn't match but were warm,
And horses that wouldn't buck. 1938

Marilee Calk Whitmer
Christmas 2000

ON THE POWDER RIVER

I left Cherokee, Cherokee County, Iowa, May 8, 1883, with my parents, who were expecting to go to Coeur d'Alene, Idaho, to try the West. They had thirty-six cattle, three covered wagons, and one three-seated spring wagon for the family. My job was to drive the cattle on a buckskin pony with a dog. We ferried the Big Missouri River at Pierre, South Dakota, on the fifth day of July. I was left on the cattle barge with my pony; while crossing it, it seemed the biggest body of water I had ever seen. [Moreau was eleven years old at this time.]

The ship pulled up the river, it seemed a half mile or more, and then struck across, and the current carried it downstream. It could hardly make the landing and had to turn so short that the cattle barge, on the end I was in, dipped water and most one foot of water ran across it. I thought I was a goner, but we made it okay.

At that time all the freight for the Black Hills (then in the big gold excitement) came over that trail by ox or mule teams, usually about twenty head of stock hitched in a team with three wagons trailing. We came from Pierre to Rapid City, on to Fort Meade and to Spearfish. Met up with Nation Hockett, and we all traveled the stage road that ran from Spearfish to Miles City.

By the time we got to Powder River at Powderville on August 3, Pap Hockett had my folks talked into locating on Powder River, as he had come out the year before (1882) with three hundred cattle and turned them loose on the range, and they had wintered well. He went back to Iowa and brought five hundred more, which he was taking to Powder River when we met him. On reaching Powderville, we went down the river twenty-eight miles to the mouth of Alkali Creek, where we squatted on government land and built a home.

The next year I went to work for the outfit belonging to Moran Brothers and Thompson. My first roundup was at the horseshoe bend on Powder River. At that time in Custer County there were twenty-six different outfits that met there to start the roundup; and after the first roundup they split. Some worked up the river, and the others down.

There were perhaps three hundred cowboys. Each outfit had from three thousand to fifty thousand head of cattle on the range. After the spring roundup I had to go home to help with the stock, as Dad thought stock should have a dry place to stay in. By this time he was about out of money, so we got our meat by hunting deer, antelope, chicken, and sometimes a buffalo.

I stayed at home part of the time and worked for different cow outfits until 1886, when I went to work for the HashKnife outfit. They

Moreau "Roe" and Lacy Speelmon, circa 1900. COURTESY OF SANDY SPEELMON

were at that time trailing their cattle from Texas and New Mexico, mostly yearlings and two-year-olds. (However, I worked on the range most of the time.)

(*Editor's note:* By "range" Mr. Speelmon means riding as a cowboy taking care of the cattle in southeastern Montana.)

We would do the rounding up, brand the calves, and gather the beef as their (the HashKnife outfit) range covered all the country from the Sioux reservation on the east to Powder River on the west, and from the Northern Pacific Railroad on the north to the Wyoming line on the south. And they had representation on the trail clear through to Texas.

They would work with cow outfits on the range near the trail and gather stock that was lost out of the trail herds, or any stock with the HashKnife brand on, as that outfit would not sell any stock, only on the market.

On the range we quite often gathered the beef and got a herd (perhaps two thousand head), and when the trail outfits turned their herd loose, they would take the beef herd to the RR most of the time to Dickinson, North Dakota; ship them to Chicago; get their pass changed; and ride the same distance to Texas. And some of them would come up year after year.

Meanwhile, we would work on the range until we got the work all done, which would be about November 20; then we would get laid off until the next spring. We were always welcome to make the ranch our home in the winter.

They generally had four or five outfits' wagons on the range in the summer. Each wagon would have about twelve men, including boss, cook, and nighthawk to herd the saddle horses. Our sport was seeing the boys get thrown off, see who could catch his horse or chase a horse that got away with the rope on while catching a fresh horse. Sometimes we'd catch a team that was running and go to town when we could.

The spring of 1888 I was put with the beef wagon to issue beef to the Sioux Indians at Fort Yates on the Missouri River. We would take a herd about June 15 and start to the reservation, about four hundred miles away, and have to be there to issue beef every two weeks from three hundred to five hundred head at a time. When we ran out, we would come back along the trail and meet another herd that had been started so we could get to the agency in two weeks.

I was sent back in 1890 on the same job, and now they were to issue five thousand head to them for their winter beef. My boss started me back to meet another herd to pilot them to the agency. He said they would be at the Deadwood and Mandan stage crossing, about eighty miles away.

I put my bed on one horse and my saddle on another. The cook fixed me up a dinner, and I pulled out. At noon I ate my dinner. What I didn't eat, I threw away. After resting a while I started on. Went to Grand River—no herd in sight. Started up the river and rode until dark. Was afraid I would miss them in the dark, so I staked my horses and went to bed without anything to eat.

Got up at daylight and rode all day. Stayed all night again and did the same thing next day. No herd, so I stayed another night, all this time without anything to eat. Started the next morning and had made up my mind I would ride to the ranch without any more stops, but about 9 a.m. I ran into the herd. Stopped the wagon, got some cold steak and biscuits, and had to turn around and make the trip over. Made the trip okay.

Then the Indians were getting on the warpath. Sitting Bull was on the fight, but we got away okay. Made it to the ranch, got what little money we had coming paid off for that year. So I went home to Ekalaka.

My parents were keeping a little hotel there. I had not been home long when Sitting Bull, with some of his warriors, got away from the guards and started west. Fort Keough was notified and started troops out to get ahead of him. They sent couriers out to notify the settlers. One came to Ekalaka about 11 p.m. Father came to the bunkhouse and awoke me and two brothers and said we had better saddle our horses and leave at once to tell families that we knew of.

We divided our route. I rode to Spring Creek to what was later the

Newbury Ranch and around the Chalk Buttes and back to the pine hills to different places and on to Ekalaka. When I got there most of the settlers were there. It was my job to scout the country to see if there were any Indians in sight. They stayed about ten days before we got word that Sitting Bull was killed and the rest returned to the reservations.

As not many of the neighbors brought much to eat, food soon got scarce. It was 125 miles to the RR so I decided to furnish the meat. I would go get a HashKnife beef, bring it to Ekalaka, kill it in the streets where all could see what it was, as I figured we had just as well be killed by Indians as to starve. I sent Bill LaForce word of what I was doing. He was the foreman of the HashKnife. He sent me word to kill all we needed and no charge.

After a year or two, I quit trying to make any money working eight or nine months a year. I was getting to be one of the bunch and had to spend with them. Therefore, I just had enough to buy two horses, but my credit was good. I could borrow from the people that had money, so I went to speculating, dealing in stock—horses mostly.

I bought Father's ranch on Speelmon Creek and about one hundred head of cattle. Kept my credit good so I could get enough cash to turn a deal any time, and I did very well as long as the range was open—as stock wintered on the range, on government land, and did my own work.

In 1894 I sold my ranch and cattle on Speelmon Creek, bought J. P. Hedges' relinquishment on the Russle Creek, filed on it for a homestead, and bought back into cattle in a small way. Dealt in horses; by this time had a nice bunch of horses and was always looking for more if I thought I could make some money on them.

In 1896 I married and began to raise kids along with my other stock. Each year I would buy a bunch of horses and take them along with what I raised that was ready and go down across the Missouri and sell them. After a few years at this, we went into trying to raise better horses, both draft and saddle stock. Had very good luck with cavalry horses for the government.

It grew into a bunch of cattle, perhaps five hundred head, and about the same of horses. I would buy small ranches or farms, use them for pasture mostly, as the country was beginning to settle up, and water holes near the feed homesteaded and stock crowded back.

After about 1916 it reached the peak and went the other way on account of settlers, dry seasons, hail, winter, drop in prices (horses especially), high taxes, high cost of living, so by 1922 I was out of business. Gave up my land to my creditors and left Montana.

Moreau B. Speelmon
Sandy Speelmon, Grandson of Moreau
Miles City, Montana

(*Editor's note:* Moreau Speelmon was fourteen years old when he rode on the Powder River spring roundup with three hundred cowboys and seventeen when he took beef to Fort Yates from the HashKnife outfit.)

A MIDNIGHT RIDE

T'was midnight in a lonely cabin,
Far distant from the busy throng.
A mother's life was truly ebbing
A faint surmise of what was wrong.
Her children stood around her bedside,
And tried to soothe their Mother's pain.
A Father too, much worn and worried,
Did what he could, but all in vain.

A knock. "Come in." A Cowboy entered:
The cowboy said, "I thought it strange,
To see a midnight light a burning,

When coming in from off the range.
Oh, yes I see, a doctor's needed."
The cowboy said in firm like way,
"The horse I'm riding won the races,
A doctor'll be here 'fore break of day."

The clock struck one and all was quiet,
Save sounds of hoofs of the cowboy's horse.
Soon faintly sounding in the distance,
As rider sped along his course.
O'er rugged hills and down the valley
The rider rode that chilly night.
At race-horse speed he kept on riding,
Until he saw a dim town light.

A doctor soon received the message,
And long before the break of day,
Could have been seen the full moon shining,
On doctor and driver on their way.
For miles and miles they kept on driving,
The farther on, the faster they rode,
And finally reached that lonely cabin,
The sick woman's place of abode.

Instead of sadness there was gladness
A mother's life was saved that night,
And one more little member added,
Which filled that home with much delight.
'Tis like a dream to one remaining,
Who bore the trials of frontier days,
But such was life on Western Prairies,
O those who braved to blaze the way.

A friend those days was like a brother,
They faltered not, nor did they fear,
To save a friend in time of trouble,
To heave a sigh or shed a tear.
Those friends so true beneath the clay,
Their valiant deeds will be recorded,
'Til generations pass away.

Corrydon W. Wilson
1904

William Brandt, the cowboy in "Midnight Ride" in the 1880s.
COURTESY OF SONJA CROCKER

C. W. Wilson came to Montana in 1880, settling east of Miles City in what is now the Sheffield area, where he and his brother established a ranch. He wrote of the history and the true stories of the area in the form of poetry. He was "cowboy" with pen in hand. In 1931 one of his books of poems was published.

"A Midnight Ride" tells of his brother-in-law, Charles F. Brandt, who was a cowboy for the XIT Cattle Company, and of Dr. Bruning, a doctor of Miles City.

Sonja Crocker
Great-granddaughter of C. W. Wilson
Rosebud, Montana

A natural poet, Corrydon (C. W.) Wilson illustrated in rhythmic verse the early years of cowboying and ranching in Montana.
COURTESY OF SONJA CROCKER

BEN WILSON

I thought I would record a few old history stories from northern Garfield County, where my dad and mom both homesteaded in the early days. My dad left home when he was fifteen years old; he had a fight with his dad, and he went and lived with his brother in Kalamazoo, Michigan, that winter. The next spring he got with a circus and headed west 'cause he'd had some uncles that were buffalo hunters that hunted out here for the forts, and he wanted to get out West. He got as far as the Dakotas with this circus, and then he got on a threshing crew and threshed through the Dakotas. He lied about his age, claimed he was twenty-one when he was only sixteen then, and wound up here in Montana around the Park at Livingston. He worked for ranchers around there and drove the stage in the Park one summer.

Well, there was a small rancher up there who decided to go down to northern Garfield County where it wasn't surveyed yet, where you had squatter's rights to homestead. Dad took the rancher's horses down there for him, and he kinda liked the looks of the country. He went back to the mountains and then went back down to Garfield County in 1912 and got squatter's rights on this land next to Charley Crane's. Dad had gone to the Army in World War I, then came back to settle in Garfield County. Dad packed for the surveyors, and they surveyed that rough country, and then he homesteaded.

My mom came out to visit her girlfriend, Agnes Crane, who had married Charley Crane, and brought her little boy because her husband was stepping out on her and she wanted to get away from him. She came out to visit, got a divorce, and then Dad and her got to going together and got married. So that's how they got started together in Garfield County, and they put a pretty good outfit together there, for most of their lives.

One day Dad was out helping the neighbors saw, getting some lumber for his cabin, and a guy rode up there and asked the way to the Missouri River. He was wanting to go across the Missouri, and Dad told him to go down the Trotter Ridge, which went by his cabin, and right there at the mouth of Seven Blackfoot, he could cross the river without swimming a horse.

The Seven Blackfoot creek was named after seven Indians that were hung there for stealing horses in the early days. The guy thanked him and went. Dad went home that night—they were having a dance at the schoolhouse for the Fourth of July—and there was this guy's dirty clothes in the middle of his cabin. And Dad's new overalls, shirt, and the pair of socks that his mom had made him were missing.

So Dad got back on his horse, and he went down to the mouth of Blackfoot where Trotters lived, and it just happened that Jim Trotter was deputy sheriff of Garfield County then, Dawson County I guess it was then, it wasn't even Garfield yet, and Dad rode up there, and he said, "Jim, that son-of-a-gun stole my clothes and we're going after him."

And Jim said, "Well, Ben, let's stay and go to the dance. We'll go after him in the morning."

Dad says, "No, we're going after him now."

They rode all night, and they caught him over on the north side, right in Phillips County then, and they took him into Malta, which was about sixty miles from where they started, and took him to the sheriff. He was wanted, this guy, and they were glad to see him. Dad said he didn't look so damn smart standing there in jail in his underwear.

Can you imagine riding that far for your clothes? Well, that's all the clothes Dad had. He didn't have any others, but what he was wearing.

This is a story about my brother. It was in December, the ninth of December; he wanted to go out with his dogs and look for rabbits in the horse pasture there, and Mom dressed him real warm and she let him go. A fog came up and came in, and Raymond got lost. Then it started to snow and covered up his tracks.

They started looking for him the next morning and couldn't find him anywhere. They really alerted everybody, and they had thirty riders looking for Raymond off in that Seven Blackfoot, which is a pretty big rough country on both sides of it, and they rode there, every dang place up and down those ridges, and they couldn't find any sign of him.

It was snowy, and it was down fairly chilly at night, got down to about ten above. The third day they were riding down in the creek, and Charley Phipps and Ed Nickoles saw this track come across, going towards home. And it was a dog track. Dad thought it was a coyote track, and Charley said, "No. That's a dog track, that's not a coyote track."

So they backtracked that darn dog track, and they got clear up on the east side of Blackfoot, and right down in some cedars, well, here was Raymond with the other dog setting in there and still alive. So they gathered him up and brought him home, and he come out of it, but he was out there two nights in that cold weather and survived, and the dogs kept him warm.

My mom's hair wasn't gray when this happened, and her hair was snow white when this was over with; she really worried and done a lot of walking herself.

Dad was selected for jury, for sheep stealing. At that time Glendive was the county seat, and Jordan, well, it wasn't even Garfield; they hadn't split Garfield and McCone counties off of it, so he rode horseback from home to Glendive, which is 150 miles. Took an extra horse, of course, and there were quite a few people who lived along the way where he could bum a meal, I s'pose. It took him three days to get there, and they turned the sheep stealer loose, the judge did, so he rode back home again. I s'pose he drawed mileage, but it would be kinda slow mileage.

About 1960 Dad and Mom were getting older, and they turned the ranch over to me and moved out to California and bought a home out there. I operated that ranch for about twenty-five years, and then they were getting to where they were going to force me off the lake, and that was all of our summer grazing. So I found a guy that wanted to buy, and I traded for a ranch up here in the Judiths. I operated that for three years, and then I retired here in Lewistown. I still own the ranch, but

I've got it leased to a nice young couple. That was the hardest thing I've ever done in my life was to sell that ranch down there, but I was gittin' too old to ride that rough country; there was quite a bit of it—we had about twenty-seven thousand acres of it, lot of it government land all right, but I was getting too old for it, and so I traded for this one up here, which was a lot easier.

Tom Wilson
Lewistown, Montana

C. L. ASKIN

C. L. Askin was born in the Ismay area, September 4, 1914, to George and Cora Foster Askin, one of ten children. His parents homesteaded south of Ismay in 1909, moving there from Sioux Falls, South Dakota. When he was a young lad, C. L. began breaking horses, along with older brothers Hank, George, and Bob. Roping intrigued him from the time of his youth, most especially team roping, and he became one of the best team-roping heelers and horse trainers in Eastern Montana. When he grew older he worked with his brother George, drilling water and gas wells in the Baker, Montana, area.

On December 28, 1936, C. L. married a beautiful young lady by the name of Shirley Belle Ruenholl. They lived in the Ismay area until 1958, when they moved to Baker, Montana, buying some acreage a quarter of a mile north of Baker in 1959, where he moved a house and a barn and eventually built his arena of life, spending the next thirty-seven years there with his children, Sharon, Rodney, Shirley, Peggy and Connie Jim; his grandchildren; great-grandchildren; and hundreds of friends.

C. L. was very well noted for his great quarter horses. Among these were Steve Reed, which he purchased at the Denver Stock Show in 1954. Later on other great horses were Scooter, Stormy, Zipper, and, lastly, his pride and joy, Roanie, which in 1988 was named Fallon County Super Cow Horse.

Over the years C. L. won several saddles, bridles, bits, spurs, belt buckles, and other prizes. In 1967 he won his first saddle in the breakaway roping in the Northwest Ranch Cowboy Association Finals. Others followed, but his most prized was the saddle that Guy Howell won while riding Roanie, which he presented as a gift to C. L.

When seventy-five years old, C. L. competed in the Century Roping held in Richardton, North Dakota, and won. Five years later at his eightieth birthday party held in Baker, C. L. roped against over a hundred teams and posted the fastest time of the competition.

He also had a talent for braiding headstalls, reins, and other horse gear and tried his hand at making saddles, one of them being a trick riding saddle that he made for his niece, Birdie Askin. One of the saddles that he made for his kids has been used by both his grandchildren and great-grandchildren.

C. L. followed all ages of people in their rodeo careers. He would always be there to cheer you on, give helpful advice, loan you a saddle, let someone rope in his arena anytime, and, if you were lucky, ride his

C. L. and Bob Askin's mother, Cora, riding sidesaddle on Main Street in Ismay, Montana.
COURTESY OF SHARON ASKIN FERREL

horse. If he heard someone complaining about a judge, flagger, etc., he would always say, "That's the way they saw it, so don't fret over it. Just go on and do better next time."

Sharon Askin Ferrel
Baker, Montana

MY GRANDDAD, STEVE MARMON SR.

Steve Marmon Sr., my granddad, was born in 1862 and at the ripe old age of thirteen ran away from home and took the steamboat *Far West* to the Dakota Territory, arriving at Fort Abraham Lincoln soon after General Custer left to get his just reward in southeastern Montana. He spent his early years engaged in various cowboy occupations in both the Montana and Dakota Territories, finally settling near Williston before the turn of the century.

The following are several events in his life that have become family stories.

Steve ran about 750 head of horses on government land north of Williston. He thought it would take a century to fill up the country with homesteaders. The Norwegians did it in less than ten years. He was forced to move.

In 1915 homesteading opened up in Montana, and Granddad settled twenty miles north of Wolf Point, taking his herd of horses along.

While trailing his herd of horses and one milk cow to Montana, one of the disgruntled hired hands asked Steve why he brought a milk cow along. Steve replied, "I just wanted to keep you boys from running the horses too hard."

In 1882 Steve was freighting for Frank Whitney. The origin of the freight lines were steamboat landings or railroad depots. As the Northern Pacific Railroad was being built across southern Montana, the gold camps north of Lewistown needed supplies, as well as the town ahead of the to-be-constructed railroad. They used bull teams to haul freight. They were slow, but oxen were strong and could pull heavy loads.

They also kept mules with each freight train. At night they would tie the mules close to the campfire, where cowboys would take shifts watching the mules. As mules are an intelligent and perceptive animal (believe it or not), they possess the uncanny ability to detect movement in the distance. With mules on guard, no Indian could sneak up on the sleeping cowboys. All one had to do was watch the mules, and when they appeared to be interested in some movement out on the prairie, there was something or someone out there sneaking around in the dark.

As a side note for the history books, one mule was named Holey Nose, as he had a bullet hole clear through the nose, going from one side to the other.

One night the freighters were camped near Custer, Montana. There was a schoolhouse dance going on, and Steve and the other teamsters stopped in for the doings. One of the "barflies," as Steve put it, was Calamity Jane, and she was not sober. Remember, she was not famous at that time.

The dance was in full swing when two fellas got into an argument. They decided to go outside and shoot it out. Well, they did just that. They buried the dead one and never stopped the dance until dawn.

Granddad told about stopping down to the Crow reservation and racing horses. They would take a break from freighting and ride south for some fun. Well, they had a plan. Not that the races were rigged, but kinda sorta was.

You see, they would race their fastest horse against the Indians' fastest horse and deliberately lose by a nose. Then they would retire their horse until the last race. In the meanwhile they would race their other horses against the Indians' fastest horse, tiring that horse out. Then on the last race they would race their horse again against the Indians' fastest horse, betting all their money. Naturally, they would win, as their horse was still fresh.

In the winter of 1885/86, Granddad hired on to help move cows for an outfit. The ranch boss told Steve Sr. that if he got busted up while moving cows, they would have to leave him there on the frozen prairie up to several days, until they could get back to pick him up. So he'd better be dressed for it.

The rest of the story takes place in the middle 1940s, when Granddad was kicked by a mule in the barn and his leg was broken. Dr. Knapp X-rayed his leg before setting it and commented, "Looks like you broke your leg before."

Steve replied that he'd never had a broken leg. Then Dr. Knapp showed Steve the X-ray, revealing a mended area of the bone.

"Back in the winter of '85/'86," said Steve, "I was kicked mighty hard while trying to mount a horse."

In the spring of 1916, my dad, Steve Jr., was born. He came three months early, and the timing couldn't have been worse. The milk cow was dry and going to have a calf in a couple of weeks. Well, milking range cows was a bit of a chore. One would have to rope the cow and cinch her down to a post, then lay a rope around the hind legs as she fought and turned and twisted. And if she did not fall on her side fighting and choking herself, you were in position to straddle the bucket between your legs, wedge yourself under her udders, and hope she would give down a quart of milk, provided one of her hind legs didn't come free.

It so happened that Charlie Myers, a homesteader that lived ten miles north of Steve, had been in the habit of letting his milk cow graze the prairie during the days and towards evening bringing her in to milk. A couple of times he couldn't find her, but she would show up the next morning, needing to be milked.

This time she didn't show, and Charlie was too busy putting his wheat crop in to go out and find her. He figured some neighbor would return the cow and wasn't worried. A couple weeks later he finally had the time and rode south looking for his cow. As he topped a hill, he saw a rider on a green broke horse getting the ride of his life. This horse was doing his best to rid himself of the rider.

Being a good neighbor, Charlie rode down to help. As he approached Steve Sr. on the bucking horse, Steve went a-flying and did a midair flip. He landed on his feet, saw Charlie, and without breaking motion took off his hat and bowed.

Several times Charlie told me this story. As Charlie put it, "That was the most unique welcome I ever had." Yes, Charlie got his milk cow back as Steve's cow now had a calf and was giving milk.

When the automobile came into its own, many of the old-timer cowboys had a devil of a time adapting to it. Little things, like using the rearview mirror, befuddled them. As everything in the mirror is backward, Granddad chose not to use it. He would look back, deciding where he wanted to go, then look straight forward and back up. He backed over several of my toys.

One night, long after Steve and his wife, Tony, went to bed, there was the noise of a motor car outside and someone shouting their names. It was Art Christman, a neighbor that lived four miles west, up Dry Fork. He was driving his Model T car around and around the house. Well, Steve went to the front door to see what the matter was. Here came Chris around the house going lickety-split. He drove past Granddad and tossed him some mail. The next time he came around, he tossed more mail. Again and again he looped the house delivering "air mail," then drove home.

Art and these newfangled cars didn't mix. Evidently, Art never got the hang of starting this finicky early car; thus, he didn't shut it off, unless he was at home or in town where he could get someone to start it for him.

I asked Dad how he got the car started at home. Dad said that Art would harness the team and hitch them to the car. Then he would turn the knob on the dash back and forth and move each lever on the steering wheel up and down until the car started. Then he would pull a slack rope that untied the knot, thus freeing the horses to graze while he was gone.

Dad told a story of one old cowboy who decided to buy a car and drive it home from Wolf Point with little to no instruction. Upon arriving at his ranch, he realized that this newfangled car wouldn't stop when he yelled "Whoa." He then pulled up on the steering wheel. Of course, all good horsemen know that if a horse doesn't stop for you, you just turn the horse into the corrals, and he will stop. Well, the corrals stopped the car and darn near killed the cowboy.

When my dad, Steve Jr., was a youngster in the early 1920s, Chief Frank Redstone gave him his Indian name. Granddad and several wranglers were breaking horses to sell. Steve Jr. was there on the corral fence watching and wanting to ride a colt. He finally convinced one of the wranglers to let him get on one of the tame colts. So he wouldn't be in the way, they let Steve ride the colt outside the corrals.

The colt ran off into some buck brush and bucked Steve off. Seeing what happened, the cowboys ran over to him. Poor Steve was all scratched and bleeding from the thorns. They took him to the house.

In the days to come, Steve's face was covered with scabs. Frank took one look at him and called him "Scabby Bear."

I remember as a kid there were times when talking with the older Native Americans, they knew Scabby Bear, but not Steve Marmon.

In the early 1930s Granddad Steve was in his early seventies. As the Fort Peck Dam was beginning construction, he decided to take his family up to see the dam construction. As a young man of about seventeen, my dad Steve Jr. remembers his dad making the comment, "Hell, they'll never dam the Missouri River. They might just as well try to go to the moon."

You ever had apple pie that was so good that you had to brag and brag about it? Well, back in the 1920s, my Granddad, Steve Marmon Sr., and wife Tony had been to Wolf Point and were returning home in their Overland car, packed with mail and groceries. You got to remember that back then we didn't have radios, TV, computers, and the like. Plus, if you lived out on a ranch, you were lucky to make it to town once a month, if not twice a year.

I won't use their names, but the neighbors along the trail done seen Steve and Tony passing. They hurried out and waved for them to stop and invited them in for pie. They wanted to hear the latest news and just visit.

The two-room tar paper shack was swept clean. In the woodstove were two pies cooking. Their table was little more than a homemade square flattop affair covered with a green oilcloth, with a vase of freshly picked yellow flowers from the prairie. Sunflowers. The chairs were nondescript high back, probably bought through a catalogue. In the rear room Tony could see a made bed, covered with a home-sewed brightly colored square patch quilt. All in all, the lady was a good housekeeper.

As they were visiting the Mrs. pulled one pie out of the oven, cut it, and served it. Sadly, the crust was on the soggy side. The apples were crunchy. Also, it could have used a little more cinnamon.

Being polite, Tony ate, not commenting about the pie, but Steve had more to say. He praised the pie up and boasted on how good it was. This irritated Tony. Still, she said nothing.

Later, on the way home in the privacy of the car, she turned to her husband and, like women sometimes do, shot him with a pointed question. "Why did you brag on her pie? My pies are better than hers. Even my worst pies are than what we just ate."

"You are right," Steve replied. "You make the best pie in the country, and none taste better."

"Then why did you praise her pie? It was horrible."

"You're right," he said. "Her pie was so bad that the only way I could make it taste good was to praise it up a whole lot. Don't think I could have eaten it otherwise."

The last year of Granddad's life, he was out checking cows when the fuel pump in his car went out, leaving him stranded north of the ranch several miles. That evening Dad looked for him but couldn't find him. As it was getting dark, he drove to the neighbors to get help.

They formed a search party, all saddled up, and went off riding in different directions from the ranch. Two of the Shumway boys spotted the taillights and found the car. There was Steve Sr. sitting in the car waiting.

"It was a long ride south, but we found you," said one of the boys proudly.

"Hell, boys. I'm not the one that is lost. You are. Look up there. There's the North Star. You two been riding north, not south."

Jim Marmon
Wolf Point, Montana

DAVE HUSTON

Dave Huston, the son of Harry and Susie Huston, was born April 23, 1917, at Hazny, Montana. Dave was the first of three children. He has two sisters, Peg Childers and Carol Umland. Dave's parents homesteaded in the Devil's Creek area in 1914, after being married in San Diego on February 4, 1914. They had many hard years, as did most of the homesteaders, but they were happy years, and while for months at a time there wasn't a dime in the house, it didn't make for a big problem as no one else had a dime either, and they didn't need money to be happy. There were not the monthly expenses to cope with then as now either.

Dave's father, Harry, was originally from Kansas but was working in San Diego, California, before coming to Montana to homestead. He worked for the company that installed the first electric elevators in San Diego. He was one of the most knowledgeable sheep men in the county, and while he never made a fortune to leave his family, he gave them a far more important legacy. He always told his children to never create a debt that they couldn't or wouldn't pay and to always tell the truth no matter how painful it was.

Dave's mother, Susie, was a far-reaching, influencing factor in the development of the schools throughout the area. She always had the interest of the children at heart and did much private tutoring after she retired from the teaching profession. She drove new cars in the days when she received from $40 to $50 per month as teacher's wages. She owned a new 1926 canvas-topped touring car with wooden spoke wheels. She had a new 1929 Chevy that was the first six-cylinder they made. She had a new 1931 Chevy that cost $700. That was the one that Dave used a hammer and a spike on to pound a hole in the muffler to hear it "bawl." She responded by taking him to the ground and pounding the dickens out of him when she discovered it. Quite an accomplishment for a forty-one-year-old mom.

Dave borrowed money from her many times but always paid her back in full. How much she is missed is impossible to measure. She was a walking encyclopedia for facts and information. If she didn't have the answer at her fingertips, she'd soon get it. Her lessons were invaluable to family and friends, and her loving memory will be forever with us.

Dave spent his early years after high school on the ranch, and his first job away from home was working on the Fort Peck Dam in 1936

Many hunters came from out of state to bag big muleys on Dave Huston's ranch. COURTESY OF KATHRYN HUSTON

and 1937. From there he went to western Montana, Wyoming, and Idaho until the fall of 1939. He was drafted into the Army in 1941 and was honorably discharged in 1943. After returning from the Army, Dave decided to pursue ranching as his lifelong career. He bought some land and leased some but had to still work at various jobs to supplement his income because his ranch was small.

In 1945 he and Kathryn Haney were married. They had two children, Sam and Peggy Del. When the children were small and before they were in school, it was possible to get away to work on various jobs. In 1953 he logged in the Stanislaus Forest in California in the summer. A humorous incident took place at Wells, Nevada, on his way to California. He got a hotel room over a saloon about midnight, and when he got up the next morning to go on, he'd lost his comb and went into the saloon to buy one. When he asked the bartender if he had combs for sale, and he did, Dave asked what they cost. The bartender said, "To everyone else, they're 10 cents, but for you they're a dollar!" Dave fussed up a bit and asked, "What the hell is the deal?" The bartender said with a grin, "Because you look like you need one worse than anyone I've seen!"

During the summer of 1956, he worked on top of the Continental Divide in western Montana. It became increasingly more difficult to keep up on the ranch work and be away from home working part of the year, so he saw an opportunity to supplement the ranch income and still be at home most of the time. He started buying canner horses around the county and other areas of the state. For the next twenty years, while the market for canner horses was good, he bought thousands throughout the area. He had several good outlets and managed to do well at something he always enjoyed—working with horses.

After putting together somewhere between a hundred and two hundred head, he'd deliver them to Ingomar, selling them to Ed Vaughn. He trailed them to the rail, and the trip took three days from the ranch to Ingomar. Ed Vaughn was the most respected horse buyer in the state. He bought thousands of horses through the Northwest and Canada and furnished the bulk of the bucking horses for the world-famous Miles City Bucking Horse Sale for many years. While handling so many horses, it was easy to pick a load now and then for some outfitter or dude ranch, and Dave once sold a carload of bucking horses to a rodeo producer in Oakdale, California, and sent them by rail. The rodeo producer's name was Ray Kohrs, nephew of the early-day prominent Montana rancher Conrad Kohrs.

Dave broke and trained horses for people for many years. Back in the '40s, he got $10 a head and usually had about five started and going at one time. There was endless amounts of country to cover, and they gentled quickly. He "caked" the cattle in the wintertime with a packhorse. He'd ride a broke horse into the hills and lead a bronc loaded with cake. After the cake was fed, he'd ride the bronc home and turn the other horse loose. When there's a foot or so of snow with temperatures as low at times as forty and fifty degrees below zero, broncs break out fast!

Dave has had mares and stallions most of his life since he settled down in one place. A few years he raised buckskins and palominos, then, as the public choice changed to Appaloosas, he changed, too. Some of the prettiest colts imaginable are pictured in old photo albums. When the two children were young, they helped show the horses by riding the gentler ones through the sale ring. There's nothing more appealing to the public than a small child on a big horse, and it proves the reliability of the horse better than any other method known.

Before the popularity of the four-wheel-drive pickup as a mode of transportation, Dave took hunters out on horseback. It was an experience to remember and afforded the hunting party many hours of posthunting fun. One particular incident was an early-morning experience a Minnesota preacher had. He said he was an old hand on horseback. All the horses Dave used were gentle because they had to be. Well, the preacher mounted the horse with his rifle over his back in a sling. The horse got frightened and ran over the hill with the rifle beating the preacher across the back. It was swinging wildly, but the poor man finally thought to pull up on the reins, and he came back over the hill. They continued on the day's hunt with everyone still intact.

Another humorous incident that took place during the course of the guiding and outfitting years was also quite scary. Dave had a Thoroughbred buggy team that he'd bought in Canada, and they were both broke to ride. He had a party of hunters from Wisconsin scheduled to arrive at 4:00 p.m. on a particular day. As often happened, they arrived about noon. Dave had one of the Thoroughbreds tied to the corral fence and was preparing to lead him to another pasture while hunting season was on because he was not gentle enough for dudes.

When the hunters drove in, they saw this horse, and one of the fellows who had a skin full of "wobble water" made a run for this horse, mounted him, and took off over the hill like a streak with coattails flying. Well, Dave was afraid of what the outcome would be, but it's said that God takes care of fools, and it proved true in

Dave Huston was an excellent horseman and always had some good horses, like this palomino. COURTESY OF KATHRYN HUSTON

this case. Back he came shortly, at the same speed as he left at, with a screeching halt at the corral fence. He threw both reins in front of the horse and dismounted. Dave wasted no time in taking the horse to pasture!

Dave's wife Kathryn and the two children, Sam and Peggy, were working beside him throughout the years and giving support in every way they could. The success of a ranching business takes cooperation and hard work with the blessings of the Good Lord, which we've certainly had. The retirement years are a reward of a kind to enjoy the grandchildren, Sam's in Helena—Janice, Mike, and Jamie, and Peggy's—Bo, Samantha, and Tacy.

Kathryn Huston
Brusett, Montana

HERB AND OTHELIA CAYER

My dad, Herb Cayer, was born in Frenchtown in 1900. He moved with his parents and sister to a homestead at Three Buttes, near Lambert, two years later. Upon his arrival, his uncle, Herb Bell, gave him a horse. It was the first of the many horses he would have all his life.

As a young boy Herb would ride to Lambert. When riding back home he would often encounter wolves. They would surround him and his horse. He would always know, especially at night, if his horse was acting nervously, that wolves were close by. They would be bold enough to bite at his feet or his horse's heels or tail. He found riding fast would only make them more aggressive. They enjoyed the chase. Riding at a slower pace was better. Luckily, he was never harmed.

When his parents left the farm to move to Detroit, he stayed in Montana working on the McCone ranch. After serving in the Marine Corps from 1921 to 1924, he returned to the Lambert area, where he bought, broke, and sold horses. He also rode broncs in rodeos, including riding in Madison Square Garden, where he won a prize to go to England and ride. However, having recently returned from the Marines, he didn't have any desire to go abroad again.

My mother, Othelia Schwartz, related something she had seen at a rodeo while they were dating. There was a bull with long horns that the cowboys were having trouble getting out of the arena. Another cowboy rode in to help. The bull charged this cowboy and his horse, and his horn went deep into the horse's chest. The blood squirted out in a stream.

The cowboy dismounted, took his handkerchief from his pocket and stuck it into the hole, but to no avail; the horse began to tremble and died, having bled to death. After she finished the story, my dad said, "I was that cowboy."

Their honeymoon was spent near Frenchtown for three months, where Herb helped round up and break horses out of the mountains.

In the '30s, while many farmers were going broke in the dust bowl era, Herb bought and sold their horses in and out of state. One time the horse buying could have cost them their lives.

Herb and Othelia Cayer on horseback in 1932. COURTESY OF PAM DREWRY

Herb was asked by a bank to buy some horses on the Fort Peck Reservation. He was told they would only deal in cash, so he had a large sum of money on him. Herb and Othelia arrived at the prearranged place and time to make the deal. The man living there said there was a change in plans; they would have to wait until morning. The man they would be dealing with couldn't come until then, and they could sleep in the bunkhouse.

Herb was leery, so they didn't go to sleep right away as the man in the house thought they had. Soon they saw a lamp go back and forth a few times in the window of the house. They figured it must be a signal—sure enough, a short distance away they saw a flashlight blink on and off a few times.

A noted rodeo rider, Herb Cayer was a good friend to his fellow cowboys and neighbors. COURTESY OF PAM DREWRY

Herb said, "We're leaving." Then they heard a click of a rifle being cocked. They drove as fast as they could without lights, so as not to be a target, thinking they maybe would be followed, but they weren't.

The next morning Herb took the money back to the banker, told him what had happened and that the deal was off.

After purchasing a ranch in eastern Montana, part of which was the Roy McCone ranch, Herb raised palomino horses, the first in the area. A governor of Oregon owned one, and he rode it in the Pendleton Roundup Parade.

Pam Drewry
Savage, Montana

WILLIAM C. "BILL" HUNTINGTON

William Clarence "Bill" Huntington was born on June 27, 1876, near North Platte, Nebraska. When Bill was young, his parents separated. His father went to Idaho, and his mother filed on a homestead in Cherry County, Nebraska. The claim was close to the C Bar Ranch, so when his mother took a cooking job on the C Bar Ranch, Bill got his first riding job as a horse wrangler. He was probably ten. It was during this time that he learned to drive a team and wagon, a skill that would serve him well in later years. Bill also spent a lot of time with his paternal grandparents in North Platte, Nebraska. Most of what little schooling Bill got took place in North Platte. One notable school acquaintance was Buffalo Bill Cody's daughter, Irma.

Before he was fifteen, Bill had cowboyed, driven a horse-powered baler, raked hay, and ridden racehorses. When he was about fifteen, his mother gave him a black horse, which he used to head for Oklahoma. Within the next year he'd made it as far north as Lander, Wyoming, where he saw the infamous Calamity Jane "taking whiskey straight at Coulter's Saloon." This was during President Cleveland's administration [1892–1896]. To make a buck, Bill did a lot of odd jobs, ranging from washing dishes and waiting tables to cleaning saloons and banks. When he got the chance, he cowboyed. By this time, it would be fair to say that Bill had achieved his growth and was a handsome, slim-built, devil-may-care cowboy who wanted to ride and cowboy with the best of 'em.

In Douglas, Wyoming, Bill met his future bride, Ella Daylong, whose family had arrived by wagon from Missouri. By the spring of 1899, Bill and Ella were engaged. After building a log cabin and a set of corrals on Basin Creek south of Billings, Montana, Bill married Ella on July 30, 1899. Bill was 23, and Ella was not quite 18. Their possessions were few: "Ella had a horse called Indian and a saddle. I had a saddle, $1.35, and a grubstake. We were in love and happy and felt we had the world by the tail on a downhill pull."

Before matrimony Bill never had settled down into one occupation, and wedding vows didn't change that. He continued to turn his hand to whatever presented itself. He did, however, at this period in his life concentrate on hauling freight with teams of horses. It can be said that all his life's laboring was horse connected; he was either breaking them, cowboying with them, looking for them, driving them, or telling about them.

The Boer War took place in 1899, and the English government bought a great quantity of horses in the United States for its cavalry. Bill had a part in that endeavor, which perhaps got him started in the Wild West show business, as all the horses had to be bucked out. Each man rode twenty-five horses a day, earning $10 a day for his efforts, and it became readily evident that a crowd always gathered and, wonder of wonders, was even willing to pay for the pleasure of watching! Bill and his close friend, George Williams, started with loosely organized bucking contests, which evolved into more diverse "Wild West" shows. Eventually, Bill and George took their show on the road. Bill and George Williams continued giving shows for quite a few years until they just ran out of steam.

About 1920 the whole business of freighting was running out of steam, too, as mechanical power began to come into its own. Things looked bleak for the entire horse market, so Bill bought a bunch of cattle. Bill and Ella moved about sixteen miles east of Billings in the fall of 1924. In 1928 their daughter Georgia married Donald Blake, and they put together a ranch just up the creek.

In June of 1948 Bill's wife of forty-nine years died. The small log cabin, which had been their home for twenty-five years, suddenly became large and lonely. Bill spent more and more time up the creek with his daughter's family, until he was no longer living in his own home. Bill entertained at every meal with stories and eventually was encouraged by his family and friends to put the stories he loved to tell about his youth and life in the Old West down on paper. In the corner of his daughter's big, well-lit kitchen, Bill sat by the hour at his table, painstakingly writing down the details of his life. He did this in pencil on reams of white typing paper. He was prolific and churned out one story after another as fast as his arthritic old hand could form the words. However, it was a challenge to read what he wrote. His handwriting wasn't anything to brag about, and his spelling was unique.

Although his efforts were originally intended as a family keepsake, when a local ag paper became interested in doing something with his stories, Bill jumped at the chance to make a little money. When it became readily evident that Bill's handwritten scrawl would have to be typewritten, Georgia got a small Underwood typewriter and started typing. Out of Bill and Georgia's joint efforts evolved two books: *They Were Good Men and Salty Cusses* and *Both Feet in the Stirrups*, which were published originally by *Western Livestock Reporter* in 1952 and 1959, respectively. The books were filled with delightful illustrations, historically correct and wonderfully humorous, by the noted Montana cowboy artist, J. K. Ralston, who by good fortune lived in Billings.

In 1952 *Western Livestock Reporter* began running Bill's stories every week in a column called "Bill Huntington Spins A Tale." Bill kept churning out stories right to the very end, and Georgia kept typing them. To fill his idle hours, at age seventy-two Bill had started a new career that lasted the twenty-one remaining years of his life.

W. C. Huntington, described in July 1958 by Lyle Harris as "storyteller, author, and one of the West's last living landmarks," died on October 15, 1969, with many family members at his side. He was ninety-three. It pleased the family when the funeral home was crowded for his service. Bill was buried next to his beloved wife, Ella, in Mountview Cemetery in Billings, Montana.

Sadly, little to none of Bill's cowboy gear remains. Fortunately, Bill left his mark in a much more indelible manner, having created an easy-to-read trail leading his reader straight back to the Old West.

Linda Grosskopf
Great-Granddaughter of Bill Huntington
Huntley, Montana

SUSAN QUINN HAUGHIAN

In 1905 newlyweds Dan and Susan Haughian arrived in the United States from County Down in Ireland. On October 31 they left Miles City, Montana, in a wagon loaded with supplies, for a three-room log cabin many miles to the north. As Susan came through the door of her new home, she was greeted by a room full of men. Afterwards they described her as a "rose in a garden of thorns." She was petite and had red hair, later to become famous as "Montana's Favorite Redhead."

She hadn't had any experience with housework, having been raised in a large family with older sisters, a maid, and an aunt to cook, wash, and iron clothes. She had been taught to mend, knit, and crochet. One day she cooked so many dried beans that she even buried some out in the yard. She learned to soften water with lye and bake twenty-four loaves of bread several times a week for her ten children, the hired men, and the herders in the sheep camps. Sometimes she took the dough along to bake in the little sheep wagon stoves.

During the Depression years, drought forced the family to move their livestock about two hundred miles to the west. A milk cow was trailed along and household goods hauled to a dugout camp there. Susan was back and forth between Jordan, Montana, where her daughters attended school, and to where the boys cared for the stock.

When eggs were scarce, Susan used turmeric powder for color or cooked a large rice pudding with one egg. A lot of molasses was used, also salted pork and beef cured in barrels. Good food was always taken to the sheep camps, such as bacon, canned goods, and jam. For cuts, turpentine, coal oil, Epsom salts, and carbolic acid were used. Treacle, a good grade of molasses, was used for sore throats. Castor oil was the principal remedy at that time, though.

Dan Sr. passed away in 1931. The family immediately pulled together, with Susan in command, dealing with bankers and acquiring more land. The ranch soon extended from the Little Sheep Mountain to the Yellowstone River in Eastern Montana. Later, at her home in Miles City, her door was always open to her family, as well as cowboys, sheepherders, and bankers alike. She made many a cup of tea and served her tasty home-baked bread to all. Susan passed away in August of 1972, leaving many grandchildren and great-grandchildren. Her grandsons continue to operate ranches formed from the original one.

Mary R. Haughian
Daughter-in-Law to Susan Haughian
Terry, Montana

DAVE WILLOUGHBY

Dave Willoughby came to Montana with his family in 1909 to live on a ranch forty miles south of Poplar on Muskrat Creek.

"I got my start working at different ranches in northeastern Montana," he said. "I especially remember riding with Charles and Jack Evans and the Doc Atkinson bunch."

He recalled an attempt to drive five hundred head of cattle across the Missouri River at Poplar for the Calligan ranch.

"Some of the cattle in that herd had managed to evade crossing the river year after year and were threatening to live to a ripe, old age. We were determined to get the whole bunch across this time.

"About twenty head managed to turn back after being driven into the river. Ropes flew in all directions until all of the reluctant cattle were roped and tied to every available tree or rock. These were transported across by ferry. Even then a few managed to escape, including one old cow that jumped into the river in the middle and swam back to shore."

Another exciting event he remembered was a shooting at the homestead shack of his sister-in-law in the timber country near Culbertson. Her brother was one of the feuding Hatfields from Tennessee who had come west to escape the famed feud between the Hatfields and McCoys.

"One night while Hatfield was at the cabin, some Indians dropped in for a visit. During the evening one of them became angry about something and pulled a gun. Hatfield tipped over the kitchen table to throw him off balance while he dodged behind the kitchen stove.

"The fight continued with the Indian using the table as a shield and Hatfield the stove. Some of the bullets passed through the table, wounding the Indian but not killing him. When the fight was over, Carrie's stove and stovepipe and skillet were full of holes, and so were the utensils hanging behind the stove."

In 1916 Willoughby bought horses throughout northeastern Montana for Gilmore and Love of Miles City, who had a contract with the U.S. Army. Just before Thanksgiving he purchased sixty-seven horses in the Scobey area. That Thanksgiving eve he attended a dance and won a turkey. The next day he put on a Thanksgiving dinner at the old Smith and Boyd Saloon. Among the guests were Mr. Gilmore, of Gilmore and Love, who personally decorated the tables.

The following day Willoughby and three other riders started the sixty-seven horses across country toward Poplar.

"The horses had been purchased in groups of from two to seven at various farms, and now they all took a notion to go home. Horses headed off in all directions, and every car and horse in Scobey took off across the unfenced prairie to head them back. It was the next day before the last of them was rounded up."

Horse relay racing was popular throughout Montana at that time, and Willoughby had a team of three horses that he raced at local events. In 1916 he took them to Great Falls and won a $400 purse.

As a trick rider Willoughby displayed his talents at fairs throughout the western states. One of his favorite stunts was a Roman ride between a horse and a car, going up to thirty-five miles an hour.

In 1955, after a forty-five-year career as a Montana cowboy and a Hollywood trick rider and horse trainer, Willoughby chose a young black-and-white pinto stallion, sixteen hands high, to "retire with." He named the horse Klickitat, which means "dancing feet" in the Yakima Indian language. He trained Klickitat to dance and for several years performed with him at fairs and rodeos in many western states, including Montana.

Dorothy Rustebakke
Area Historian
Scobey, Montana

ORD AMES

The Steve Held Foundation Committee selects both a living and a deceased cowboy each year for a "Cowboy of the Year" award in Broadus. At the July 4, 2000, Ranch Rodeo, Ord Ames was honored posthumously, forty-one years after his death.

Ord was born at Lawn, Nebraska, in 1889, the eldest son of Clint and Maggie Iron Ames. The family moved to Hutton, Montana, on the Rosebud in 1898. Clint Ames bought and traded ponies with the Indians. When Ord was ten, Clint took fifty Crow ponies from Hutton to Lead, South Dakota. The ponies were sold there, including the horse that Ord rode during the drive. When Clint decided not to return to

Hutton, Ord was abandoned in Deadwood, where he spent the winter in the care of the girls from the red-light district, who returned him to his mother in the spring. Ord was put on a train at Edgemont, South Dakota, and sent back to Crow Agency. At the train stop he caught a ride on a freight wagon hauling food out to the Indian agency. Ord never saw his dad again.

During Ames's rugged and adventuresome life as a cowboy, he experienced both the days of the open range with the long trail drives

As a young man, Ord Ames rode the open range across Wyoming and Montana, working for the big cow outfits.
COURTESY OF LINDA NYBAKKEN

of cattle and the transition to fenced pastures and cattle trains. At age seventeen, in 1906, Ord went to work for John Holt's LO Ranch on the Mizpah. During his apprenticeship with the LO, the ranch ran about thirty thousand head of cattle. In 1913 he went to work for the 79 Ranch at Stacey, and it was at the Stacey Open Rodeo (one without a fenced-in arena) that he won his first saddle in the bronc riding contest. Following his debut as a rodeo hand, Ord continued to rodeo while working on various ranches. His family has a collection of bits, spurs, and bridles awarded to him at rodeos.

Ord returned to Nebraska and married Nellie Yarger in 1914. They had three children, Marguerite Huckins, Montana Cook, and Delbert Ames. After marrying they returned to Montana, and he went to work for Osborne Pemberton on the Little Powder. In 1917 he worked for the Laurel Leaf Outfit, where he rode the "rough string." In that same year he filed on a homestead on Buttermilk Creek (named for the palomino horse that had roamed there). Buttermilk is now a part of the Lewis Ranch, and Lewis has restored the homestead site.

In the years following 1917, Ord worked for several cow outfits as their cow foreman or trail boss. In the '30s he went back to the LO, then on to Wyoming, where he worked for the Bar C for Charlie Orchard at Big Trail, Wyoming. In 1942 Ord worked for the DDD outfit at Forsyth as cow foreman. The Three D shipped thousands of cattle in from Mexico. This era followed the Depression, and the owner, John McNierney, loaned money to many cattlemen so they could get back into the cow business.

Ord's ranch work included many hours in the saddle in Powder River, Custer, and Rosebud Counties, as well as much of Wyoming and a winter in Marfa, Texas. He was a true range rider, who could relate many interesting incidents to the landmarks in Powder River County. Ord explained that there were two professions in this territory: You could be either a cowpuncher or a sheepherder. If you were the more ambitious type, you chose cowpunching. If you desired a plush, easy life, you took up sheepherding.

Ord's happiest times were spent on the back of a horse or visiting with the many friends he acquired in his various travels. His unhappiest times were spent behind the wheel of a vehicle. His driving skills were so poor that when he lived in Broadus during the '50s, he chained up in late October and only removed his chains after the last snowfall in the spring. It wasn't uncommon to hear his little Ford clattering and thumping through Broadus on a dry winter day. Ord's last ranch work was for Vic Rue and Sam Smith at Broadus in the '50s, and his last job was as Deputy Stock Inspector in Broadus in 1958. Ord passed away in April 1959 at age 70 and is buried at Broadus.

Steve Held founded the Posthumous Award, and the committee comprised of Bob Robinson, Charles Patten, Louise Popp, Jim Sanborn, and Slug Mills made the selection. In a 1956 *Powder River County Examiner* article entitled "Ord Ames Chose the Open Range," Ashton Jones wrote, "At age 68, Ord is still able to hold his own with the best when it is time to ride. Though his life was not one of spectacular achievement, it was one of a lifetime of work which exemplified western values both in the heart and on the range."

Linda Cook Nybakken
Granddaughter of Ord Ames
Nashua, Montana

"ARE YOU RIDIN' OR HANGIN' ON?"

"Daddy! Daddy!" I hollered, running past the bunkhouse and around the corner to the old log house Grandpa had built at the ranch.

Bursting through the door, I skidded to a stop in front of Daddy and blurted out, "Patches tried to kick me!"

Without a word he stood up, reached for his Stetson hanging on the wall, and headed for the corral. Stepping inside the gate, he lifted the blacksnake off the post and turned to face the pinto he'd bought for us kids to ride.

"Patches!" he ordered. "Get around."

Patches turned his head and looked back, ignoring Daddy and his stern command—he didn't have to obey anyone; he was the boss around there. One fast strike with the whip and Daddy began his education. Dust flew as Patches raced around the corral, trying to escape the deadly accuracy of Daddy's aim, leveled on his hide after each order to get around. I do have to say this: That horse learned fast, and after a short but thorough whipping, he turned and stood stock still as Daddy walked up to him. Patches never turned his rump to us again.

That was Daddy—knowing what needed to be done and doing it. Quickly. Effectively. To the end. He grew up a cowboy, but before us kids were born he became a water-well driller and never rode again. The last ride was on Patches, when he first brought him home, a two-year-old bought off an Indian kid on the reservation, green broke. Green is right; he blew up with Daddy when he stepped on him, but Daddy just wrapped his long legs around him and I'm pretty sure laughed at him. He got off and turned him over to us kids. Patches was really a pretty good horse, and after we moved to the ranch, we tore around the hills, checking cows, dodging rattlesnakes, and trying to outrun each other through the creek beds.

Daddy's saddle was an old Miles City Coggshall, the most comfortable saddle I've ever ridden. Us kids would fight over who got to ride it and who had to take Uncle Spike's, quite possibly the worst saddle ever made. I don't know that it made us any better riders, but Daddy's orders to "Sit up straight" as we left the yard and "Don't touch the saddle horn" probably did. I'm still amazed when I see people hanging on to the horn. Five minutes with Daddy would have straightened them up.

But the one I remember most was, "Are you ridin' or hangin' on?" It took me years to figure it out, I'm ashamed to say. What was the deal with that riding and hanging on anyway? Well, it's pretty simple. When you're riding, you are in control. The horse may be doing his best to oust you, but it ain't going to happen. At the end of the day, you will still be horseback.

Hanging on, however, means you are desperately trying to stay in the saddle. Defeat is imminent, and the horse knows it, and you know it. It will only be by a miracle that you will retain your seat and do not land—splat!—in the sagebrush. Oh, boy. It's better to be ridin' than to be hangin' on.

Daddy rode all over eastern Montana in that saddle, including catching wild horses on the divide west of Glendive and breaking them to sell. Fences are the bane of riders, and once I asked him what he did when he came up to a fence he had to go through. "I had a big Appaloosy," he said. "I'd ride up to the fence, throw my coat over the top wire, and he'd jump it." A pretty slick, efficient gate. It was only after I'd spent six months riding English and learning to jump that I appreciated Daddy's simple but dangerous method of getting over a three-strand barbed-wire fence with his horse carrying a heavy western saddle.

Roping was something I always wanted to learn how to do, and I never thought that the best teacher in the world sat at the table drinking coffee every morning. When we were in high school, a mare and her colt, along with a beautiful blue roan, came in the yard in the stock rack of the truck. She was a wild thing, but the roan was crazy. Impossible to touch, handle, catch, do anything with. After being around him a while, Daddy realized what was wrong. He was blind in one eye. Therefore he was constantly afraid and trying to protect himself from what he couldn't see.

Daddy wanted to catch him one day, so out to the corral he went with my brother. Building a loop, he flipped his arm and snagged the roan in one catch. Unfortunately, my brother wasn't aware of the skill of the roper and hollered out, "Lucky catch!"

"Luck, hell!" Daddy swore, throwing down the rope and stomping out of the corral, black as thunder. Yeah, that catch was no more luck than I was. How many? A thousand, ten thousand times he'd thrown a rope? And it curved where he put it.

Daddy wore black Tony Lama boots, real ones with red stitching on the uppers and low-slung leather heels. About every three months I'd see they were all scuffed and faded and dig out the can of shoe polish to shine them up again. His hat was a black Stetson with a narrow brim, just enough to keep the sun out of his eyes but not so much as to catch the wind. He had a pair of bronze spurs hanging on a nail in the joist of the basement, a lady's leg etched on one side and a five-sided star for a rowel. I loved those spurs and took them to the saddlery one Christmas to have new straps made because the original ones were so cracked and worn. Today I wish I'd never done that; those old leathers told the story of the miles he rode, the broncs he broke, the years buckled to his boots. Like an old cowboy, Ray Krone (whom I've had the pleasure of knowing through working on this book), says "Too soon old . . . too late smart."

I never knew the prowess Daddy really had until long after he passed away, his death due in part to an accident suffered years before as a young man, at the feet of a horse. Because of his ability to handle horses, Grandpa put him in charge of all the stock on the place. One day Daddy went to go into the door of the barn, but one of the workhorses was standing directly in front of him. Not realizing the horse didn't know he was there, he put his hand on his rump to move him aside so he could pass by. Startled, the horse kicked back with both hind feet, hitting him square in the chest with a powerful force.

For days Daddy lay in his bed, so injured Grandma did not know if he would live. Finally, he healed and was able to go back to work. But years later, after being operated on for an aneurism at his heart, from which he died, the doctor asked my mother what had happened to him that caused this unnatural aneurism. Only then did we learn from his family of the terrible summer when he'd been kicked by the horse and Grandma feared for his life. Now we knew where that other rule came from. "Always speak when you come up behind a horse so he'll know you're there."

I went to Grandpa's house after the death of my uncle, to choose some things for my brothers and sisters. There, in a little box, my uncle had put some remembrances, a couple of letters, some photographs, and on a piece of paper a few words for us about Daddy.

"Boone could do anything with a horse."

Wanda Rosseland
Daughter of Boone Weber Whitmer
Circle, Montana

 CHAPTER 6

YOUNG SQUIRTS

KIDS AND COLTS

Erwin Miller must have liked kids; he always had a few working for him. He never had none of his own, so I guess he more or less adopted us. We were absolutely no use to him at all. The old saying, "One kid all kid, two kids no kids" is all truth. We thought we was hellish good hands, but the fact was, we caused more damage than we were worth. When I was a kid, I went to most of the ranchers in the Cleveland area to get a job. Nobody wanted a kid. I was too young. But when I asked Erwin Miller, he hired me. I have a soft spot for him on account of that.

I was born on a sheep ranch and raised on a farm, so I didn't know much about what I wanted to learn. My buddy, Duane, was my first and worst teacher. Duane was going to teach me how the cowboys broke horses. He was thirteen or fourteen years old, and to me he certainly sounded like he had years of experience. He talked Erwin into letting him start three two-year-old colts, and it turned out I was his helper.

In due time we headed to the horse corrals at the upper Hansen Ranch. The first horse we get aholt of is soon named Shanghi. Maybe Duane named him, I don't remember, but he later becomes quite a bucking horse at times. We finally get a hackamore on Shanghi, with a long lead rope. These colts have already been halter broke by someone, so that chore is eliminated. Duane says the first thing we have to do is sack him out. So he gets a long willow and ties a gunnysack to it. While I'm holding the horse by the head, he starts beating him with the sack. Soon the situation is: I'm running in the lead, the horse behind me, and Duane is beating him over the ass with the gunnysack. Finally, we are all played out.

The colt is in the best shape of us three. I'm tired out from trying to keep from getting run over by the horse, and Duane's arms are tired from swinging that sack. I never realized before what a bronc buster had to go through. All this shit, and we haven't seemed to gain anything. This horse is now so wild we can't even get close enough to throw the saddle blanket at him.

Duane has his wind back by now and says to me, "I'm tired of being good to that outlaw son of a bitch. We will tie a hind leg up on him, and then he will let us saddle him." This takes about an hour and has us all exhausted. By this time Duane and me are rope burned and skinned up, and the colt is in the same shape. But like Duane says, "The son of a bitch is standing still now." We throw the saddle on. Duane says, "I'll ride him first and you second, okay?" "Okay," I says. Duane fixes himself a set of reins, and we let Shanghi's hind leg down and take off the rope.

All cowboys wear spurs. Duane is no exception. He is wearing a pair with big Mexican rowels that Erwin has given him. Duane eases up on Shanghi and gives him a little nudge with his spurs, but Shanghi won't move. He just stands humped up. He must be afraid we are going to tie some more legs up. Duane looks over at me and says, "This is one of them son's a bitches you just can't be good to." Then he raises his legs and buries his spurs in Shanghi's belly.

Shanghi bucks around the corral, but he can't buck hard, he's too tired. After wooling him around a bit, Duane gets off and tells me to get on, which I do. Shanghi bucks a little more and stops. He won't even move. Duane says, "Hell, Jim, he's a little stubborn, but he's broke good enough; let's turn him out." And that is the way the cowboys at the reservation received Shanghi.

Jim Halseth
Chinook, Montana
Cowboy Ways: On and About the E—Y of Chinook, Montana

A GOOD PLAN

One winter Ham Signor and I were hired to take care of thirty head of cattle located about forty miles north of Blackfoot on the south fork of Milk River. Our lodging was in a small log cabin without electricity or running water. A drafty four-hole outhouse served as our bathroom. We were sixteen years old, both grade school dropouts.

Our main task was to feed and water the herd. That meant chopping a hole in the iced-over creek every day with a single-bladed axe and scattering broken bales of hay to the cows in the pasture. The temperature got down to about thirty below and stayed below zero for a week.

We left the water bucket full at bedtime one night and the next morning found the bottom popped out. It had frozen solid. The cabin was almost as cold inside as out because neither of us got up to feed the fire in the stove.

After a breakfast of snow water, coffee, and bread, we set out to catch the team of giant Percheron workhorses, which took the better part of the morning, chasing them from corner to corner in the twenty-acre pasture. We needed them to feed the cattle using the stone boat sled.

After that, we decided to try to start the 1920s McCormack-Deering tractor. Our plan was to use it instead of chasing and harnessing the horses every day. Why didn't we leave them in the corral? We were sixteen. Our thought of the future was about fifteen minutes. The crank would not budge because of extremely cold oil. So we hitched the team to the tractor and pulled it around the yard. The rear wheels slid fine on the snow because of the thick cold transmission oil, which wouldn't allow the gears to move.

Ham got the idea of soaking a couple of rags in gas and oil, tied on to two pieces of baling wire, then holding the flames under the engine and transmission until the oil warmed enough to allow the gears to turn.

It was a good plan. Ham suggested we go in the house for a cup of coffee while the thawing process went on. It took a while to get the cookstove hot enough to boil water. That was the flaw, the fly in the ointment, as the saying goes.

Ham glanced out the window and saw the left rear tire starting to burn. We ran out, and since we didn't have a usable bucket or shovel, we frantically threw handfuls of snow on the rapidly mounting flames, all to no avail. The team spooked from the odor of burning rubber and pulled the tractor into the makeshift barn, which was really an open-ended shed, and stopped, letting the fire catch the scattered hay on the dirt floor.

Luckily, Ham had a sharp pocketknife and cut the rope holding the doubletree to the tractor. The team escaped through a hole in the side of the barn, enlarging it considerably. The two horses speeded up quite significantly when the gas tank exploded.

We had hastily followed the team to safety. The tractor and barn were a total loss.

The boss showed up the next week to see how his hired hands were doing. He saw the charred remains of the barn and blackened tractor. Over a cup of coffee, we truthfully told him what had happened. He stood with hands on hips and said somewhat gruffly that in view of the circumstances he would not pay us for the work we had done. He figured the incident made us even. We agreed, glad to be let off so easily.

He took us back to town and said he hated to do it, but he would have to hire a man to spend the remainder of the winter with his herd. He emphasized the word "man" as he glanced at us in the cab of the pickup.

Ham's and my wintertime job was over.

In my later years looking back, I came to accept that a boy's thought of the future is about ten or fifteen minutes and the thought of accountability is practically nil.

Henry Boyle
Great Falls, Montana

THE HOLLOW TREE

People are always asking me if I knew anyone that had come up the trail from Texas. The following is a little tale about the two that I did know.

When I was a kid, there was two men on the upper Big Horn Valley that came up the trail from Texas. One was a white man. One was a black man.

The white man's name was Charley Binion, and he was full of BS stories. For instance, he said the herd he came up the trail with was so big that the riders in the lead never did get acquainted with the drag riders.

He was also the first to tell the old story of the hollow tree. The herd boss supposedly sent Charlie ahead to find a crossing on a bad quicksand river. Charlie couldn't find a crossing, but he did find where a big tree had fell across the river. When he looked the tree over, he seen it was hollow, and he rode his horse through it, no sweat.

Charlie hurried back to tell the herd boss, and they crossed the herd through that hollow tree. However, when they counted out on the other side they were short a hundred head. They went back and looked through the tree, and wouldn't you know . . . that hundred head had turned up a limb!

Charlie was a top hand, and like many cowboys of the time, he didn't work in the winter. Charlie wintered in a shack at the livery barn in the tiny town of St. Xavier. Too bad I can't tell you the rest of the stories I know about this old trail rider.

The black man's name was Jim Simpson. When I was five years old, my mother said, "There is a black man helping your dad, and they will be in for dinner."

I couldn't imagine anyone being black, so I was all eyes. Finally, I spotted my dad and three or four riders coming down our lane. Sure enough, one of them was black. This scared the hell out of me, and I ran and hid in the closet. I frightened my mother, as she couldn't find me, and she thought I might have fell in the creek.

The cowboys all said Jim Simpson could rope better with a soft-twist rope—like a clothesline rope—than most hands could with a good hard-twist lariat. For years any soft-twist rope on the Crow Rez was called Simpson's Rope.

When I was twelve years old, Jim was living in a dugout just below our upper ranch on Soap Creek. One evening on my way home, I stopped to say hello to the old guy. Jim was cooking two pork chops in a skillet, and he said, "Stay for supper, boy?"

"You bet," I replied . . . but then I got to watching him turn the pork chops. He'd turn one, then pick what was left of his teeth with the fork, then turn the other one. I couldn't stand that, so I said, "I gotta go," and out the door I went and rode home. After a while I realized that the smart old black man had put on that tooth-picking bit for my benefit. He ran that fool kid off so he could have both of his pork chops for supper!

Too soon old . . . too late smart.

Ray Krone
Augusta, Montana

RAMRODDING THE BUGGY

Lee Stafford was going to school at Spring Creek, too, and we always seemed to get into trouble when we were together. Lee suggested we go up to this ranch that was abandoned; they had an old buggy there that we could borrow to ride down the hill on. We could take the seat off and turn the tongue up over the back and one of us could ride the tongue back there and guide it and steer it off the hills.

I finally agreed to go with him, and we went up and got this old buggy and took the seat off, and we run down the hill to the cabins. There were two or three hills, and we made it without any problem. But there was quite a hill after the schoolhouse. You had to make a sharp curve right at the bottom; if you didn't you'd run right over the creek bank into the creek.

So the first episode, well, I was the driver, out on the tongue. And Lee was the passenger; we'd put the seat back on, and he was setting in the seat. We went off this hill, and there was a bump about halfway down it. Give you quite a jump on that tongue, but I was well enough loaded that I stayed with it, and when we got down there towards the bottom, why, I run sideways and turned the side on the flat down by the cabins there, and it worked fine.

So the next flight we had, Lee, he decided to do the driving, and I was going to be the passenger. We started off, and I was a passenger up there then without a driver. We got down the hill, went right over that bank into the creek, and boy, I tell you, it bounced me plump off that seat, and I run a leg through one of them wheels. It went around with me till it kind of stopped and tore my brand-new pair of pants from the cuff clear up to the crotch. I took matches and sewed up the cut, thinking maybe Mom wouldn't notice what happened, but she did.

Tom Wilson
Lewistown, Montana

56 BELOW

In the summer of 1886, there was such a scarcity of grass and hay on Alkali Creek that my father and brother, Jacob and Billy Speelmon, moved the cattle about sixty miles away to Box Elder Creek, where they set up a camp near Speelmon Creek and stayed with the cattle.

Winter came with lots of snow. Mother wanted me to ride to their camp to see how they were faring, so I borrowed a horse that had foraged on greasewood and brush and set out. The snow was up to the saddle skirts, and the horse was near "played out," so I knew I could not go all the way.

I turned away and went to the Wear horse ranch, where I stayed overnight. The next morning the temperature was 56 degrees below zero. I got my horse and started for home, about twelve miles. The going was hard and slow, and before noon a windstorm came in. The blowing snow got me disoriented, and I found I was riding in circles.

That poor horse was about to drop when I thought I saw what looked like a man pitching hay from a stack. I knew there were no haystacks in this area, but I rode on over. I found I was in the middle of a band of sheep, where the herder was swinging his coat trying to turn the sheep into the wind.

If ever a cowpuncher was glad to see a sheepherder, it was me. I helped him with the sheep and stayed overnight in his wagon. Next morning here came some cowboys from the Wear ranch, looking for me. I managed to ride most of the way home before the horse gave out. I just left him there and walked the rest of the way.

Editor's Note: Roe Speelmon was fifteen years old at the time.

Moreau B. Speelmon
Sandy Speelmon, Grandson of Moreau
Miles City, Montana

WILEY KING

When I was six years old, in 1927, it was my job to help with the yearly roundup and branding. I would saddle up one horse to ride and tie a bedroll on the other and head for the hills.

One day I was told to search a certain bunch of coulees for the cattle and wait at a designated meeting place for the other riders.

After waiting quite a while, I disobeyed orders and took off. I got lost and ended up at Wiley's log cabin, five or six miles north of Myers, Montana, on Alkali Creek, after dark.

His greeting was, "Come on in, sonny; crawl up under my navel and spend the night." After I'd slept a few hours, the bedbugs won the battle, and I spent the rest of the night outside, covered with my saddle blanket.

Donald L. Nansel
Billings, Montana

THE WILL-O'-THE-WISP

We were fifteen miles from the school, so Dad built a cabin down there about a quarter of a mile from the school on a flat little place there. A couple of other neighbors did, too, that were a long distance from the school, and then us kids walked from there to school. It wasn't even a quarter of a mile, I don't s'pose, probably an eighth of a mile to school.

This one kid was riding horseback; he was a part-Indian kid, and he'd been going to school a long time, I don't know how long. I might have been in the first grade, when this Indian went by there after school and stopped and stayed till it got dark. So he stopped with us, and he got to telling about these will-o'-the-wisps that were a bouncing light out on the prairie, and nobody could catch up with 'em to see what they were. They were really wondering what in the heck they were because they were pretty scary.

He said us kids had seen 'em because we'd been up on the ridge by the schoolhouse and we could see a bouncing light south of us over there. We just knew that it had to be the will-o'-the-wisp. Well, what it actually was was a car light over on the Gibson divide, going in and out of sight. But we just knew it was the will-o'-the-wisp.

That night I had to go do my duty in the outhouse. Dad had built this outhouse, above the cabin. I went out there, took care of my business, and I got ready to leave. And something had me down that outhouse hole. I couldn't get loose. Boy, I jerked, and I tugged, and I pulled, and I finally made one hell of a lunge and got ahold of both edges of the door sill of that outhouse and tore loose. And I went squalling to the house.

"That will-o'-the-wisp had me down that toilet hole!"

They all armed themselves with a flashlight to go out and see what had happened. I had them damned bib overalls on, and they both had got caught in the crack of that seat and I'd tore 'em off right at the top of my pants. I never had any use for bib overalls after that.

Tom Wilson
Lewistown, Montana

TWO BOYS ARE HALF A BOY

In June of 1948 I was part of a family haying crew working for a rancher on the south fork of the Milk River, about thirty-five miles north of Browning and west of the Duck Lake road.

The ranch house and a stack of lodgepole pine logs—firewood—sat near the creek at the bottom of a two-hundred-yard hill that had about a thirty-degree slope.

This Sunday the boss took the family to town, leaving my almost-fifteen-year-old cousin and me to cut and peel corral poles. I was sixteen.

Cliff said, "You know that big old tractor tire by the wood pile? I wonder how far it would go if we rolled it down the hill? We can use Dan to pull it to the top."

Dan was one of the team of Belgian workhorses taking the day off, feasting on hay in the barn alongside his teammate, Lipstick. I harnessed him while Cliff rounded up a lariat and singletree.

The huge horse had no trouble pulling the tire up the slope. I disconnected the tugs and untied the rope. We ground-hitched Dan to let him crop the springtime bunch grass.

We stood up the tire and pointed it northeast toward the empty prairie, then gave it a push. Our experiment was in force. About a third of the way down, it hit a shallow coulee and turned left, heading straight for the house. We panicked and started running after it. The tire impacted the woodpile, flattened out, sprung back to shape, continued on, and skimmed the peak of the roof, then rolled across the creek, where it hit a cottonwood, bounced backward into the water and slowly fell over.

Dan must have spooked when we started our dash down the hill and headed for the barn. I saw him pass by out of the corner of my eye, his dinner-dish-size hooves pounding the ground. I had neglected to stow the tug chains to the britchen hooks, and they were hitting him in the hocks, causing him to panic further. He went right through the closed corral gate, breaking the poles into jagged ends. Cliff and I stopped and stared at the damage our experiment had wrought. "What do we do now?" he demanded.

"Unharness Dan and go cut the poles," I replied. "But first we better patch up the gate with baling wire. We can claim ignorance about what happened." After we did that we left the scene of the morning's disaster in the '34 Ford flatbed truck, motoring to the mountains with axes and drawknives on the floorboard.

That night at supper, the boss, Cliff's father, asked us how the corral gate got broken, the tractor tire ended up in the creek, and how the logs in the woodpile became scattered. I stared at Cliff, waiting for him to answer, to disclaim any knowledge of the events, but he remained silent. After a few moments had elapsed, John glanced at Cliff, then me, and continued. "The kids found a singletree and my best hard-twist lariat on top of the hill." He was referring to the two younger boys. "Just what in hell did you guys do today!"

We had no recourse but to own up to our experiment. The corners of John's lips quivered as he tried to maintain a straight face. "I want that gate fixed with new poles and the woodpile squared away tomorrow night after evening chores, but you can get that tire back to where you found it tonight. By hand and before you go to bed! It seems like every time I leave you guys to do a job, you get into trouble. I guess what Uncle Joe says is true: 'One boy is a whole boy and two boys are a half a boy, and they don't get a damn thing done when they're left alone to do what they're told to!"

After baling out the water from the tire so it would be light enough for us to roll up the hill to where we found it, with the little kid audience looking on, the sun had winked out behind Triple Divide mountain and we were exhausted. It had been a long, tiring day. Fixing the gate with new poles took quite a bit more time, a couple of days, especially with John supervising.

That night in the bunkhouse before we went to sleep, Cliff said, "I'll bet that old tire was going a hundred miles an hour when it hit that woodpile. Damn! We're lucky it didn't hit the house!" We started giggling and didn't stop until our stomachs hurt.

Henry Boyle
Great Falls, Montana

 **CHAPTER 7**

RANCH LIFE

THE CALVING SEASON FROM HELL

CALVING NOTES 1996

April 8—Sometime in morning

Big bagged cow can't seem to find her calf. She thinks it's over the riverbank or elsewhere.

Found dead calf on feed ground. Tried to blame wife for running over it with the feeding tractor. Cows probably trampled it, or I ran over it with grain pickup. Called neighbor and found new calf for mother. Paid $150. Probably worth $125 next fall. Wife went to get calf. While neighbor was trying to figure out how to load big calf and keep it loaded, wife got impatient and threw it on tailgate and hogtied it.

Big bagged cow still can't find calf. I decided she hadn't calved yet and she was confused. We looked all day, off and on.

We moved some heifers and their calves to dryer ground. That went pretty good, except a few calves jumped in a drain ditch full of ice chunks and had to swim to other side, and cows got bogged down in mud, and some heifers ran off and left their calves behind, etc.

Looked for Big Bag's calf again. I decided she *had* calved and I was confused.

Bankers showed good timing, showing up to do annual cow check while there's a dead calf on feed ground and I'm looking for lost one.

6:30 p.m.

We put heifers in night calving lot. Put a bug-eyed heifer and a dark red heifer in calving pen. Heifer's calf from this morning is sick. I think maybe it was stepped on, but I doctored it for everything else anyway.

I went to house.

Wife got in another heifer, a Brangus-Hereford-Gelbveih cross (another bad idea).

Checked heifers at 9:30. Ones we got in, doing nothing. New one in lot doing fine.

Checked again at 11:00, nothing. Checked at 12:30. Bad Idea calved in barn. She likes her calf, but she hates me. Bug-Eye doing nothing. Dark red heifer has toes (pointing right direction).

Checked about 2:00. Red heifer has tongue. Bug-Eye doing nothing. Bad Idea is still owly.

At 2:30 I decided to pull red heifer's calf, tongue was starting to swell. She couldn't get up. She's lying against door outside calving barn. Had to crawl over door with calf puller. Got heifer pulled away from door to let Bad Idea and her calf out. She chased me. Had her nose in my pocket while I pulled red heifer's calf (tough pull). Bad Idea's calf was crawling all over red heifer in meantime. Dragged red heifer's calf in front of her, so she would recognize it later.

Decided to investigate Bug-Eye. Nothing dumber than a bug-eyed Angus heifer—except maybe me and other guys who raise them. Calf was dead. Pulled it. Been dead a while. Cow didn't care. Let her out, drug calf out. Checked red heifer. 100% PROLAPSE. Caught Bad Idea's calf and put in pen in barn with cow in hot pursuit. We dueled for a while. I used shovel.

Finally got red cow up. She staggered into barn and amazingly into head catch. I haltered her and gave her a tail block. Pondered on if I should wake up wife to help me. Decided against it. Threaded my needle. Readied my syringe and found some boluses. Rinsed uterus and proceeded to stuff cow. After about 30 minutes I succeeded.

First time I'd done that without assistance (full prolapse). Sewed her up tight with boluses inside and gave her a shot. Milked her and tubed calf. Opened chute and she fell down. Won't get up. Drug calf in front of her so she'd know it. She'll probably try to get up and fall on it and kill it.

5:57 a.m.

Checked heifers in lot. Another new one (doing fine). Noticed neighbor's open heifer had sucked out two pregnant heifers.

Need some coffee.

6:20 a.m.

Checked two pair that calved in night calving lot. One calf had managed to get two fences away into roping arena. Her mother was in a dither. Finally got them together, but mother wouldn't let the calf suck. She'd decided she wanted other calf in lot. Put her in the chute—she's a kicking witch, and calf is head shy. Fed calf, hobbled cow, and put them in pen outside as I needed barn.

Pulled big calf out of a 3-year-old who has only one gear, reverse. Think I broke calf's lower leg when it hip-locked and strap slipped to lower joint. Milked cow, fed calf, and cast the leg.

3:15 p.m.

Checked heifers. Red heifer with head only out—calf dead. Decided to try pulling it before readying my surgical tools. It came with medium-hard pull. Cow is jiggered. Two more heifers calving. Checked 45 minutes later. Two new ones doing fine.

7:00 p.m.

Milked cow and fed calf with cast foot. Decided to feed bulls at Dad's before checking old cows. When I got to cows, I found one with calf half out and cow half dead. Headed to barn to get puller and strap. Pickup quit four times but kept starting again. Been a case of bad gas going around.

Tied cow's front legs together in case she tried to get up. Hooked on and pulled calf. Biggest calf I've ever pulled. Probably around 130 lbs. Haven't had good luck with these particular purchased cows. Genetics say, "Have big calf." Size sez, "No, you don't."

Started to take rope off feet of cow when she started to prolapse. Stuck my arm in up to my shoulder in cow. Took a break and hoped someone would come along. Family will be back Sunday. Sometime later my Dad was headed to town to help my brother (he's got a real job, gets paid and everything). I waved Dad down and sent him to barn for needle and cord. Stitched her up and took rope off feet. She couldn't get up anyway.

Went home to check heifers. Put two new ones from lot in new pen. Jiggered cow got up, but it took me half an hour to chase her out of lot. She'd either go the wrong way, fall down, or chase me.

Moved dithered cow and calf. She has let her calf suck but won't mother it when I'm around. Calf is as stupid as its mother.

Resplinted calf with weak tendons from the other day.

Went back to give sewed-up cow in pasture a shot of LA 200. Picked cactus out of her bag and milked her for calf at barn. She still can't get up.

Checked heifers.

Fed everything.

Doctored yearling filly in barn (wire cut). Explicit instructions on how to from wife. Can't find everything. Will improvise.

Checked big pen of calved-out heifers. Blind calf wandered out in trees for 723rd time. Found and returned it to its mother. Pulled calf out of round bale feeder.

Checked mare about to foal and went to house for breakfast or dinner or whatever it is.

Ron Haynes
Saco, Montana

A COW CAN BE CANTANKEROUS

By Lucile Canfield

Now C. C. Clark and Bob Candee aren't cowboys
chapped and spurred.
And yet this little incident I was told once occurred.
A big old cow belonged to Bob, I guess she was Charolaise,
Her sunburned bag they noticed so they went to doctor her that day.
Now Bob, he drove the pickup and C. C. swung the rope,
And in the pasture raced around, to catch her was their hope.
At last the loop went round her neck, but C. C. had no dally,
And so the cow with rope and C. C. went charging up the valley.
So Bob baled out and grabbed the rope and all three went around,
They finally choked the old girl and she was on the ground.
They didn't have a piggin' string so they never tied her feet,
Just thought as long as she was down they'd fix her quick and neat.
So Bob got out his spare tire and tied it to her tight,
He thought the weight would anchor her
and she'd stay down all right.
He used it like a picket pin and then sat down on top,
While C. C. got the bag balm out to use it as a sop.
He walked up to the old cow and muttered, "Now you Witch."
But that old cow had got her wind, she took off without a hitch.
A skidding Bob and tire behind, a regular runaway,
To add some more excitement to the checkin' cattle day.
Now the moral of this story, as a cowboy said long past,
Is to always set your dallies or else tie hard and fast.

Dedicated to a couple of my neighbors. Lucile.

Bob Candee
Richey, Montana

BACK TO THE PAST

There aren't many cowboys who subscribe to the science fiction philosophy. They tend to be realists, with both feet solidly planted in the here and now. But from time to time, a person runs head-on into a situation involving a portal into a different time. My first experience happened when I was a junior in high school.

I had gotten a summer job on a ranch up in the Jordan area, the Brown ranch, Bill Brown Jr. and Bill Brown Sr., proprietors. Both men would merit their own story, if not a book. However, this story wasn't about them; it's about me and my encounter with time travel.

I was up in the breaks of the Musselshell, mainly because I didn't get along all that well with my dad, so he farmed me out. But it was just what I wanted. I had told Bill Jr. that I was looking for a riding job. No fencing, no farming, just cowboying. And I got just that. I arrived after dark with my bedroll and saddle, and we left before daylight in the morning. Not exaggerating, it was two weeks before I saw the ranch buildings in the daylight. I had an old Miles City saddle, which I completely wore out that summer. That fall when I left to go back to school, I was in about as good a shape as a person gets.

The Calf Creek ranch was a combination of rolling prairie and steep draws and badlands running down to the Musselshell. The area had more than its share of characters, and from time to time I would go help the neighbors, branding or gathering anything that could be accomplished on horseback, and in the process I met men who would have fit in just as well a hundred years ago as they would today.

As time went by I was really enjoying the summer, and it was not hard to imagine myself on a ranch in the 1800s. In fact, one morning, while I was riding through the cows, doctoring calves and thinking how the rolling hills and tall grass probably looked just like this a hundred years ago, I rode over a hill, and to my surprise there, scattered out over the prairie, was a herd of buffalo. Now this was in the 1960s, and private herds of buffalo weren't anywhere as common as they are today. Ted Turner didn't own a single bison. But there they were, and for a long moment I mulled over the idea that I had somehow rode into the past. But as it turned out, a wealthy "out of state" man had bought a ranch in the breaks and had populated it with buffalo, exotic goats and antelope, and other nonindigenous species. The buffalo did not recognize a fence as native to their habitat and went wherever they darn well pleased. And I was pleased to see them that day, as I traveled back in time, at least in my imagination.

My next encounter with time travel was quite some time later. After a three-year tour of duty in Vietnam, I found myself working for the Vale Creek ranch located on Pryor Creek, out of Billings. They were running three or four thousand head of cattle, both cows and calves and yearlings. We had a good crew, and I was enjoying cowboying once again. I found myself hanging my hat out on the reservation, in a camp with an older man, Jack Rich. He was a real nice man, and we got along well, but after Vale Creek had finished branding that spring, I was sent out to rep on John Scott's wagon.

Vale Creek's ranch on the reservation was right in the middle of the Scott ranch. Scotts were running over ten thousand cows, I was told, and I think that was probably pretty close to the truth. They ran a wagon just like in the early days, complete with a cook tent, bed tent, rope corral, fifteen to twenty men, a cook (Bill Sanford), some fifty head of horses including a rough string, and an actual rough-string rider, Wade Cooper.

When Doc Appell, the Vale Creek foreman, informed me I was going to the wagon, I was excited for the first time in a long time. I had heard of Scott's wagon, but now my imagination was running wild, thinking about what I was going to encounter.

The morning finally came, and I caught up my string, five head of colts, well started, and educated in the ways of a roundup cavy. I had spent some time with them in a big round corral, teaching them to line up facing out, just as they would be required to do in the rope corral, and I would take them to neighbors' brandings as much as possible, getting them used to being around strange horses and staying with the cavy rather than heading for home.

There were two of us going, Dave Diley being the other. The time finally arrived and Dave and I tied our bedrolls on the gentlest colts, saddled up another, and we were off on a great adventure. It was a day's ride out to the wagon, and I got there just at sundown. I stopped on a hill overlooking the wagon, camped on Bovey Creek, and I was sure I had stumbled on paradise. Truly, it was a look into the past.

I wrote a poem about my time on the wagon; it turned out to rival the *Iliad* in length, but I am including a short excerpt (see back of book) describing my first encounter with the wagon. I hope you enjoyed my journeys back in time. I know I did, and they remain a constant part of me even as I am retired and not able to live the life I have led this past fifty years.

Joe Charter
Billings, Montana

NOT QUITE THE HOLIDAY INN

Bunkhouses are a necessary feature of nearly every ranch. A place to be in out of the weather, they are all types, sizes, and shapes, but none are very fancy. Most of the earlier ones were built of logs, with a rough board floor covered with dirt. Nearly all of them were only one room, with the size being dictated by the number of year-round men that would live there.

The bunkhouse might have a couple of small windows, but usually, if you could see through them, it meant the glass was missing. Cowboys don't do windows. The door was homemade and fit close enough to keep out most of the big critters.

I think every bunkhouse I was ever in was heated by a stove made from a 50-gallon barrel. A spot on the top was hammered flat for a space to set a bucket to heat water in. A 2 x 4 wooden frame surrounded the stove on the floor and was filled with about 50 percent sand and the rest cigarette butts. Nobody ever accused the cowboys of being great housekeepers either.

The furniture consisted of a table, homemade or salvaged, and several chairs, no two alike. Most had guy wires holding the legs in place. There was also a great variety of beds, reclaimed from most everywhere, but a good share of them were single army cots, with the standard, comfortable three-inch-thick mattress. Some of the earlier mattresses were a large sack made from a canvas-type material called "ticking." They were filled with hay, usually changed about once a year.

Most of the men had their own bedrolls, consisting of all types of blankets, quilts, and so on, that they had accumulated, and covered with a fancy gray canvas bedspread. The ranch nearly always had spare bedding for someone who didn't have any, and it was mostly secondhand army blankets and others made from retired Levis. Most pillows had nice flour-sack covers.

Along one wall, preferably close to the door, was a bench that held a couple of granite washbasins, three gallon buckets for water, and a sardine can for a soap dish. A large nail held a cracked and discolored mirror hanging by a piece of wire. Other nails held towels of assorted colors of gray.

Close by, hanging from the wall, was the Laundromat—a large, round, galvanized washtub and a scrub board. Wires or ropes strung across the room served as the dryer. Lighting was obtained with maybe a couple of barn lanterns hanging from the ceiling or a kerosene lamp on the table. All had badly smoked chimneys. Wooden apple boxes, either nailed to the wall or stood on end by each bed, were used to hold each owner's personal belongings. A row of large nails driven into the wall held extra clothes.

At least one guy had a large windup alarm clock. A collection of old newspapers and magazines covered the table. All of that served as home to a great many men for many years, and lots of places still do.

Over the years the buildings improved, and some were made out of wood-frame construction. One bunkhouse at our ranch was that type, and cheesecloth was tacked up on the inside in preparation for wallpaper. The wallpaper must have been back-ordered, because after eighty years it's still that way.

After electricity came to the country, bunkhouses got wired, usually with a single bulb hanging in the center of the room, with extension cords strung in all directions. Eventually, water lines were put in and a small lean-to room added as a bathroom. Some even had a water heater.

During my years of living on the ranch and trailing cattle, plus many years in the construction business, I became acquainted with many bunkhouses. I wasn't ever in one that wasn't comfortably warm, probably because of the not-too-large room and the large barrel stove.

One place where we stopped over with cattle we were told to pick out an empty bed and make ourselves at home. I took the top blanket off the bed and leaned it against the wall. It didn't even bend. I slept that night with my chaps on.

One rancher decided I was too young to stay in the nice warm bunkhouse and put me in the upstairs guest room in his house. It must have been ten degrees colder up there than outside, and I nearly froze. A couple of ranches were notorious for having bedbugs, but fortunately, I never stayed in those. All bunkhouses had large calendars with pictures of pinup girls but very seldom had the current year on them.

Gradually, ranches acquired more power machinery, which required fewer men to operate it. Also, there were fewer single men that wanted to do ranch work. Married men, some with families, required a whole different set of facilities, but in most places the old bunkhouse still occupies a corner of the barnyard.

Jay Nelson
Jackson, Montana

LIFE IN A COVERED WAGON

My job was riding bog on Fort Peck Lake, looking after seven hundred cows and fifteen hundred sheep and a lot of wild horses. It was one of the first years Fort Peck was full of water [after the dam was built]. The water would go up and down on the shore, and the cattle, sheep, and wild horses would bog in the mud, so I would have to look after them and pull them out.

I lived in a covered wagon. Not your best of homes, but it got me by.

It was a freight wagon with a treated tarp stretched over some iron bows on top. It had walls built out at the bottom, then up about five feet. It had cupboards built in the back corner, a clothes closet and drawers on the other side, and a bunk bed in the front.

Gale and Pamela Cayer Drewry, 1989. COURTESY OF GALE DREWRY

The stove had a tin plate around the chimney to keep the tarp from getting too hot. Where I was camped all summer there was a lot of sagebrush and dried cow chips to burn. One day a storm came up, and as I had the wagon parked under a big cottonwood, I took my saddle horse and pulled it out on the flat till it was over. I was afraid of lightning hitting the tree. Then the next day I pulled it back into the shade.

It had a window in the front and a door in the back to open, but that was the extent of my air-conditioning. It got darn cold in the fall after frost. You would build a fire in the stove to fry eggs, bacon, and spuds in the morning for breakfast. Then the frost would thaw off on the tarp and leak in. Oh, boy, what a life of a cowboy.

An accomplished singer and musician, Gale Drewry performed with country music bands and has written and cut his own songs. COURTESY OF GALE DREWRY

You knew when the wind came up at night because the tarp would whip and wake you up. A mouse would come in because it was better than what he had. I had to run a mousetrap line to keep them down. I had a lot of blankets and a tarp over them. I had a horsehide to put over that if I needed it.

I took my clothes down to the lake to wash them while taking a bath there, too. The water was always warm until the middle of September. It gets darn cold when you're getting in and out. But after riding eight or ten hours in the sun or the wind, it was nice.

When you had to go out in the middle of the night for a potty break, one would bang on the floor with a boot to wake up the rattlers, so they could get a head start. There were a few that came after the mice that were after my food, which was delivered once a week.

You'd listen and think and look before you would leap, because if you got hurt it was a twenty-mile ride to the ranch or a week before someone would come with food to check on you. So if one tells you the life of a cowboy is great, just show them this story and then see if they say it is great.

Living alone like that with no one around to talk to is a great experience by itself. My horses knew what kind of a mood I was in. I talked to them all the time. When they start talking back, you've been there too dang long.

I had my guitar and did a lot of singing. I had a clothesline from the tree to the wagon wheel. I got seven dollars a day and my Bull Durham to smoke, and of course my room and board. I had no electricity or gas bill to pay. They brought me two five-gallon cream cans of water as the water in the lake was not fit to drink.

When we took the stock to the ranch in October, I was done. But I missed it later. On to playing and singing in a nightclub. Boy, what a change.

Gale Drewry
Sidney, Montana

CAVED IN

It was a very hot, sunny day about noon, and we were running horses in the badlands. I was riding a horse that we were breaking for someone. As we were running, my horse fell, throwing me forward. When I looked back, my horse had disappeared into the earth. I looked down and could see nothing except a black hole and dust. I did not hear him land, thinking he was still falling. My sister, Lorrane, rode up and jumped off to look. I jumped onto her horse and went to get Dad.

My mind was numb, as I thought the horse had fallen into a bottomless canyon. When I got back and had a look and my eyes got used to the dark, there the horse stood below, trapped in a washout. He was standing below the ground; it was a few feet above his head.

He had slid rear first, only leaving a small hole in the earth. The water had washed away the dirt below the ground and left a shallow covering. When we hit that spot, it caved in. Rex or Rockie rode home to get Mom and shovels. I think it took a couple of hours to dig him out.

Kathern (Taylor) Adkins
Bullsbrook, Western Australia
Australia

ON THE ETCHART RANCH

My father was Charles Wood, who was born in 1912 on Rock Creek north of Hinsdale, Montana. He grew up on a homestead and lived in a sod house. He worked for ten years for Dick Nelson, who had a large ranch. Later he went to work for the Etchart Ranch, another large ranch. My uncle, Clayton Wood, was a top working cowboy and the cattle foreman on the Etchart Ranch. Because Clayt was the foreman, I was hired to work in the summer of my teenage years. Clayt's daughter Faye and I were the only girls who worked with the men. We had to ride right with them and do whatever they had to do. Clayt always said he liked us better because at the end of the month we didn't run to town to spend our paychecks. The bad thing was, most of the men never came back for a couple of weeks!

There are a lot of stories I could tell about those summers. One I remember real well was when our horses were being shod. There was a large shop that had a cement floor. At one end was a bed that the nighttime cowboy would use to rest while watching the heifers that would calve soon. We had two thousand two-year-old heifers to calve out.

Being seventeen years old, I had a lot to learn. While I was waiting for my turn to get shoes on my horse, I decided to tie him to the headboard of the bed. Dee Stockton, an old-time cowboy, was shoeing another horse. I went over to watch Dee, leaving my horse behind. At that time my horse moved a bit and the bed came with him. The next thing I knew, all heck broke loose. My horse went flying out the door with the bed tied to him. There was a bog with some water in it behind the shop. That horse hit that bog running as fast as he could. The bed parts were flying in pieces all across the bog. The last I saw my horse he was going over the hill with just the headboard tied to him. I was lucky, and he finally got untied and didn't get hurt.

In the winter my folks and I would live at a winter camp south of Glasgow Air Base on Porcupine Creek. It was about the coldest place to have a cow camp. We had one room, with no running water or electricity. We drank from the creek and used lanterns to see with. We used a woodstove to heat and cook on. That one little room would really be cold by morning when it was forty below. Our water pail would be froze in the morning.

The cattle were not fed hay in the winter unless it was a tough winter. I remember the winter of 1965 so well! It was cold and so hard of a winter we couldn't even get feed in for the cows. The snow iced over, and the cattle lost all the hair around their faces trying to break through the snow to eat. Etchart's airplane had to drop our food for us. We never saw any people. The forty and fifty degrees below zero nights were too hard on the cattle. They would be lying down like they were asleep, but they had died in the night.

One day my dad said that a young cow had a calf about four miles from our place. He said there was no way to save the calf. I was such an animal lover I couldn't stand leaving the calf to die. So, not telling anyone, I got on my horse and took off to find the cow and calf. It was twenty below, and it wasn't long before I was very cold. I went the four miles and found this little black whiteface calf and a skinny little cow. The calf couldn't move very fast because he was half froze. I soon got ahold of him, and the next thing I had to do was get him up on my horse. I was freezing cold and had quite a time getting him on the horse. I knew we had canned milk by the case in a hole under the house, so I wasn't going to try and get the cow to come. The funny thing was, that skinny cow just started following me. I was so cold I didn't keep watching to see if the cow was coming or not.

I put my hands under the calf's belly, and we used each other's heat to keep from freezing. I remember that as being one of the coldest rides I ever took. That little calf was so cold he never moved. When I came riding over the hill by our camp with the calf in my arms and the cow coming behind, I was sure happy I made it. But there was my dad, mad as a wet hen for me taking a chance on my life for a $40 calf. The cow was so skinny she had no milk, so the calf had canned milk until the cow was fed enough to come to her milk.

The winter was bad right into spring. I remember seeing a baby colt running with the wild horses. About two weeks later I saw the horses again, and there was no colt with them. I don't know how many animals died that winter, but there were a lot of them.

Our horse training is so different now from when I worked at Etchart's. I remember a young horse I was breaking. I was working it in the round pen. I got on him and had no control but just ran around the pen. There were a couple of hired hands watching me, and they just opened the gate, and away I went! That horse took off as fast as he could go. Over the hills we went. I couldn't even get his head around.

I just hoped we wouldn't hit a hole and end up in a pile. All I could do was ride it out until he got tired of running. At the end of the run, the horse was ready to go back to the ranch. It just seemed like a lot of long rides, and we made pretty good horses out of them. The horses that are trained today have a much better handle on them, but maybe they are not as tough of a horse.

Lynn Ediger
Wolf Point, Montana

HENRY, THE STUD HORSE

I found a three-year-old Quarter horse stud I liked, but I had no money to buy him. I related my problem to my mother. Well, the only one in the family that had any money was my old grandpa, who lived in Chinook and was about ninety years old and a hard man. I told my mother, "I'm going to ask Grandpa to loan me the $300 I need." Mother told me, "Grandpa will never give you that money."

"Well, Mother," I said, "all he can say is no. I'll try it anyway."

So in to Grandpa Kuhr I go. He is glad to see me until I ask for money to buy that stud horse. Then that old gent throws a fit worse than any horse I ever saw. He hit me with his cane and hollered at me, "Horses, horses. I'm not loaning you any money to buy a Goddamn horse." He threw several other words in that I neither remember nor even understand.

The old fellow finally ran out of wind. I said, "Grandpa, are you going to loan me the money or not, just say yes or no."

"No," he said, "and get the hell out of here." Just as I'm going out the door, Grandpa hollered at me, "Come back here. I used to like horses, too. I'll give you the money, and remember I want to take a look at that horse I bought." Grandpa was pretty tough, but I knew in his heart he still liked horses.

That's how I got Henry. That's what I named him. His pedigree was so long I just shortened it all up. Henry was three years old, and we had our trials and tribulations. Before I was done, I found out he likes to buck, just as well as those scrubs I had, but we got along after a fashion and I took in a few mares to breed. Also, I found out this horse had an eye for a cow, which means he liked to work cattle, so I decided to make a cutting horse out of him, and I did. I don't know how they train cutting horses, but this is how I trained him.

I'd have cattle in my big corral, and I would cut one out and see if I could keep it away from the others. At first I was patient, and if the horse made a mistake, I overlooked it. After a while he knew what he was doing, but being lazy, he would let too many cattle get by him. This is how I corrected that: I got some baling wire and made a whip about two and a half feet long by twisting it together. Then when, out of his laziness, he let a cow get by him, I would hit him on the thigh just as hard as I could, only once, and it wasn't long before he had it figured out. If he let the cow get by him, he got whacked, and this hurt, as sometimes he had three or four big welts on him where I had hit him. That's the only punishment I gave him. One mistake, one whack.

Now Henry became the best cutting horse I ever rode. No cow could get by him, but during his gentle training when I whacked him for missing a cow, he got mad and bucked me off, and about the time I hit the ground, he was bucking so hard he fell down himself. That's the first time Henry bucked me off. I rode him all the other times, and Henry was a very gentle horse, as long as he was ridden regularly. Let him have a week's rest, and he wanted to buck.

As he was a stud horse, every so often he got pushy and wanted to test you a bit to see if he could be dominant. About once a month he would do this, and then I would have to beat him up to keep his respect for me. Seems a little mean, but stud horses are strong willed, and if babied too much, they can be dangerous.

Joe Fay was a rich oil rancher and bought the best of horses. I helped him once on the reservation. There we had to cut out a lot of other people's cattle. Joe Fay had his two professionally trained cutting horses cutting out cattle, and I was also cutting out on Henry. I knew I had the best horse, and when we were finished, Joe Fay came up to me and said, "You know, I paid a lot of good money to have those two horses of mine trained, and that little horse of yours is better than both of them." I was proud then, and I am yet. He was the best cutting horse I ever saw.

Other than that, he had a lot of failings. He was so lazy he was no pleasure to ride any distance. He loved to outthink cows and was never lazy doing that. Also, he liked to buck. Other than the work he loved, Henry was a pain in the ass. Being a stud horse, he had to be kept up. When he was out with mares and you got him and took him away from his ladies, he was mad, and usually, you had a bucking ride before he would settle down.

This Henry horse I suppose I loved, or at least he was in my heart. One time my wife and baby son were trailing our cattle to a lease I had on the reservation. I did the trailing of cattle with Henry, and my wife drove our pickup and set our camp up. We had a pretty cheap camp, a bedroll and some grub. When we went to bed, we rolled our bed out on the prairie and put the baby between us and went to sleep.

This one night we were camped on the east side of the Three Buttes. It was a beautiful night. My cattle were on water a quarter mile or so below us. I had hobbled Henry, and he was grazing grass for the night. About 2:00 a.m. I am woke up by something nudging against my body. I wake up somewhat startled and find my horse standing over me with his head about a foot above me and he is dozing. I don't know what to do. One jump in the wrong direction and Henry will kill us all in our own bed.

I don't want to scare my pony, so I lay still and say his name softly to him. "Henry, Henry, wake up. You're almost standing on us." My wife, hearing my mumbling, wakes up and thinks I am talking in my sleep. I say, "Hell, no, I ain't talking in my sleep. My horse is about standing on top of me."

Anyway, we are all awake now except the kid. I get up, unhobble Henry, and lead him out a little ways, hobble him again, then go back to bed, as I am tired, and go right back to sleep. Again, I am woke up. This Henry is right back where he was before, right over the top of me. I am laying out there wondering what to do this time. It comes to my mind, mares don't step on their colts, and Henry must know what he is doing, so I don't bother him and go back to sleep. I feel his hooves against me and roll a little ways away from him.

When we wake up in the morning, I have about pushed my wife and son out the other side of the bed. Henry's hooves are still against me. I think he would have followed me plumb across the bed. I guess he was just lonesome. Once you got Henry, the stud horse, away from home, he was really quite a friendly fellow.

Jim Halseth
Chinook, Montana
Animals I Knew, Dogs and Horses and a Cat or Two

THROWING THE HOOLIHAN

The hoolihan is thrown while you're on the ground for the purpose of four-footing horses mainly. You start out with your rope in your roping hand on your left shoulder, if you are right-handed, bringing your rope around across your body to behind your back, throwing it overhand while leaning forward a bit. The purpose is that your loop gets there faster and is standing vertical instead of the traditional way, which makes it pretty hard to catch the front feet.

I learned mostly by watching Shirley Bridges (he was foreman of the CBC Prairie Elk Ranch) and Sid Vollen; he was foreman of CBC Miles City Ranch. Also, Hobart McCain was very good at it. He four-footed them, then watched, catching their front feet in the air, jerking up the slack in the rope before their front feet came to the ground. When they hit the ground, you ran around behind them, pulling their front feet up in the air. The horse almost always would kick with his hind feet, and one of the feet will go between the front feet, hence being hog-tied, without anyone else to help.

That is the way I've done it, too, while working alone. I also learned a lot from Leo Taylor, a CBC ranch hand, whom I worked for.

Gale Drewry
Savage, Montana

THE FURSTNOW SADDLE #700

I was born at Lane, Montana, which is between Manrock and Enid. Lambert is where I grew up and went to school. (We had our fiftieth class reunion on September 6, 1997, which was a great success.)

Shorty Crockett was down the road a ways, north of Richey. I knew him as long as I could remember. He was really good people. They didn't come any better than Shorty.

In 1942 Shorty gave me an Al Furstnow saddle with the catalog number #700 stamped on the seat. I'm sure it was built sometime between 1910 and 1919, for that was the only catalog I found it in.

The way Shorty happened to give it to me was during the war, and I didn't have a saddle. Shorty needed a couple of horses broke, so we made a deal even up. Shorty said the saddle had a cracked tree in it, but if I wouldn't tie onto anything too rough, it would work. But you know how an ol' redheaded thirteen-year-old kid is (and freckle-faced, too) . . . well, I ended up with a broken tree.

Having the best dad ever, he wrote to Al Furstnow at Miles City. With the war on, we didn't know what to expect. As luck would have it, they had one tree for the #700 on hand. It didn't take long, and the cost wasn't too bad. It came back like a new saddle—woolskin lining, latigos, cinch, strings, the whole ball of wax. I rode it steady for about twenty-five years.

Then I sent it to Furstnow's and had them round the corners on the skirts and put in a three-quarter rigging. It was a good saddle and still is. I rode it in the Montana Centennial Cattle Drive from Roundup to Billings in 1989, which was the biggest event I ever took part in as far as people, horses, cattle, wagons, and anything else I might have left out.

I might add old #700 never looked out of place one bit, and I'm sure seventy-five years before, it would have been an eye-catcher.

If I didn't tell you that it leaked a few times, I'd be lying. I learned a long time ago not to use the word "never." I might not throw it on another horse, but I sure wouldn't take a lot for it. It's in good shape, wool lining and all.

I only had one new saddle in my life, and it was a Hamley bronc saddle. The last few years I got to thinking that I would like to have one more new saddle before I tip over, but that all changed this last summer. I spent about three days with my oldest grandson, Joe Blankenship, who was picking up at that night rodeo for Jim Ivory in Cody, Wyoming. Joe was looking for another saddle so he wouldn't have to change saddles when he switched horses, so we were going from saddle shop to saddle shop in Cody, looking for saddles. We walked into one shop, and there amongst a dozen or more saddles, old and new, there was this one saddle that really stood out. Before we got up to it, I said, "Hey, Joe! There's quite a saddle!"

"Yeah," he replied, "that's one of them Cliff Ketchum saddles."

That really got my attention, as Cliff was a good personal friend of mine, and I wasn't too interested in a saddle for Joe right then, but for myself!

Cliff had the San Fernando Valley Saddlery in California. He built saddles for some of them actors, and he put saddle seats in a Cadillac for one of them guys.

Yep, I walked out of that shop with that saddle! Several people thought I paid too much for it, but I'm sure I would have bought it even if it would have been quite a bit more. This saddle has the San Fernando Valley Saddlery stamp on it and also the "Cliff Ketchum

Custom Leather, Ralston, Wyoming" stamp . . . I wouldn't take a lot for it.

Fritz Rehbein
Rozet, Wyoming

I LEARN TO MILK A HORSE

Many cows had felt my fingers squeezing milk from their udders during my life, but never a mare. I had to learn to do it to save my younger stepdaughter's colt from death. The colt was attacked by a mountain lion one very dark, sultry night at about eleven o'clock.

I was sitting on the porch of my single-story log house drinking a cup of tea before going to bed, when I heard a horse squeal and the thundering of hooves. There wasn't a breath of air moving. Sound seemed to be magnified a hundredfold. Fran, my elder teenage stepdaughter, rushed onto the porch and whispered, "What was that noise?"

"It sounded like a scared horse," I replied. "Get the flashlight." I loaded my .30-30 rifle.

Near cliffs in the pasture, we found my younger stepdaughter Cher's thirteen-day-old colt, Lineback, standing by his mother's side. His head hung down to the ground. At first glance he seemed all right, but upon closer inspection we saw blood oozing from two puncture wounds in his neck, near his mane.

He was able to walk and broke to lead, so we led him and his mother to the makeshift barn I had built three weeks previously.

Fran and I applied a compress bandage to the wound to stop the bleeding.

Two neighbors arrived by all-terrain vehicles. They had heard the commotion and motored over to see what had happened. They said they had seen a large black bear the week before and thought maybe he was causing harm to the area livestock.

After closely examining the colt, we found scratches, as well as the punctures, on his neck and shoulders. We figured he'd been attacked by a mountain lion. One of the men knew horses better than I and told me the importance of the colt's getting his mother's milk at his age to keep his bowels moving.

By now Cher and her mother, Diane, were at the scene. We moved Lineback and his mother, Dusty, into the dirt-floored basement of the house, which was built into the side of a hill. Since the colt could not turn his head to nurse, I had to somehow get him to drink his mother's milk.

While cows have quite long teats, those of horses are very short, less than an inch long. The mare was extremely gentle. I got milk from her bag with my thumb and forefinger. She was very patient.

First I tried to feed the colt with a glove, filling it with the life-giving fluid, figuring Lineback would treat the finger as a teat, but he would not take it in his mouth. In retrospect I think it was probably because of the taste of the material.

As an almost last resort, I tried a pie-pan full. He drank. I set the alarm clock for three hours. According to my neighbor, that was a must. On the third day after the attack, Lineback was well enough to turn his head to nurse. He eagerly sucked away.

We put him in the corral and doctored him for two weeks with combiotic antibiotic and hydrogen peroxide. We had to make sure his wounds did not get infected. It was the end of May and quite hot. Fran and I held him while Cher applied the medicine with a large syringe.

We found out how serious his injuries were one day when the medicine shot out the opposite side of his neck. Apparently the lion's fangs had met in the middle. Why wasn't his nervous system damaged? The girls and I looked up a horse's anatomy at the library in town and found that his spinal column ran through the center of his neck. The lion's fangs had only caused a flesh wound. About a month later one of the neighbors said that a mountain lion had been seen with a mashed face. Could that have been from one of Dusty's hooves?

Lineback healed fine, and Cher sold him when he was a three-year-old to a girl who was fascinated with his "colthood" history.

It was a new experience for me. I had been raised on a ranch and considered myself a pretty knowledgeable cow and horse hand. I had learned to milk cows before I was ten years old; it took me forty more to do the same with a horse.

This happened about two miles up Haywire Gulch, which is located ten miles south of Kalispell, during the spring of 1983. The mare, Dusty, was a kid horse, about ten years old and therefore quite gentle. She was a lineback buckskin.

Henry Boyle
Great Falls, Montana

GATHERING THE BLACKFOOT

In 1956 Tom, a friend and neighbor, had recently taken over the management of his father's ranch and needed help to gather and ship cattle because there was a drought and his aging father had not been able to gather and ship everything that should have been sent to market the previous year. Tom and Dave would gather the ones to ship until they had four truckloads and would then load a couple of trucks as early as possible in the a.m. and take them to the sales ring in Billings, which was two hundred miles away.

They'd double back and each take another load; it would be midnight before they'd get to Billings with their second load, so they'd go to bed. It made a long day after all the work, besides driving six hundred miles, and it didn't take long to stay all night!

Gathering wild cows and yearlings and two-year-old bulls out of the breaks in Blackfoot is not exactly a picnic in the park. It took a lot of good horseflesh and many miles of riding and roping. They had a number of the wild bulls tied to trees along the way to soften their disposition. After a night of those bulls being tied to a tree, Tom and

Dave managed to get them on into the corral and shipped. They did this steady for a full two-week period before wrapping the job up.

There are no guarantees in a situation like this, except for a few bruises and minor wrecks along the way. Dave felt they were lucky to accomplish the mission.

Kathryn Huston
Brusett, Montana

ROPING THE CAT

This was probably, oh, late '50s, early '60s, and it was up north, in the breaks north of Snow Creek, northwest of Jordan.

Ray Beecher and I were riding up there horseback. His son Glen, when he was a kid, would run a trapline, and we come across one of his traps that had a bobcat in it; he had one foot snagged. This cat was pretty feisty, and we didn't want to kill him because his hide was no good. It was getting on towards spring and too late in the season for his hide, so we were going to turn him loose.

So Ray roped him, dallied on his horse, and kinda stretched him out a little, and I got a forked stick there, pinned him to the ground, and got the trap loose off his foot.

Well, then he got loose from me. He run up the hindquarter of the horse Ray was riding, and he was right behind the cantle—you know how your skirts come back; he was partially on those skirts, setting there, swatting at the back of Ray. The big commotion, of course, was Ray trying to knock him off with his elbow, because he had his back to the bobcat. It was funny—I got to laughing, as the cat was hanging on behind him , with Ray grunting and trying to knock him off. He finally got it done. But it was funny to watch. Of course, he wasn't amused.

Ray was riding a buckskin horse that come out of one of Binion's studs, one of the best horses I'd ever been around for temperament, a good cutting horse, rope horse, you could do anything on him, and that horse didn't throw a fit when that cat jumped up there behind Ray, so he was lucky—most horses would have had him bucked off by then.

The bobcat didn't make it up in one bound; he went right up that horse's leg. Most horses would have thrown a tizzy. I was surprised at that. It happened pretty fast, that part of it. Then the cat just kinda set back on his haunches and swatted at Ray with his front feet.

But Ray got him knocked off, and the cat still had the rope on him. I'd got a stick with a yoke on it like a slingshot, and I finally got him pinned down and got the rope off him. We turned him loose. He kinda . . . took off. He wasn't hurt too bad, just that part of his foot in the trap; if he'd of been hurt bad, we'd probably have killed him. I don't think he'd been there too long because he was pretty feisty.

Of course, the cat was stationary; you didn't have to chase him down and rope him. That trap was staked down, and it was Glen's trap. He was just a kid yet in high school. I don't know if he'd remember us telling him about it or not.

Anyhow, mine's a firsthand account. There were just the two of us there. If they challenge me on it, I'll just tell them I'm senile.

Hank Green
Circle, Montana

A TOUCH OF ROMANCE

Time for romance? "No," most cowboys or ranchers would quickly reply, "the work has to be done first, then . . . maybe."

However, that gentle side appears in subtle ways.

We were young and trying to establish the ranch in the 1960s, and there wasn't a lot of time or money for luxuries or romance, at least not as the movies portray. But in those years, in the spring, the gumbo hills would come alive with wildflowers, and as Denzil checked on the cows, he would reach down from his horse and grab a handful of color. When he came home, he would hand them to me with a grin and never say a word. By the time he finally reached the house, they were usually wilted, even though they still had their roots and gumbo dirt attached, as time didn't allow for getting off the horse to be selective!

But to me they were a dozen roses from the finest flower boutique. For over thirty years I received flowers from those gumbo hills. I never found out their names, but it didn't matter; they always brightened my kitchen in a special glass vase—wilted or not!

Though Denzil is gone now, God still seems to allow at least a few of the wildflowers to bloom, even during the droughts, and for me it keeps that precious memory of a touch of romance alive each spring.

Sonja Crocker
Wife of Denzil Crocker
Rosebud, Montana

Denzil Crocker on the Crocker Ranch, east of Rosebud 1964. COURTESY OF SONJA CROCKER

RANCH LIFE IN THE BEAR PAWS

Down by the windmill, next to the well,
I have a story, I'd like to tell.
It's springtime in the Bear Paws, in north central Montana land,
And me, just a cowboy, or sometimes called a hired hand.
It's calving time down by the willow flats,
It's time to take off our felts and put on our summer hats.
As the snow melts from the mountain tops,
and the meadowlarks begin to sing,
Winter is behind us and now, we know it's spring.
As the crocus and the cactus begin to bloom and show,
It won't be long before the hay will be ready for us to mow.
The grass in the bottomlands and hayfields are lush and green,
And the prettiest part of the world, I don't think I've ever seen.
The cows are in their summer pastures growing fat and fast,
If the market holds, the rancher will make a profit, I hope, at last.
And hopefully he will see his way clear,
To pay a little bonus to the ranch hands this year.
As summer is ending and fall is getting near,
We are getting into the busiest time of the year.
Trailing, sorting, shipping, bawling cows and dust,
Before it's over, it's a wonder it doesn't get the best of us.
Saw a few snowflakes the other day,
So it kinda tells me winter is on the way.
Better get the teams ready and patch up the hay racks on the sleigh.
I hope this winter isn't too cold,
I've been on this ranch for over forty years and I'm getting kinda old.
It won't be long before I'll probably move to town,
Cause this is one old ranch hand they won't need around.

Victor R. Mord
Birchdale, Minnesota

CHAPTER 8

RANCHING LOG

All stories in this chapter are by L. D. (Dean) Switzer, contributed by Dean's wife, Pat Switzer, Richey, Montana.

BADLANDS TERRAIN

To describe the badlands and the outlying mountains in the Missouri River country of Montana is a task that must be aided by a ready imagination on the receiving person's part.

There is a brief area that seems to act as a moderator between the rocks and timber of the mountains and the gumbo crags and timber of the badlands. By the people who live in the Missouri River country, these insignificant areas are rather carelessly called "the flats." True enough, some parts are quite level, but the "flats" are apt to abound with cut coulees that make a running horse or steer do a quick rehash of his plans and either call off the chase or take a new start.

Still, they are the flats because looking one way the country falls abruptly and the other way are the many small mountain ranges that give that part of Montana its own complete little history.

The coulees that fall away from little hogbacks and round pinnacles on the flats start their riotous trip to the river sedately enough, but that soon ends!

Soon there appears a juniper bush or two and maybe a couple of bull pines, then a couple of sharp turns, and you can no longer see out of the coulee. About now, you begin to notice the gumbo is quite loose and porous, and the banks of the coulee have begun to funnel out toward the top and have a scattering of timber along the slope facing north.

In the bottom there is a growing gash that begins to dodge boulders that block the way and gnaw along a big overhanging wall. The bottom may begin to show traces of water, and in the larger coulees a small alkali stream sometimes develops.

In the big coulees there will be a trail show now and small patches of buffalo grass will cover the edges of the coulee bottom. A look up now and the north slopes are covered with a dense growth of fir and juniper thickets. The fir timber is tall and straight and the juniper a small twisted wreck that looks as if the firs had just finished tramping it down.

The south slopes are mostly bare and loose, shaley gumbo that seems to defy timber or grass. They rear menacingly to heights of a

The badlands of the Missouri River Breaks are so rough, the only way to get through them is horseback. COURTESY L. D. "DEAN" SWITZER

thousand feet in places and give a saddle horse a stiff half hour to reach the top.

Very abruptly, the bluffs along the edge of the coulee end and a green bank of cottonwood trees and willows appears, bordering the Missouri River.

The river varies from one-eighth to one-quarter of a mile wide, and to the river cowboys there are only two depths, "wading water" and "swimming water." The measure is on a horse, of course, though it would be about the same on a man.

The river itself makes a lasting impression, winding through what almost constitutes a gorge, breaking around islands, easing out into five-hundred-yard expanses, to rush over a reef that lies across the riverbed.

These reefs of rock are what make the fords that the river cowboys learn to know as well as they know the inside of their hat. Their horses get to know the fords as well as or better than the riders do.

To get back on the flats now and head for the mountains, instead of starting in a coulee, the route starts following hogbacks and benches. When the foot of the mountains is reached, after very few miles, the trail will lead into a canyon where cattle and horses have grazed. The canyons have sparkling little creeks that water abundant growths of serviceberries and chokecherries, also plum and thorn thickets, which the cattle love to scratch their backs in. Many a cowboy has lost half a month's pay in shirts and Levis torn off in a battle trying to dislodge a stubborn critter from these little bovine forts.

As soon as the grass and water play out, the cattle trail ends and one used for climbing the mountains begins. It's much less comfortable, but also more efficient.

In no time you can see a day's ride laid out below, leading toward the river. The higher you ride, the deeper you can see toward the river, and at the summit it seems you can almost see the water.

The panorama below is a great confusing mass, where ridge meets ridge and coulees join and form a creek, all ending at the river many miles away and thousands of feet below.

During cloudbursts, water falling where you stand will be in the river and on its way to the Mississippi in a few hours.

A unique twist to this country is that the panorama is remarkably similar on either side of the river. The Breaks, as they are called locally, are about the same, and the mountains are very similar—short, complete ranges in themselves and still forming a pattern as if the river were the center of a great amphitheater hundreds of thousands of acres in size, with a gateway to the east.

MOVING IN

The last reluctant, bunch-quitting steer hopped over the log, and Mac said, "Well, boys, we've got 'em. They're home."

We led the packhorse and our saddle horses over the log and dropped the reins. They immediately began grazing on willow leaves

L. D. "Dean" Switzer at the cabin where he and his brother, Bob, summered in the Breaks.
COURTESY L. D. "DEAN" SWITZER

and the fresh grass. The rest of the brush and light limbs were piled on the log to constitute a barrier, and the little bunch of "Southerns" had completed a journey from the Arizona deserts to the banks of the Missouri River in Montana.

We mounted, and Bob caught up the packhorse's halter rope. "Where you gonna camp," he asked, "in the old shack?"

"I'll look first," I replied and loped up the trail the steers had taken.

The old cabin was a relic of homestead days and made of cottonwood logs, with a dirt roof. It had been abandoned for ten or fifteen years, and the weather had given it a pretty good working over.

I tied my horse to a big sagebrush by the door, stomped the step with a boot heel and listened for the buzz of a rattlesnake. They think very highly of old buildings for summer camps.

I didn't hear anything, so I took a stick and shoved the door open and rapped the log above the door and listened again.

Still no buzz, so I stepped gingerly through the door and looked around—first for snakes and then to size up the prospects as a camp.

One corner of the roof had fallen in, and the foot of dirt that had been on top was now inside and spread over the floor by rainwater. All in all, it looked much less inviting than a clean patch of grass under one of the big cottonwoods.

I said as much to Bob and Mac, so we rode over a couple of hundred yards and spooked some steers out of what they and we thought was a likely looking spot.

A big cottonwood spread branches out over a thick stand of bluejoint grass a foot high and nice and green. It was only a hundred yards from the river, and dead limbs provided wood. Everything looked fine for a long or short stay. We jerked my bed and grub off the packhorse and stowed it in the edge of some rose briars and prepared to leave again.

Bob and Mac had to go back out of the breaks to where the pickup truck waited. We'd come as far as possible with the pickup, then packed on into the river. I was going along to see if I could pick up a steer we lost in the timber before we hit the river.

They had to go down the river to a ferry to cross and get on to the ranch. It was June, and the river was way high from the June rains and snow melting in the Rockies. I had to camp with the cattle until they located on their new range; then I could cross to the ranch.

During the rainy part of June in that country, it rains every afternoon or evening, and we had been soaked every day while trailing out from the railroad.

This day was no exception, and when we hit the top after climbing an hour or so, there was a big black shower headed for us from the west. Mac and Bob were in a hurry immediately! In the gumbo country a pickup either stays on good footing or doesn't travel when a thunderstorm strikes.

They left with very little ceremony—Bob said, "Mac, you lead my horse." And Mac said, "So long. I'll holler across tomorrow." In a couple of minutes, the timber hid them, and a big drop of rain spooked me into a thick bunch of fir trees. I got under a big one and put on my slicker just after I got wet instead of just before.

I hunkered down and thought about my camp. Maybe the rain didn't reach that far north. Maybe the tarp was tucked under the grub, where the wind couldn't get it. Maybe the wood wouldn't be too wet. Maybe it was the other way around, too.

In an hour the sun was showing low in the west and I was five or six miles from camp, so I got on my horse and let the tail end of the shower chase us down the trail toward the river. Water was running everywhere, and I wasn't too hopeful for a dry camp.

When I hit the river and started up the trail through the narrows, I could see a lot of drift running on top of the water. I knew my camp was wet!

It was. Also the steers had come back and tramped on my bed. The nice, green, foot-tall bluejoint was nearly covered with water, and the labels off my canned grub were floating around in it. From then on I opened cans by the sound of the contents and found that beans, tomatoes, and peaches all sound alike.

The old shack looked quite a lot better now. I packed my bed over and hung the blankets around on sagebrushes and rose brush and hoped they'd dry a little before dark. Then I brought over the grub and found some dry sticks and made a fire in the old stove. The stovepipe lacked about four feet of reaching the roof, but the other end of the roof was gone, so I guessed I could stand the smoke.

My only water receptacle was a two-quart coffee pot, so I took it and headed for the river. The water was so muddy you'd have to chew a little to drink it, so I tried a cactus, split the flat way, for a settler. It gathered some mud, all right, but there was plenty left when I pulled it out and put the coffee in. That coffee didn't change the color of the water at all, but it smelled different, so I just decided the mud was coffee grounds and liked it fine.

Before I got my coffee boiled, the smoke had me hunkered down on the floor, where there was a little breeze, and I'd heard pack rats quitting the logs in the roof for half an hour. Once in a while one would take the usual route, which was via the old stove, and give a squeak and take off like a flying squirrel. The stove wasn't very hot, but the pack rats were barefooted.

I was pretty well convinced that there weren't any snakes in the house by then, so I gathered up my blankets and tarp and made a bed up with the edges tucked clear under and the only opening at the top, and it quite small. All the varmints I'd been hearing made me give quite a lot of care to tucking under the tarp.

I saddled up and loped up to the other end of the bottom to see if any steers had started to climb out. They were all bedded down on some buffalo sod, where it wasn't muddy, and looking full and happy. That made me feel pretty good, so I went back to camp, staked my horse, and went to bed. The old shack didn't look like it was on fire any more, and the pack rats had stopped making a racket, so it seemed a little more friendly. I had put my tobacco sack and some matches on a little shelf close to the door, which is where the head of my bed was, just to have 'em handy.

We'd been in the saddle at daylight that morning, and that's about 3:00 a.m. in Montana in June; dark comes about 9:30 in the evening, so I didn't toss and turn any; I just went to sleep.

I awoke scared and just as wide awake in an instant as I could have got in an hour. I couldn't hear anything, but I knew something had wakened me because I was spooked and tense, listening. I was thinking "snake" and afraid to move, when something scratched my bare leg right about the knee. I came out of that bed like a shot, and if the door hadn't been right at my head and open, I'd have torn the whole east end out of that old shack.

I stood just outside and listened. All I could hear was my shirttail flapping. There may have been a breeze, but my heart was pounding hard enough to pop my shirttail.

I was scared to walk around, barefooted, and couldn't see anything except stars. I could hear something scratching around in my bed then and decided my companion had been a pack rat. I didn't see how he could be fatal, so I stepped in and groped for my matches. I found a couple and lit one just as a pack rat climbed up on the old stove. He was probably the wrong one, but I settled for him—I picked up a willow cane the homesteader had conveniently left and lambasted him. He squeaked and immediately was answered by his relatives. I was pretty mad then, because I'd been so scared, and pounded around on everything to spook them all outdoors.

I think the only thing I spooked was my saddle horse. He snorted and blew like a wild horse every few minutes for an hour or two.

Morning finally came, and was I tired! I'd listened all night— between catnaps. My Bull Durham was missing, so I didn't have a smoke until I packed my bed out to finish drying. That pack rat had been carrying it when he crawled in with me.

SWIMMING WITH A STEER

The grass and clover were getting scarce on the bottom we had the steers running in, so we decided to move 'em over to Cow Island. We wanted to cross the river as easily as possible, so doing it half at a time looked good.

Cow Island is in the middle of the Missouri and about a mile long, half a mile wide in the middle and pointed at each end. It has a couple of thick groves of cottonwoods and acres and acres of rose briars and willows.

Horses hate the briars, and men hate the willows and briars both. The briars are just about the height of a critter and will make a horse bleed across the forelegs and chest while following a steer who is trying to brush up and give a rider the slip. Once in a while an old pony gets to jumping over the tops, instead of tearing a trail in them and is about as hard to "set" as a bucking horse.

The willows average about twelve feet high and are as "thick as the hair on a dog." Most of 'em are about the size of a fifty-cent piece in diameter and flexible as a buggy whip. They'll gouge you, whip you, pull you off your horse, and above all, they blind you. A horse puts his head down and follows the cattle trails in the lower part of the willows, and a rider sticks up in the thick part, where they've woven the new shoots together. Let a horse follow a critter into that on a lope and keep on loping until he and the critter have come into the open. If you're not missing and still have your hat, you've the makings of a river cowboy. Half of my first summer on the river was spent hunting my hat and occasionally my horse.

To get back to the steers: We gathered the brush last so we wouldn't have to work it twice, and also, the cattle in the open wanted to go to the brush.

Bob and I were working it together, and every now and then we would get out in the open where it was quiet and lope back a ways to listen for something moving in the brush. We found plenty of 'em doing the sneak before we got out in the open with the bunch.

We pushed the steers out on a big sandbar and held 'em there, yelling and crowding until the lead started to cross the hundred yards or so of water to Cow Island. As soon as the lead hit swimming water, we began to alternate our own positions from front to back of the herd, trying to hold them straight till they started coming out on the island shore. That is a job always referred to as "hell on horses." It is, too. They have to swim their utmost, then turn back and outrun a bunch quitter going for the wrong shore. Their sprints are made in water that's belly deep as well as in shallows.

If you're in the river by design instead of by accident, you're nearly sure to be riding your best, and pet, horse. That makes for more consideration of how you're using him. The green horses get their best experience when you get in by accident; they think a critter on dry land is a snap after a few sessions in the river.

The water was warm and clear, it was late in July, and we hadn't any

Mac Bethune and Bob Switzer fording the Missouri River. COURTESY L. D. "DEAN" SWITZER

trouble. We had lost two or three but figured they'd cross easy enough when they saw the others on the island.

We were sadly mistaken. We'd reckoned without a little, snaky two-year-old. He was an artist at hiding in the briars and fast as a deer. He would run full tilt through the worst briars until he'd get tangled and go down; then he'd want to fight. We tried everything we knew: Ropes he'd tangle in the brush and under a horse's tail. A stick across the horns, and he'd fight harder or sulk, and he wouldn't run until he could sprint for cover again.

After so long a time, we had worked him to the water's edge under a cut bank. Then we got upstream and downstream a hundred feet or so and ran our horses at him simultaneously. His nerve broke, and he jumped into the river and hit swimming water immediately.

We hit right behind him and gave a little encouragement with a couple of green willows. He finally took the hint and started swimming for Cow Island. We were congratulating each other on our good luck as we climbed out onshore again. We began to wonder how wet our tobacco and papers were as we looked back toward the little two-year-old.

To our disgust and amazement, he was about halfway to the island and standing in water less than belly deep. He was looking right at us shaking his head a little, then taking quick, short steps with his front feet. All the while his tail was switching both ways. He was about as mad as seven hundred pounds of steer can get.

He showed signs of coming back any minute, and we could see he was on a semisolid sandbar. One foot after the other kept breaking through the solid sand on top into quicksand. He'd walk a few steps and repeat the performance. Also, he was trying to work up courage enough to come back where we were. We threw rocks and waved our hats and yelled our heads off, but he stood pat. Our horses with us and our saddles would weigh 1,250 pounds, and we knew that quicksand would bog a horse, and there was enough water over it so he'd drown as soon as he got down. The steer had our "tail in a crack," and he knew it.

We sat in the shade of some willows for half an hour or so; then I said to Bob, "I'm gonna take off my clothes and go out on that bar and try to spook him. He's cooled off a lot now."

"He'll probably spook you, but you ain't gonna spook him," he stated.

Then, of course, I had two lessons to teach—one to Bob and one to the steer.

I lack webbed feet, but I dog-paddled out to the sandbar a couple of hundred feet below the steer. By now I could see there was going to be no surprise for the steer. He showed fight a-plenty.

I had three or four little rocks to open hostilities. When the water was about knee deep, I could see it was time to start gettin' in my bluff or else start gettin' out.

My first little rock splashed water in his face, and he started taking up the slack I had to work in. I still wanted to run my bluff, so I threw the rest of my rocks and charged him, yelling and screaming my loudest. He thought, "This is it" and took a bead on my belly, and he charged, too.

He won right then, but quitting wasn't any too easy. My first dodge I fell down, but as luck would have it, so did the steer. We were ducking around in two feet of water, which didn't improve our footwork. The steer got just as much water and sand in his eyes as I did, I guess; anyhow he didn't see me immediately. I was still lying on my side with only my head showing, and the steer evidently didn't see me.

He was looking toward the bank where Bob was hollering, "Give him hell, spook him, grab his tail. He can't hurt you."

Then he'd laugh till the horses he was holding would start backing away.

About then the steer ducked his head my way and blew his nose in my face. I splashed water in his face, and he hooked at me with a horn and took off downstream, kicking at me as he passed. I was glad to see him go.

That day I named that steer "The Little Wringy," and he was still wild the last I saw of him. He was charging a gate man in the Sioux City stockyards.

Yes, he went across to the wrong side of the river—missing Cow Island entirely.

HORSE "WRASSELING"

We had a neighbor, two creeks up the river, who had a couple of hundred Thoroughbred and "Thoroughbred-cross" horses. They were fast, smart, and thoroughly wise about avoiding being corralled. The local terrain lent itself admirably to their will unless several riders were working together.

The trails were in the best possible route of travel, which was often very bad, and the possessor of the trail was in command of the situation. A rider couldn't pass a bunch of horses, and they couldn't pass him.

Most of these horses answered every qualification of a wild horse except that they carried a lazy S six on their left hips. Only "slicks" and some old renegades were called "wild horses" locally. These old renegades were usually carrying the brand of an owner long since gone from the breaks. The offspring of these were considered the property of the man who was "hand" enough to corral and brand them, thus ending their career as "slicks."

These wild bunches were usually led by some wise old mare or a cagey old gelding running with some fillies and young studs that the old stud had whipped out. They get whipped out of the bunch the spring they are two-year-olds. Most range stallions clean out the two-year-old fillies, too. That seems to be nature's way of keeping away from destructive line breeding.

This neighbor of ours we'll call Bill. He is one of the oldest and best of our Montana friends. We could never have found a better neighbor. He helped us with our work when we were shorthanded, showed us fords across the Missouri, taught us in such a way that we thought we figured it out ourselves, and then, when work grew tedious, he showed us how to play. He is as full of sly little jokes as he is of good humor. He has been a good cowboy for nearly fifty years and still takes calf-roping money home from rodeos.

Bill dropped a word about branding his colts, and we both said, "When?"

"Pretty soon, I guess, about tomorrow morning."

"We'll be over. What time?"

Bill started riding off. "Oh, not too early." He grinned and added, "About four," and loped away.

We felt pretty good. We were going "filly chasing" with one of the best of them all.

We "jingled" the saddle horses and caught two good ones and let them fill that night on good bluejoint hay so they wouldn't gaunt so bad on the next day's ride. "Filly chasing" is the toughest work a saddle horse can draw in the breaks.

Next morning we had an early breakfast of venison and sourdough

Wrangling the horses on People's Creek. COURTESY L. D. "DEAN" SWITZER

pancakes and pulled out, up Cow Creek. There were five of us, all well mounted. Bill's grandson Cayuse was one of us, along with his dad and Bill, plus Bob and me.

Cayuse was the best mounted of the lot. He rode a little pinto pony—half Shetland and half Thoroughbred. Cayuse weighed about seventy-five pounds, wringing wet, and was ten years old. Tough as a boot and not much bigger.

We began to split up after three or four miles, and single riders would go up a ridge. We aimed to throw all the horses we could find into Cow Creek and hold them together till we had enough to go in.

Well, when you get behind that kind of livestock, you'd better be horseback or you'll lose 'em.

An hour after we had split up, little bunches of horses were showing, running down the ridges toward the creek. They'd stop briefly for a few sips of water, splash a little, and start climbing out the other side. When that kind of horse is disturbed, he won't fill up on water. He knows he may have to run, and a belly full of water would sure hold him back.

Climbing out of the creek, they'd meet horses coming in, and they'd all whirl and come back. Then the old wise mares began acting up. They'd spot a rider or two and try a trail those riders couldn't reach in time to turn them. Then they'd hit another rider they hadn't seen. That would confuse them long enough for the men to kind of bunch the whole herd, and two riders would take the lead and a couple more bring up the rear.

Due to washouts, cutbanks, boulders, timber, etc., the riders couldn't do much outside of trail, so the wise old mares had a chance to escape again. They followed in a lope or fast trot pretty well, but now and then one would make a break for a trail leading out of the creek. One such break was made by a sorrel bald-faced mare—with her gang right at her heels.

Cayuse was the only one in position to cut her off, and he was right on the job. He and the lead mare were racing for the trail, and the mare beat him by a few yards. Cayuse and the little paint pony didn't hesitate: They took to the rough going and kept in the race; the little black and white speedster was gaining, too. The mare was the first to notice he was coming up on her, but she had no intention of giving up and turning toward the creek again.

At last Cayuse got a break; the trail turned sharply his way, and he got the good going, putting the bunch quitters at a disadvantage. When he got ahead of them, Cayuse began waving his hat and yelling. They checked and whirled back the way they'd come with Cayuse right at their heels, piling them off that hill.

Cayuse was riding a "single rig" saddle. Going up that hill on a run had slipped it back a ways and his blanket was coming out from under the saddle skirts. When he started back down the hill, his pony was hitting hard with his front feet to brake himself a little, and that single rig bounced right over his withers and pitched Cayuse down over the edge of the trail. He rolled a time or two and came to his feet running.

He had lost his reins and wasn't aiming to be set afoot if he could help it. He was just in time to stop his pony. The saddle had dropped down over his head and thrown the little paint, too, giving Cayuse time to get in front of him.

Cayuse was a good little cowboy—he didn't waste a moment. Leading his pony back up the hill to his saddle, he slapped it back on and cinched it to stay. He stepped on and quirted his pony down the hind leg and highballed down that hill with a grin. He had got the bunch he was after, and the spill didn't matter—he saw that we had held up a little so he could catch up, and what hide he had lost would grow back.

In less than an hour, we reached the mouth of Cow Creek at the Missouri and pointed the horse herd into a wing that led to the corral. One side of the wing was the river and the other side a fence half a mile long.

The experienced old mares and the stallions knew the futility of any shenanigans now, and jogged along getting their wind back. Not so with the two- and three-year-olds. They darted here and there through the herd and raced from the "lead" to the "drags," making a lot of commotion and whinnying for the pals they'd lost track of.

Once in the corral they quieted down after the old "boss stud" had cut the young studs and a sprinkling of geldings over to one side away from his mares and colts.

As if that was all they'd come for, all the young colts butted their mother's flank and proceeded to have a lunch. Thus reassured and fortified, they began looking over their new surroundings with a reckless disregard of other horses' opinions, until a frown from a stranger would send a colt scuttling back to his mother. She'd always look him over with nose and eyes to be sure he was her colt and all okay.

We ate dinner with a lot of talk, all horse talk, and Cayuse was right in the thick of it saying, "Gran, I could have got the 'Bally Mare' if she'd gone clear to Squaw Creek." Maybe he could have, too.

We all had good laughs when Bill told us of an old-time friend of his who was always in great demand at horse roundups. This friend could bulldog horses up to husky two-year-olds and never hesitated to tell strangers of his unusual ability.

Bill knew Bob and I had been around horses all our lives, but he also knew we hadn't much experience with raw broncs, and he went into much detail as to how this old friend of his took hold of a horse to throw him. That was Bill's way of giving advice—he made it available, and you could take it and nobody need know you were learning.

Everyone was anxious to get back to the corral and do the branding, gelding, and sorting of a few three- and four-year-olds who would be held and broken for saddle horses.

The big fellows we had business with were forefooted and hog-tied because of their size. One would spook past, and Bill's catch rope would snatch the two forefeet; the bronc would land on his side with a grunt. He'd be seized by one ear and his nose immediately and his head held until he quit struggling. Then he'd be hog-tied and ready for a lazy S six or whatever was his due.

When we started working on the yearlings and the "suckers," or baby colts, they were necked by a man on a horse and dragged, squealing and fighting, a few yards clear of the bunched horses by a rope dallied around the horn of a saddle.

Bill showed us the bulldogging hold to use, and from then on all we needed was practice, and we got all we could stand.

Theoretically, it goes this way: A man grabs the taut rope, holding the little bronc, and goes down the rope hand over hand, slips an arm over the colt's neck, reaches down, and grasps the lower jaw right behind the chin. Then the other hand loosens its hold on the rope and seizes an ear. The chin is lifted and turned out and back. The colt leaps, is overbalanced and falls flat on his side. The man is then in perfect position to hold him down, kneeling at his head with a nose hold and a knee on the colt's withers.

That's the theory. After *lots* of practice, it works that way and is very easy on the colts.

However, here is how my first one did: I went down the rope too fast, and the colt jumped forward before I touched him. Both of his front feet went over my shoulders, and his chest struck me full in the face. Needless to say, we both went down (especially me), and the colt made little, dollar-size tracks all over me before he got in the clear again. When I got up I was a little subdued and much chagrined. No one was sympathizing, and there were some poorly hidden grins. My next approach was more cautious, and I got a mane hold on the colt at the same time he got a finger hold on me! I'd left my hand too far out on the rope, and he grabbed it with his teeth. I jerked it loose and put the jaw and ear combination on him. He leaped, and sure enough! Here he came down—right at my feet. He didn't stop there, though; he had slipped out of my grasp and turned too far toward me. He kept on turning and knocked my feet out from under me, kicked me with all of his feet, got up and stepped on me some more, and was rid of me again! This time I didn't need to look; I could hear those grins.

I approached the colt and went down the rope, the third time a chastened and wiser man. With what I imagined to be great deliberation, I waded into those flashing front feet and past them, got my hand full of ear first, reached way down the off side for that jaw hold—and then it happened! I was overbalanced, with weight on the colt's withers; he sat back on his neck rope, then jumped mightily ahead. I stood on my head on the opposite side of him. He had me down again and was definitely the winner. There was lots of noisy grinning by then, and Bill said, "Guess we'd better send in a sub."

He walked over, though, and said, "Try it this way," and showed me slow and easy. I said, "That's the way I tried, Bill. I guess that colt doesn't know how."

We all took turns throwing the colts, and by night Bob and I could get by, too.

A couple of years later we got into a "colt wrasseling" experience that was out of hand from the very start.

We were summering our cattle on the Milk River, close to the Canadian border, and had some accommodating neighbors who knew a cowboy enjoys a meal cooked on a kitchen stove after a few months of cooking over a campfire. They also could use a little help occasionally, and we were glad to oblige.

This particular neighbor had a little bunch of spotted Shetland mares that he had crossbred to a burro, such as they use in Mexico. I guess the offspring are called Shetland mules.

Whatever they're called, they're so active they make a cat look "bogged down" by comparison. The fellows we were helping didn't profess to be experts handling broncs, although they were at handling a tractor or irrigating shovel. We, however, were considered and referred to as cowboys and hoped to remain as such.

We expected to take the lead in roping and throwing these little mules. They were "as cute as a bug's ear" and only about waist high to us. Most of the little mules were yearlings and "twos," pure white in color.

The first little mule, I necked. Bob was going to wrassel him. As soon as my loop settled around his neck, I realized we were not in for a snap. The little mule said, "Wah," and put up the fanciest job of wringing himself out we'd ever seen. He went through acrobatics that were intended to buck the rope off his neck, which was impossible. Had he not had foot-long ears, he might have kicked the loop off, though.

Bob was a little cautious at approaching such a dervish and got a good hold, called "Slack," and flipped the little fellow on his side. Then the commotion started again. The mule didn't care to have his long ears handled and could do something about it—he kicked Bob's hands loose, his little pointed hoofs fairly drumming. Bob leaned forward and pressed down on the mule's withers; promptly, he got kicked in the stomach and sat back on the seat of his blue overalls. The little mule leaped up and darted into the bunch of Shetland mares, skidding me along on the end of my rope.

Willing hands helped pull him back out in the clear, and Bob got ahold of him again. This time when he said, "Slack," "willing hands" went right on holding, and the little mule didn't fall. He braced his front feet against the pull of the rope and proceeded to kick up past his ears. He kicked past on one side, all right, but on the other his hoof was hitting Bob in the south end (as he faced north). One sharp little hoof cut through Bob's pant leg, and the next kick ripped it clear around and tore it off just below the pocket. After losing a lot of hide besides his pant's leg, Bob began losing interest also in that method of holding those little mules.

He let go after they'd both been up and down some more and picked up his hat, saying, "Give me a rope; I'm running out of clothes."

From then on we "head and heeled" the mule colts with catch ropes and hog-tied them down. Jogging back to camp that night, we were laughing about the day's events, and Bob said, looking down at his bare leg shining in the moonlight, "That first little mule! Boy, he turned me every way but loose!"

SNAKE-BITE MEDICINE

Rattlesnakes are numerous in the breaks and in the brush along the Missouri River. Being alert to their possible presence comes naturally after seeing many and having their sudden buzz startle you half out of your skin.

As a rule they want only to escape a person, and the buzz of their rattles quite often is a prelude to flight. Sometimes it's quite the opposite—a buzz and the flash of a striking head come almost simultaneously. This is apt to be the attitude of a snake in an area with good cover. Big sagebrush, rose briers, thick willow, or large boulders are excellent refuges for snakes. The caution they inspire in a person who is fifty or seventy-five miles from a doctor also makes their hiding easier. Many a snake is killed that is a half day's ride horseback from an automobile, let alone a doctor.

You never see a fat cowboy! Bob Switzer and Jim Kincaid. COURTESY L. D. "DEAN" SWITZER

Very seldom will a cowboy pass up a snake if there's a chance to kill it. I know one cowboy, a rider for a big outfit on the Belknap, who scuffs dirt at a snake to make it coil, then jumps on it with both boot heels. It's very effective, but I've no desire to use that method. My snake killer for the past several years has been a .22 caliber pistol that is carried in a holster permanently attached to my saddle skirt. I've also killed many rattlers with a lariat rope—just double it and pop the snake. It either stuns it or breaks its back. I've known fellows who cut a foot or two off the end of their lariat after killing a snake with it. They say they're afraid a snake might bite the rope and leave a broken fang sticking in a strand. A scratch from such might contain poison enough to be very uncomfortable, if not more serious.

Several persons were bitten by rattlesnakes in the Missouri River country while we were there, one a sheepherder whose horse, being loose in the daytime, excited enough curiosity to save his life.

His niece looked off the ridge, hundreds of feet above the river bottom, and spotted the loose horse. Deciding to investigate this slight variation of the usual, she rode down and found her uncle unable to move and near death from a snakebite. Because of her visit and subsequent medical attention, he recovered.

An Indian was leaving our neighbor's ranch after a brief stay. From the first gate he came racing his horse back, as pale as a white man. In a shaking voice he explained, "I got off at the gate and felt something on my boot. I thought it was wire and kicked it loose. Then it buzzed. I think I'm bit, Bill."

Bill got him quieted down with some one-hundred-proof "medicine" and looked his feet and legs over. After some more medicine the Indian began to think a snakebite couldn't hurt him and pulled out a second time. He lived, too. He hadn't been bit, but he had sure been scared.

I know about how he felt. One summer I got a snakebite scare. Bob and I were repairing a fence in Big Warm Canyon. We could drive to a bluff, right above Big Warm Creek, in our pickup truck. From there we had to walk into the bottom and repair the fence.

At one point we had to splice a wire that was broken. Quite a lot of rosebushes grew along the fence, and I was clawing them away with a claw hammer. I was kneeling to reach them easily, and when finished I rocked back on my heels. Bob was a few feet to one side and said quietly but distinctly, "There's a snake!"

I knew he had to be close and craned my neck one way, then the other, before asking, "Where?"

"Right under you," was the answer.

That was enough! I knew which way to go—and I went! When I came down I couldn't see any snake, and I thought he had said "snake" just to see me jump.

"I don't think that's so damn funny," I said, stepping back toward the fence.

"Look out or you'll get bit. Maybe you are anyhow," he added. "He's coiled right where your knee was."

Then I saw him! He was coiled about as big as a dollar and flattened out, trying to look like he wasn't there and doing a good job of it. In the yellowed grass and dead rosebush leaves, which blended nicely with his color, he was hard to see, then hard to recognize as a snake.

I "recognized" him with my claw hammer, then looked him over. He was a baby rattler about a foot long and had scarcely enough rattle to use at all.

He was squarely where I'd had my knee, and a slight depression had kept my weight off him.

Bob asked, "Are you sure he didn't bite you?"

Immediately, my knee developed all kinds of symptoms. It prickled, felt sore and any other sensation I happened to think of. The worst shock was when I pulled up my overall leg—the whole knee was discolored. Black and blue with a striking, yellow-greenish outline. Also, in places it was bloodshot with the pores of the skin like tiny red blisters.

"No little old snake did that," declared Bob. "That's a bruise."

"I know it," I replied. "That's where the Pete Mare got me the other day." The Pete Mare was the name of one of our brood mares. I was breaking her to ride that summer so she would be easier to handle on the range. She had fallen and caught my knee with the saddle horn.

"What are those little red spots?" Bob wanted to know.

"Nothing, I guess," I told him, "not snake bites anyhow."

"Well," he said, "if you're bit you'd better get to climbing that hill. I don't want to pack you out of here."

I figured I wasn't bit, but I had a notion to go on out and let him fix the fence.

We went on with our work. Every once in a while I'd sneak a look to see how my knee was doing. Several hours later, and back in camp, Bob said, "Well, if he bit you, I guess your poison was stouter than his."

One spring I had several near misses quite early, so a very kind neighbor lady fixed up a "snakebite kit" for me to carry. It contained a shoestring to use for a tourniquet, a single-edge razor blade to slash the bite, and a teaspoonful of potassium permanganate crystals to put in the wound. The crystals were to counteract or to throw out the venom of the snake, I guess; I didn't question what they'd do. Afterward I wished I had!

I carried that little outfit in a flat tin ex-lax box that would fit snugly in my buttoned shirt pocket.

I was making long rides that spring, on both sides of the river, and welcomed an invitation to help a neighbor slide some country under some broncs he had roughed out. He was a professional horse breaker. He made a business of breaking them for people who couldn't do it or hadn't the time. In an average year he'd break forty head. His name was Timmy Shannon, and he was a little black-headed Irishman.

Timmy had two gray geldings that needed riding; he gave me one, and he took the other. His was a "spoiled" horse that was treacherous, though a very good-looking animal. Mine was a big cuss and would have looked fine in a blind bridle with his head poked through a collar. He was pretty gentle, Timmy said, but plumb green. He had ridden him three or four times, and all he had done was sulk a little.

I saddled him up and started to "limber him up" before going out of the corral. I had a hackamore on him and had set it pretty high, since he was gentle.

The first time I checked him to make him turn, he dropped his head and tried to buck me off. He was so big he was awful rough, but I was gettin' by pretty well until he began to whip his head. That kept taking and giving me slack in my reins, and I got to clattering around in my saddle considerably. I blew a stirrup and was about to get bucked off when he butted a corral post and stopped.

Timmy was sure mad at that horse. He came over and tossed me his quirt, saying, "Go ahead and take it out of him."

"I'll ride it out of him, Timmy. It's too hot for a bucking horse ride."

That was right, but I got a couple more "rides" anyway, a few miles away from Timmy's. The old gray decided to go home and made it for a half a mile or so. Before I had him convinced that he should go my way, I had sweat through my shirt and my eyes were full of saltwater.

We got going again, and I had no more trouble with my steed. I was complaining about the heat, though. Timmy didn't say much about it, and I finally asked him if the sun was bothering his foot.

"No," he said. "But you had a pretty good workout."

"It's not that," I told him. "My foot in the shade is cool enough but the one in the sun is burning up."

The heat continued to bother me, and I kept hitching my belt, twisting my pant legs, and doing a lot of fidgeting, as much as the old gray would let me.

We finally came to a ranch close to the foot of the Little Rockies and stopped. I wanted to see the owner, who it turned out wasn't home. No one was there, so we put our horses in the barn and fed them. Then we got ourselves a meal and settled down in the shade outside the house.

"Let's pull our boots, Timmy," I said. "My foot is still burning from that sun."

"Mine are okay, but that's a good idea," replied Timmy. "I'll give you a pull."

He straddled my leg, taking my boot in his hands. I put a foot against the seat of his pants and pushed. We repeated the process all the way 'round.

My foot still burned, so I examined it closer. On the instep was a score or more small black spots. They looked like dirt, and I told Timmy, "I got a boot full of dirt when the old gray was bucking, I guess. It's pressed right into the skin."

He took a look and said, "I'll try my knife on 'em."

He did. I stopped him.

"I'll try to soak it out," I said. "It's smarting like the devil."

I got some water and a cloth and applied it to the spots.

"Holy cow," exclaimed Timmy, "it's turning purple."

Sure enough! Purple water was trickling away from each little black spot. We looked at each other wondering what kind of dirt that was.

About then I noticed the same stinging around my belt. I jerked my overalls off, and sure enough again! The black spots were all the way up my right leg and real thick at my belt line. The water turned purple again.

I didn't, and don't now, know anything about potassium permanganate, but I sure suspected that I'd spilled my snakebite kit. That's what it was. The old gray had shaken the little tin open and spilled the works into my shirt pocket.

I don't know if the snakebite medicine ate the hole in my pocket or the tin box wore it through. Whichever it was, I got the medicine without the bite, and I think the old gray came out on top.

I've never carried any more snake equipment than a .22 pistol since then.

GETTING OUR GOAT

Rodeos were our chief recreation in the summertime and, specifically, calf roping at said rodeos.

Calf roping is great sport and very competitive. The competition necessitates practicing quite a lot—or else not winning at the rodeos. Practice requires a calf (or several) to rope at home, and opinions vary considerably as to the effect on the calves.

Some, including myself, think the calves are just as big in the fall— roped or not. All they require is plenty of milk from their mothers and a little good judgment about how much they are used for roping practice.

Others say the calves don't get as fat or as big if they're roped, and therefore a substitute less valuable is sought.

Here is where the goats come in: They are much less expensive, and the loss is less in case of accidental laming or other injury. A goat is just as fast as a calf and much more elusive. This gives a roping horse valuable experience in following a dodging calf at top speed. Goats tie differently from calves—it's a matter of opinion whether they are easier or more difficult. The practice is beneficial from the standpoint of speed in tying.

As the boys found out, the goat always wins. COURTESY L. D. "DEAN" SWITZER

We and our neighbor Bill roped calves every Wednesday and Sunday evening. We used Bill's calves; he had three or four milk cows, and he split the "take" with their calves.

A family that lived a few miles up the ridge, toward the mountains, had some goats. They had a few too many, and the boys were trying to interest their neighbors in buying some of the kids that were weaning age.

They sounded like the real thing for roping, so we got a pair of kids. Bill took one, a male, and we took the other, a female. Everyone knows that a female goat is almost always called Nanny. We thought we'd be different, so we named ours Mary.

Mary developed to be the name of one of Bill's milk cows as well as of our goat. To differentiate between the two, we always said, "Mary-goat" or "Mary-cow." That gradually became established as one word, Maricow or Marigoat.

Marigoat was too small at first. We let her have a private barn while she grew, and she gradually came to regard it as her private refuge as well as her home. Marigoat was very friendly but also very stubborn. She welcomed a visitor in her barn and followed happily behind when walked for exercise. She grew fast and soon was eligible for roping.

We led her out from the barn a short way, released her, and sprinted toward her on horseback. She fled and entered her barn at full speed. We checked outside, and Marigoat figured the barn was impregnable. She'd stand inside the door, peering out, and "Baaaa" derisively.

After she knew where to run and how fast to start, we started roping her. After Marigoat had been roped and hog-tied a few times, she refused to lead back to the starting point. We didn't want to drag her, so we carried her! That worked fine . . . for a while. She was growing like a weed and soon was quite a load. We had to carry her about a hundred yards to give the roper a chance to throw; she ran like a streak.

She got so wise that she would jockey for position like a jockey does with his racehorse. If the roper, on his horse, was too close, she'd refuse to run and would scamper close to the heels of her "carrier."

After getting the roper out of position, or if he should get off his horse, she would be gone like a shot and safe in her barn. We admitted we'd been outwitted and quit roping her, except when by chance we'd catch her in the open at wrangling time or when coming in from a ride.

Bill had even worse luck; his goat would not run at all. The trouble was that they were too gentle and wouldn't scare.

After less than a month of roping Marigoat, I casually asked Bill, "How's your goat doing?"

"Not so bad," was his noncommittal answer.

"They seem to be lonesome, don't you think?" I asked.

Bill's ears pricked a little. "Yeah, maybe so," he said slowly.

"We ain't ropin' much now. We might let you use Marigoat—for a while," I ventured.

Bill looked thoughtful. "Well . . . I'll tell you, why don't you take my Billy for a while? I'm going to be pretty busy and I . . ." He looked sideways to see how I was taking it, and we both laughed.

From then on Bob and I tried to give Bill our goat, and he tried to give us his.

One day I caught a glimpse of a horseman below our barn in a bunch of willows. I figured he'd be up in a few minutes, and I went in the house and put on the coffeepot.

No one showed up, and I began to wonder, what was up? I ambled out to the corral and looked across Bull Creek. "Baaaaa," came a greeting, and there stood Bill's goat.

I knew then why no rider had showed.

I grabbed a horse out of the barn and hightailed it down into those willows. I found the goat, and he spooked toward home. I followed him until I was afraid I'd be seen by Bill, then went back home.

The next time I saw Bill I told him about the deer tracks in the willows below the barn—he didn't turn a hair.

Bill's son was working in Glacier Park that summer and only came down a couple of times to visit. One day he showed up and asked if he could borrow a team and wagon. He had some stuff at the top of the river hill to haul in. We always left our pickups on top because they couldn't pull out. The hill was too steep.

We got the team in for him and told him to drop in for dinner on his way home. He dropped in, and we had a chat after dinner. When he got ready to go, I said, "Say, Eddie, I told Bill he could have Marigoat. Why not lead her over behind the wagon?" He looked doubtful and hesitated before saying, "I dunno—I haven't anything to lead her with." He brightened when he thought of that.

"Oh, we've got lots of rope," said Bob. "I'll get you some."

He hurried into the barn and slashed a halter loose from its lead shank. "This'll hold her," he stated.

Eddie was looking dubious again, but we didn't give him time to weaken. Marigoat was easy to find. She was busy trying to scare the team. She departed behind the wagon.

The next time we saw Bill, he cussed us out good-naturedly and said, "I was afraid you saw me in the willows that day."

His good nature was tried by those goats from then on.

"Billy goat" got so he'd waylay Eddie's wife and chase her. She was scared to death of him and would hardly stir out of the house.

Marigoat showed Billy all the tricks she had learned at our expense: How to stop the horses from going in the corral by standing on her hind feet in the gate; how to pull the canvas off the water barrel; how to paw a hole in a screen door or window screen.

This last was their undoing. Bill and his family returned from town—a three-day trip—and found a hole in the screen door and a goat occupying each of two double beds. The flower plants were eaten. The table cloth was chewed. The drinking water was drunk—ample evidence of a couple of days' residence by the two goats.

A few days later Bill happened by a little sheepman's place. During their visit he complained of the coyotes killing his sheep.

"I wish I could git me a goat," he wailed. "A goat will run them damn coyotes away in the daytime."

"Well," said Bill quickly, "my goat is gettin' too big to run good—I'll just give him to you."

"I sure would take him, but I can't get away to go git him," the little guy whined.

"Oh, I ain't doin' a thing. I'll bring 'em up," said Bill.

He did, too! The little sheepman was surprised to see two goats but just thought that was twice as good. So did Bill.

Everybody heaved a sigh of relief when the goats were gone. We heard of them again from a rider who came down Cow Creek and saw the little sheepman en route.

He said he rode up and the little guy was cussing his dog. Inquiring, "What's the trouble?" he was informed, "It's those damn goats. One blocks the trail and won't let the sheep by, and the other stands off my dog."

THE BRONC RIDING CAT

Timmy Shannon had a very simple little outfit. He liked it that way.

He had grass enough for his own horses and the broncs he was breaking for pay. He ran a little bunch of cattle and put up a couple of stacks of hay in the summer. There was no road into Timmy's place. He brought everything in to the river on a packhorse or else dragged it from a saddle horn.

His wife, Peg, was a good rider, and when Timmy had a "pay" bronc snapped out pretty well, he'd talk Peg into riding it. She was always scared, but he'd razz her a little, and pretty soon she'd be riding the new bronc.

They didn't have a chicken or milk cow or anything that needed constant attention. Their pets, other than horses, were a dog and two huge cats. The cats were very simply named Blackie and Whitey.

Blackie was a short-haired cat and as fast as a racehorse. He either hid or ran whenever confronted by danger. Coyotes and bobcats were numerous and made short work of a cat if they caught one.

Whitey was a beauty. He was all or part Angora, and his fine, silky hair was two inches long and always a gleaming white. He feared nothing and would bluff his way through any situation.

Timmy's wife would get cabin fever every so often and go traipsing off to Great Falls to visit her relatives for a couple of weeks or a couple of months. Timmy would go along, but he couldn't stand towns very long and would soon be back in the breaks, snapping broncs.

He'd visit around among his numberless friends, helping one rancher, then another for a few days each.

Every week or so he'd drop in at his own place, stay a couple of days, then pull out mounted on a new bronc. Blackie and Whitey knew by some sixth sense when he was coming and would go up the trail nearly a mile to meet him. Then they'd scamper in and out of greasewood and sagebrush, playing hide and seek all the way back to the house. They were overjoyed at having Timmy home again and rubbed his legs and purred noisily while he unsaddled. When he started to the house,

Horses Jimmy and Flash, with Dean Switzer, on the Belknap Indian Reservation, 1941. COURTESY L. D. "DEAN" SWITZER

they'd leap upon his shoulders and ride. When Peg was returning, too, they were outdoing each other leaping from one person's shoulder to the other's.

Naturally, Timmy and Peg thought a lot of these affectionate cats and always fed and cared for them outrageously while at home. As Timmy said, "Give 'em a vacation. They hunt while we're gone, and there isn't a mouse on the place."

That was very true. Even oats, laboriously packed in on horseback, were free from mice. The cats seemed equally well fed whether on their own or being cared for.

One day Timmy was coming down Bullwhacker Creek, returning home. His horse pricked his ears and stared down the trail ahead of them. Timmy looked, too, and was expecting to see Blackie and Whitey come into view.

A moment later a coyote trotted around a crook in the trail and dangling limply from his jaws was the cat Blackie.

For one horrified instant Timmy stared. The coyote stared in return and then bolted as an enraged little Irishman bore down on him. For a hundred yards or so, the coyote carried Blackie, then dropped him and fled for his life.

Timmy followed, building a loop in his lariat rope as they tore along. Timmy's mount had enough cow savvy to follow pretty well, and when they hit a little opening in the greasewood, Timmy dabbed a loop on the coyote. He caught him around the belly and took a couple of dallies around the saddle horn.

When the bronc felt a tug or two on the rope and saw it stretched tight toward the coyote he reverted to a wild horse and stampeded. After a half mile of greasewood and then a few rocky crossings of Bullwhacker, there wasn't enough coyote left to scare the bronc, and Timmy got him stopped.

Taking what was left of the coyote out of his rope, Timmy said, "You picked the wrong time to kill my cat." Timmy rode back, found the remains of Blackie, and buried him by caving a cutbank off on him.

Both Timmy and the other cat were inconsolable over the loss of Blackie. Whitey was lonesome for his pal, and Timmy was sorry for Whitey.

The river was high for a long time that summer, and my visits with Timmy were done shouting across the broad expanse of water. We'd both get close to the edge of the water, and our voices would carry remarkably well. Unless we were at the water's edge, it was very difficult to hear each other.

I was watching cattle along the river above and below Timmy's. But I was on the opposite side of the river. Quite often I'd go up the river when Timmy wasn't home. Nearly every time, Whitey would hear my horse's hoofs clattering in the rocky trail in the narrows and come down to the river's edge and "meow" in a mournful tone. He was very voluble and would follow along the opposite side of the river for half a mile or so.

Timmy and Peg came back down to the river toward the end of the summer. Timmy pitied Whitey a lot. He seemed lonesome, Timmy thought. Determined to do something about it, he took a half-grown white kitten home to be Whitey's companion.

He usually packed grub in from the closest ranch; he'd haul it that far in his pickup. This rancher furnished the kitten; and it was up to Timmy to furnish transportation for the cat. Peg, riding a gentle horse, was leading the packhorse, and Timmy had to figure a way to carry the kitten. His mount was a half-broken bronc.

Timmy always either tied his duffle on his saddle or wore it—he refused to carry anything in his hands. It looked like he was stymied until he put the cat in a little pasteboard box, about eight inches by a foot in size. This he tied securely and then rigged a harness for his shoulders and had his friend tie the box to his back. Timmy was then wearing the box like a knapsack.

"Fine! Fine!" he said. "Couldn't be better. Both hands free."

Everything went well for the first couple of miles. The cat meowed a few times, and Timmy's bronc kind of pricked up his ears. It wasn't any worse than Timmy whistling, though, so he took it pretty easy.

They rode slowly because of the packed horses. A trot is liable to cause the grub to mix a little if a few seams are weak. Timmy's bronc got to dreaming along and stubbed a toe and scooted along on his nose a few feet. That scared him some, and he was scampering a little and looking back at Timmy. He was all set to try something, and all he needed was something to touch him off.

The cat didn't care for the juggling he was getting and expressed himself. "Yeow, meow, yeow," he squalled.

That was enough! Timmy's bronc took off on a dead run. He was going toward home and showed no sign of stopping. Timmy didn't worry much at first. The country was level enough for fast traveling. It was only about a mile to where the trail left the ridge and dropped down five or six hundred feet to the bottom of Bullwhacker. The trail down that hill was a "slow trail." It skirted shale banks, went through timber and around and among washouts and in general was a dangerous place for speed.

Timmy was the only one that seemed to care about that, though. The cat still yeowled occasionally and clawed at the inside of his box. His claws made a strange and terrible sound for that bronc, and he ran all the harder.

They hit the rim of the hill going full tilt, and the bronc caromed off a bank on the first sharp turn. There were lots more turns coming, and some had only space to carom off. The cat was silent now. He was so confused he'd forgotten how to howl.

The bronc was thinking about his own neck a little by now and doing all he could to save it. He was trying to stop, too, but he had too much speed. All he could do was miss the biggest holes and blunder through the lesser ones. Timmy was wanting to quit him all the time, but by the time he picked a spot to roll off, they'd be past it.

Just before they reached the bottom, the trail leveled off a little, and Timmy sat back on one hackamore rein and got the bronc to turning and pointed him back up the hill. That was the end of the run. That bronc was so winded he couldn't have made it up the hill in an hour.

The next sound from Timmy's pack was a tentative "mew." The cat was taking it easier, too.

In half an hour or so, Peg showed up and said, "My gosh, Timmy. What'd you do that for? You'll kill that poor cat."

"Poor cat, hell! This cat damn near killed me," yelled Timmy.

The worst was yet to come.

Timmy and Peg got plumb cheerful again, thinking of Whitey's coming pleasure at having a cat for company.

They tied their horses to the corral, with Whitey fairly roaring, he was purring so loud.

Peg got the box cut loose from Timmy's shoulders and set it on the ground. She opened the lid and stepped back to watch Whitey's reaction.

A good horse under you and you're ready for whatever the Breaks want to throw at you.
COURTESY L. D. "DEAN" SWITZER

The little white cat emerged, blinking in the bright light. Whitey made a swift dash and sprang upon it. With a vicious crunch he bit through the base of its skull, killing it instantly.

Peg squealed, and Timmy swore.

Timmy forgave Whitey, saying, "Hell, he never saw a cat that was any color but black. How'd he know what it was?" It was a long while before Peg would admit that Whitey was still her friend.

Timmy summed it up. "Should have been a black one. Yessir, should get another one—but I won't!"

CHAPTER 9

AROUND THE CAMPFIRE

O, I DEARLY *LOVED* THAT FORD CAR

At the close of World War I, about 1918, I bought a bunch of cows and rented some land in the Bull Mountains north of Billings, Montana. Cattle had been pretty high but had come down. I gave $86 a head for the cows. They was good white-faced cows, and I thought they was so cheap that I had stole them.

Then there was about five years of drought and grasshoppers and a big panic. All the old-timers know how tough it was. There is no use telling about it, as I always feel like throwing up when it is mentioned.

I had an old T Ford car at that time. I was living at Pickett Springs, forty miles northeast of Billings. As it took me three days to make the trip with a mule team, I thought if I got a Ford I could make it in one day. Times was terrible: Banks all going broke. No money. No credit. But I did manage to trade a couple of pretty good milk cows for an old Ford car.

It run fairly well on the level. It was a whiz going downhill, but when you started uphill she'd just snort and stop. The only way you could get uphill was to turn her around and put her in reverse. Sometimes you could make it on the first try.

She was awful hard to start. I always left her on a hill if possible, for if you turned her over with the crank, she generally backfired. She knocked a few fingernails off for me. I used some nasty cusswords on her sometimes. . . . O, I dearly *loved* that Ford car. But if you had plenty of baling wire, a monkey wrench, and a pair of pliers, you most always made it.

One time I left her up on the hill. When I went to start her, it was kind of cold and she rolled plumb to the bottom and never made a kick. I hitched up the mule team and drug her back up the hill. But she wouldn't give a snort. So I took a wagon box rod, wrapped it with rags, poured coal oil on the rags, and made a torch. Then I got some boiling water in the radiator and applied the torch on the bottom of the engine. She started, run a little ways, and quit. The fellow that was helping at the ranch said he thought that if we pulled her around the flat with the mule team she would probably go.

The mule team was scared to death of that Ford. As long as it didn't start, you could get along with them, but soon as she coughed, them mules went crazy! We had hauled it quite a ways in gear with the mag key turned on when we came to a little grade downhill. He got the mules in a trot. All at once she fired and jumped ahead. That slack loosened the chain, and the doubletrees hit the mules on the heels. The car backfired like a gun! Them mules was off on the dead run.

The man couldn't hold them, and they got away with me in the Ford! I put the brakes on, but by that time the mules was a-flying. I would have jumped out and let them go, but they was going so fast that I never had time to. The ground was rough, and I had too much trouble holding on. They finally made a circle toward the corral. There was a bad coulee to cross—we made the coulee okay, but after we crossed it there was a side hill. The car turned over, and somehow in the deal the chain came loose. Them mules went on with the chain sticking straight out and their ears lying on their backs!

When the car rolled over, somehow it rolled me out. I was plenty scared but not a scratch! After that I couldn't get them mules within a hundred yards of that car. We straightened up the wreck. The top was busted up, and the fenders was bent. We pounded 'em off the wheels, and it didn't look too bad. I give her a spin with the crank, and she chuckled right off. We caught the mules and took off their harness, and I started for Billings.

That turnover must of loosened up her bowels, as she traveled right into Billings going about twenty miles an hour and never even backfired! I got some groceries and started back next day. She was still on her good behavior. I just gave her one turn, and she rattled like a locomotive letting off steam. Just before I got to Shepherd, I blowed out a hind tire, and the inner tube was all tore up. There wasn't nothing I could do, only get another tire.

I caught a ride back into Billings, got a new tire, and got back just a little after dark. Some sonofagun had taken the other hind tire! I said my prayers and bummed another ride into town to get another tire, but I didn't take any chances leaving the new tire. I took it with me. Next morning I caught another ride. I thought I should be okay that time. When I got back, I saw the hood of the car turned back on the frame. When I looked, someone had taken the engine. There she set—the top mashed, two tires gone, and the fenders all pounded up. No car. Thirty miles from home. Carrying two tires.

Walter Ross, a Bull Mountain rancher, came along and took me home—disgusted, mad, and glad.

Linda Grosskopf
Huntley, Montana
Great-granddaughter of Bill Huntington

NEVER FORGET TO CHECK FOR EVIDENCE

My good friend, Sam McDowell, was a successful cattle rancher but also a talented roper. He loved calf roping and also team roping and was good at both of them. He was also a pickup man at the National Finals Rodeo one year.

Each fall, for quite a few years, Sam hosted an invitational roping rodeo at his ranch arena. Top ropers from all over came to the two-day event. The local people were privileged to see the best of them in our own home country.

One particular year I was just about done building an addition on Sam's house when the ranch rodeo time arrived, so I was sort of in the middle of things. Everything went off smoothly, and after it was all over, Sam's friend, Dean Oliver, stayed an extra day. At the time Dean was World Champion calf roper.

While they were hashing over the past two days' events, Sam happened to mention that down in the willows on the lower end of his ranch was a cow moose that had contacted pinkeye and had gone blind. She was still in good shape, but there was no chance she could survive the winter. After some discussion they decided to save her from starvation during the winter. Since hunting season wasn't quite open, they chose not to do much advertising of their intentions. They drove down through the fields, avoiding any roads, till they found their victim. After dispensing her they butchered her and hauled the meat back on the same route—not seeing or meeting anyone else. The meat was hung up in Sam's garage to cool out.

Now Sam had plans to fly early the next day with his two sons to the World's Fair in Montreal, Canada, so he asked me if I would help Dean load the meat up when he was ready to go home. I assured him it would be no problem. Sam's wife drove them to the airport and then planned on spending the next day with her parents.

Dean was packing up when I arrived for work the next day, so I helped him load the moose, which was quite a load for his station wagon. We carefully covered it with blankets and all his rodeo gear, and he was on his way home. I worked on my project all day, and since no one would be there that night, I carefully locked up before I went home.

The next morning when I arrived for work, there were several vehicles in the yard with assorted game wardens and sheriff's deputies wandering around. I inquired what it was all about, since no one was home, but they didn't offer any information.

After I went to work, I could tell that someone had been in the house, since everything wasn't as I had left it the night before. Finally, a couple of them questioned me, but having a very poor memory, I wasn't much help. About that time Sam's wife came home, and after finding out what was going on, it sort of upset her disposition and didn't take her long to clear out the yard.

Apparently, someone had turned them in, but since there was no evidence and Sam was out of the country, there wasn't much they could do.

Several days later Sam and his boys came home. After he heard of all the excitement, he went to the county judge and paid a small fine, without admitting to any guilt. In the meantime Sam's wife had called Dean, who arranged to have the meat stored in a lot of freezers, not including his own.

After all the excitement had died down, I was visiting with Sam one morning when the game warden drove up. After visiting for a while, he went to his truck and brought back a coat. He asked Sam if he recognized it. Sam said that he sure did, it was his, and he asked where he found it. The warden said, "It was hanging on the willow where you butchered that moose!"

Jay Nelson
Jackson, Montana

MYSTERY BANK ROBBERS AND ONE SIX-SHOOTER

In the north-central part of Montana, along the Milk River valley, lies the historical little town of Harlem, which has housed its share of outlaws and cattle rustlers. Among the more famous was Kid Curry and his gang. Kid Curry was well liked and known as a man who paid his bills. Pike Landusky was also a frequent visitor to Harlem. He was killed by Kid Curry during a quarrel in a saloon in Landusky, Montana. Some cattle and horse rustling is still practiced around this community almost the same as it was years ago. Most of the people here are still typical westerners. The farther south on Main Street one goes, the more western it gets. On entering two of its south-side bars, one suddenly steps into an era of the past.

That, however, is another story. This is about three bank robbers, one who was killed, two who got away, and the Colt .45 that I have today.

The bank these three boys tried to rob was Harlem, Montana's first bank, organized in 1905. On July 31, 1911, the bandits rode into town at noon on stolen horses and approached the rear of the bank. While one held the horses under cover, the other two went inside and forced the occupants to stand against the wall with their hands raised. After getting the money at the cashier's desk, one of the bandits headed for the vault; then, remembering his six-shooter, he returned to pick it up. As he picked the gun up, it accidentally fired. The noise alerted Marshall Q. R. Laswell, who happened to be on the outside of the bank.

Laswell ran to the rear of the bank and upon entering the building saw the bank employees standing against the wall with their hands raised. At about the same time, one robber came out of the vault with over $8,000 in his possession. The Marshall fired and brought the bandit down. As he fell, he fired a shot at the Marshall and missed. Several shots were exchanged between the Marshall and the other bandit before the outlaw was able to get out of the building, minus the money, making his getaway with the remaining partner, who was holding the horses.

A posse was quickly organized, and the chase began. The outlaws had foreseen the chase and had hidden some stolen horses in a sheep shed on the Putnam ranch about twenty miles southwest of Harlem. Here they abandoned their tired horses and were able to get away on fresh mounts. These horses had previously been stolen from the Putnam ranch, and one was a notorious bucker too tough for most cowboys to ride. Milo Powell, an old-timer, states whoever rode the outlaw horse had to be a good rider because he rode the horse as far as the Missouri River, where more fresh horses were cached. After they crossed the Missouri River, the trail of the bandits was lost.

The dead bandit was judged to be about thirty-five years of age. The two outlaws who got away and the dead man were never identified.

Milo Powell saw the two stolen Putnam horses drifting back toward their home range a day or so after the outlaws had used them. Milo said it looked like that old outlaw horse had met his match at last, as he was gaunted up like a thin snowbird and had dried sweat and mud plastered all over him.

The slain robber's gun came into my possession in a roundabout way. Marshall Laswell had it lying around his office for several years; then he gave it to his friend, Harry Rush, of Chinook, Montana, who in turn gave it to his friend, Tom O'Conner, to scare coyotes away from his sheep. Tom O'Conner was herding sheep for John Tilleman, south of Chinook, at the time when I met up with Tom and this gun. I was fifteen years old that winter, and I was hired to haul hay to Tom's sheep and also feed hay to about a hundred head of cattle. Tom O'Conner and I became very good friends, and he told me about the robbery and also showed me the six-shooter, which Tom had at that time. I felt I could not rest until I somehow had acquired that gun. I tried to buy it or trade for it, and I did a lot of begging for it. At first I didn't have much success, but the winter was long, and I didn't give up easily. Finally, Tom gave in and gave the gun to me on one condition; I must never fire it while we were working together, as he was afraid I might hurt him or myself with it. I promised and kept my promise, too.

The gun is a .45-caliber single-action frontier model Colt with a seven-and-a-half-inch barrel. It has such a fine hair trigger on it that when it's cocked a slight touch of the finger will cause the hammer to fall. One can readily understand why it accidentally fired when the robber picked it up, seeing he must have had it cocked. Also, on the grips there are three notches carved. What the notches are there for I can't be sure, but I suppose they each stand for a dead man. The six-shooter is still in excellent condition.

My friend, Tom O'Conner, is past ninety and is in good health but is blind. He resides at the rest home in Lewistown, Montana. I hope someone will read this to him, as I'm sure it would interest him very much to know I still own this gun and think often of him and the winter I worked with him. He is one of the few old-timers still around.

Jim Halseth
Chinook, Montana
(Written in 1968)

THE SHOOT-OFF

About twenty-five years ago (from 1995), one of the hunters who came to our guide and outfitting business, insisted that I have a "shoot-off" with him with a pistol. I told him that I had never shot a pistol in my

Cowboys ready to gather the roundup at Dave Huston's, 1968. COURTESY OF KATHRYN HUSTON

life. He was very persistent and threw an empty can out fifty or seventy-five feet away and gave me the first shot. Beginner's luck! I hit it right dead center.

Of course he said, "And you tell me that you've never shot a pistol!"

I had to shoot twice more, with the same results, and he let me off the hook. He went away mumbling something about another day, but thank goodness, he got very busy with his big-game hunting and forgot about it so I managed to hold my good record.

I guess I must have learned something from my folks, who were both crack shots. My mother used a .22 rifle, and as a number of people can tell you, my dad could shoot with the best of them. On the other side of the coin, Dave's mom couldn't hit the broad side of the barn. In about 1925 she attempted to shoot a hawk that was flying away with an old hen. She aimed, closed both eyes, and fired—the hawk flew away, and she shot the hen!

Kathryn Huston
Brusett, Montana

THE EAGLE EYES

Harvey Willcutt Sr. was wagon boss for Edd Dana's Bird Head outfit in south-central Montana until they went broke in the depression days of the '30s. One time a nester stole a Bird Head cow, and the deal ended up in a jury trial in Hardin. There was a new lawyer in town, and he defended the cow thief.

The lawyer's name was Maddox, and the main point of his defense was proving from how far away the cow's brand could be read. One rancher testified he could read the brand at twenty feet. Another said he could only read it at fifteen feet. But old Harvey Willcutt, with his eagle eye, could read the brand at a hundred feet.

The nester was convicted and had to spend a couple of years at The Home Ranch—the Montana State Pen at Deer Lodge. The nickname

"Old Eagle Eye" followed Harvey Willcutt the rest of his life. They called Harvey Jr. "Young Eagle Eye." After a while that got to be too much of a mouthful, so it was shortened to Old Eag and Young Eag.

I've always considered Harvey Willcutt to be the best cowman, next to my dad, I ever knew, and his son was not far behind. What great cow people they were.

Ray Krone
Augusta, Montana

MRS. MOO

This story is a little bit more modern day than my usual. It's about an old girlfriend of mine. We called her Mrs. Moo.

For years our Augusta ranch was pretty much a straight steer operation. We only ran a couple of hundred mother cows, but we had lots of steers. All the steer calves from the Hardin ranch were shipped to Augusta, and I grew them out until they were two and three years old and weighed around twelve hundred pounds. In those days all the cattle were shipped on the railroad, and we could only get about twenty-four of these big steers in a cattle car, so we always had fifty carloads. Fifty cars is a train, so we were shipping a trainload of beef every fall, usually in September.

Once we got the steers sold for delivery, we'd have to gather them, weigh them on our scale at the home ranch, then trail them five or six miles to another place of ours, leave them overnight, and pick them up the next morning to take them on into Augusta and load them on the rail. This all sounds easy to anyone who has never been around big steers. But let me tell you, it's not easy!

Those big steers were great cattle, much more so than the baby calves sold today. But they sometimes took some cowboying to handle them. They were great to handle on the open range, but they could be hard to pen, and there was no way you could force them to go where they didn't want to, like trying to get them to cross a spooky bridge.

Because of this, we were always looking for something to help us handle these big dudes. So when a neighbor said he had a milk cow that was broke to lead, I bought her right on the spot. I'd never seen anything like her—you could lead her at a lope! She'd lope right alongside your horse, and when you'd jiggle her halter shank, she'd moo right on cue.

When we'd pen the steers to weigh them, a cowboy would hold her inside the pen till we'd get the herd close. Then I'd wave to him, and he'd lead her out in front of them, then turn and head for the gate. He'd jiggle her halter shank, and she'd moo and suck them old steers into the pen slicker than the scum off a Louisiana swamp!

Our worst deal taking the steers to Augusta was that we had to go the last four miles down a county road, across a spooky bridge, and go right through the edge of town to get to the stockyards. We'd trailer Mrs. Moo to where we hit the road, then put her in the lead, and away we'd go down the road toward Augusta. With twelve hundred of those big steers in the road, they'd reach more than a hundred yards, and it was mighty touchy business. One bad move and they'd tear the fence down for a mile!

We'd be going along just fine when all of a sudden they'd stop and all be turned, looking you right in the eye, and the fences squeaking and groaning on both sides. This was where Mrs. Moo was worth her weight in gold. We'd lead her back and get the lead started with her help, and the whole herd would unwind like a giant centipede, and away we'd go again. That old cow could get those steers to follow her where a dozen men couldn't force them to go.

One fall when we got her in, I noticed she had a bad crack in one claw of her left front foot. I was afraid she'd go lame on the gravel road, so we decided to shoe her. I called all over Montana to find an ox shoe, but no luck, so we put a double-ought horseshoe on her. You could pick her foot up just like a horse, but she wouldn't stand for the pounding, so we had to tie her down and finish the job.

The shoe worked just fine, and she wore it till it fell off. I've often thought that if some cowboy was on a three- or four-day drunk in Augusta and was riding home all hung over and saw three cow tracks and one horse track in the snow, it might have been enough to make him quit drinking!

Mrs. Moo never knew a hungry day, and we kept her till the end.

The floods of 1953, '64, and '75 whacked out the railroad tracks, so no more trains to Augusta. Too bad. Also too bad there are no more big steers like those we had.

Ray Krone
Augusta, Montana

HEISER SADDLES

I better start out by stating that my better half's maiden name is Heiser. So when we got a sale bill for Dick Mader's Estate Auction, she noticed that on the inventory were two Heiser saddles. Ann made the remark, "I sure would like to have one of those Heiser saddles."

I'm not going to say that Ann's great-granddad was related to the saddlemaker Hermann H. Heiser, but what I will say is that they both grew up in the same part of Germany, at the same time. I suppose that's why Ann wanted a Heiser saddle.

So we went to the sale. When they started selling the Heiser saddle, they couldn't get anyone to bid, so the auctioneer gave a little spiel on how Dick Mader used the saddles rodeoing, calf roping, and bulldogging and how he made the circuit from Cheyenne to Calgary. One saddle was his, and one was his wife's. So when the auctioneer came back for bids, I started them at $100 buyer's choice.

As in all auctions, someone started bidding against me, and I paid more than I wanted to. The auctioneer asked which one I wanted. I thought how Dick bought them both new and how they both showed about the same amount of wear. I thought they should stay together, so I took them both.

Trying to keep Western heritage alive, I put them in the museum in Broadus, Montana, as Dick was well known in Broadus.

Fritz Rehbein
Rozet, Wyoming

SOME WILD STORIES!

The summer of 1934 my mom's brother, Roy Cooper, came from Sheridan, Wyoming, to our ranch in Sorrel Horse Valley in lower Big Horn County, Montana. He was riding a little brown horse named Shorty and leading two gray packhorses, Dude and Dogie. He spent over a year with my parents, Glen and Margaret Quest, my two sisters, a brother, and me. I'm sure he helped feed us, as the grasshoppers had eaten our garden.

In the dry 1930s deer were very scarce, but Uncle Roy crossed the Big Horn River on Dogie and went to the Pocket Creek area to hunt. It was scary because the game warden was always lurking around.

Uncle Roy did shoot a deer, and when his gun went off, it spooked Dogie. He got away and came back across the river. Uncle Roy knew when us kids would be in the corral, milking the cows for the evening, so he walked to the riverbank and hollered across at us, about half a mile away. He said to get our dad, who was in the field, and have him bring a horse and a packhorse.

Together they got the deer home and had it well hidden when the game warden showed up the next day. It took most of the day to catch Uncle Roy's horse, as he was running around the whole valley. All the neighbors were curious as to why he was running loose with a bridle and saddle on. In those days you learned to tell some wild stories to stretch the truth!

Uncle Roy was a Godsend to us that year. He later went to Billings and opened a gun shop and became a very successful businessman.

Peg Quest Kuntz
Custer, Montana

BRIM AND MITCH

Some of these old boys had an awful time learning how to drive a car. This Brim Barrett, he lived up at the mouth of Forchett Creek, above it a little ways. He had lost his boy when a horse reared over backwards with him and killed him, but he had several girls. A salesman from Malta was selling Buick cars, and he told Brim, "Well, we'd sure like to sell you one of these Buick cars."

"Well," Brim said, "if you bring it out to the ranch and show me how to drive it, I'll buy one."

So they did. They brought this car out to the ranch, but Brim and the girls were gone riding. The Buick people waited a while, but Brim never showed up, so they decided to go back to Malta. When Brim and the girls got back from riding, here was this new Buick setting in the yard. And the girls said, "Oh, Dad, let's drive it, let's drive it!" And Brim said, "No. We're not gonna."

They kept after him for two or three days, and finally, Brim said, "All right, we'll drive it."

But he had to have everything in the round corral. If you rode up there horseback, the first thing he'd say was, "Well, put your horse in the corral." He had a big round corral, so Brim said, "All right, we'll drive it." But he said, "We'll hook the team onto it, and we'll drag it into the corral so it don't get away from us." So that's what they did.

They hooked the team onto this new car and dragged it into the corral, and Brim got it started. He made a couple of circles around in there with it and hollered at the girls.

"Open the gate, girls! I got 'er!" And out the gate he came. But he forgot how to stop it. He ran into the garden fence and wound up a bunch of wire under it, and it finally stopped.

Another episode with him involved a preacher. It was late at night, and somebody knocked on the door, wanting to stay all night. Brim said, "Yeah. Put your horse in the corral."

The guy says, "I don't have a horse."

Old Brim says, "I don't give a damn what you got. Put it in the corral."

So the next morning Brim went out to do his chores, and here laid a bicycle in his corral. This preacher had rode a bicycle clear out from Malta. So that's kinda the way that went.

Another old boy had quite a lot of ranch holdings around Malta; he was a Basque, and his name was Mitch Etchart. He had got him one of those Buick cars, too, and the only thing is, they just had mechanical brakes and didn't stop very easy. He was in a hurry going to Glasgow, and he came over this hill and here was a bunch of pigs in the middle of the road. He plowed into them and never stopped to see if he'd hurt any or anything. He got on into Glasgow, and there was a cop standing on the sidewalk when he pulled up. The cop said, "What are you doing with that dead pig on your bumper?"

Mitch looked at it, and he said, "It's my damn pig. I can do anything I want with it!"

Maybe it *was* his, I don't know, but it was lying upside down on the bumper that wrapped around the front of them old Buick cars.

Another time he was going along the road out of Malta, on the highway, and the highway patrolman stopped him: He was driving on the wrong side of the road. The highway patrolman said, "You're not supposed to drive on the left-hand side of the road; you're supposed to drive on the right-hand side."

Old Mitch told him, "I'll drive any damn way I want. This is my road. It's my land on both sides of this road." Those individuals were pretty much individuals.

Tom Wilson
Lewistown, Montana

SILVER ENGRAVER JIM WOLFE

In a log cabin in Forsyth, Montana, Jim Wolfe places a flat piece of oval silver onto the top of a rotating stand, just the right size to cup in the palm of his hand, takes an engraving tool, and begins to cut into the surface of the silver.

From the time he was a child, he knew he wanted to be an engraver but never had anyone to show him how. "I always wanted to meet one, so he could teach me, but I never did, so one day I decided I was going to teach myself."

He began in 1987, and at first he treated it as a hobby, repairing bits and silver spurs. But as he became more proficient and skilled, his work led to an opportunity to demonstrate the craft in Grand Central Station in New York City.

That experience exposed him to the world of "custom engraving," which encouraged him to research and engrave images that have pushed his talents and skill to a much higher level.

As he stretched and learned, he found himself doing more deep relief and detail engraving. Doing more animals. More steel. Always researching deeper into the art and styles. "Basically allowing myself to make new mistakes every day!"

Whether it's a belt buckle or a concho, a hair barrette or a pair of earrings, each piece of work begins the same way, with his own original design—the swoops and curls, the animal or letters—carefully penciled onto the silver before he begins to work. Then the engraving, tap, tap, tap with the little hammer, molding, buffing, the final polish. Over the years he's made more than three thousand pieces, some of which are a part of the permanent western art and engraving collection in Elko, Nevada.

"Every piece I make, I put everything I know into it," he says. "I think my most memorable one will be the one I can look at and say, 'Excellent work.' Layout, gray scale, shading, depth, uniformity, time—everything done perfect to my standards.

"I don't see that happening in the near future," he adds with a grin. "But that's what keeps me going. I know I can produce better."

Today his son Jackson works alongside his dad, threatening to become an even better artist than his dad. Which will be fine with Jim.

"Am I a proud father? Yes, I am!"—causing one to wonder if some day it might be Wolfe and Wolfe Concho Company.

Wanda Rosseland
Circle, Montana

 **CHAPTER 10**

THE GREAT DIVIDE

RIP TANA AND BOOTS

Letter to our friends on losing Tana and Boots
RIP Tana and Boots

Well, we had the vet here Monday morning, and he put our fourteen-year-old mare, Tana, down, since we both believed that she was in much pain with the glandular disease she has had for the past five years. It was a really hard thing to do, even though we had both prepared for this time in the past few months. She had a difficult winter, and we knew it was time. It's so hard; we wanted to call, but we are in tears just writing this to you. She went down kicking at the vet, so she was a fighter to the end. But we know that she is more comfortable in God's hands now.

The really hard thing is now dealing with Boots . . . old Boots, our twenty-three-year-old gelding, healthy up until now, too. The minute that Tana died, he picked his head up from the corral where he and the colts were eating, stopped, and called out to her. He put his head down and never moved after that. I knew he was in shock, but I never expected what would follow.

I took him out in the pasture and thought it might help him to go over to the spot where Tana had been buried just minutes before, but it didn't help. He just followed me wherever I moved to. He had lost his true love and was looking to me to be his leader to comfort him. The colts have their own little subherd, and Boots had lost his herd, his life's pasture mate.

We let him stay out there a while, but he just laid down in a corner by the corral and wouldn't move. Art called the vet. He went and got some horse sedatives, and we groomed him and hugged him, and the sedative made him more comfortable. After three more calls to the vet, we gave him banamine in case he was starting to colic. He would get up and lie down and just looked miserable, but no sign of colic or any other illnesses.

I feared the worst was yet to come. I knew he had made his decision. I hugged him good night and told him I hoped he would stay and be my horse longer, but if his mind was with Tana, I knew he would be happy with her. I told him this and went to bed.

As a show of honor and respect, a horse, with an empty saddle and boots turned back in the stirrups, is led at the funeral of a fallen cowboy. PHOTO BY WANDA ROSSELAND

During the night, he just gave up, went behind the barn, laid down, and died of a broken heart. I have heard of animals grieving, and even seen it before this, but I have never seen a reaction this strong, so fast. He made his own decision that he just wanted to be with her.

Who says that animals don't have feelings like humans, nonsense.

Love to ya all,

Trish and Art

Trish Baker
Gallatin Gateway, Montana

THE BIG SNOWSTORM

The following is a story of the big snowstorm in May in Billings. I don't know the date, but my Dad, P. R. Krone, came to Billings in 1907, so I'd say this would be 1913 or '14. There were herds of cattle coming into Billings on the rail, and the outfits that bought the cattle were there with their roundup wagons to receive the cattle and move them out to their range.

My Dad was there with the Antler outfit, and they had unloaded their cattle and had moved them a little ways from the stockyards and were standing night guard on them and were going to move them towards home the next morning. However, that night it went to snowing so bad they couldn't hold the cattle and had to turn them loose. Dad said there were four or five other herds in the area, and these cattle also had to be turned loose. What a mess.

There were several other Northern outfits there, and they of course had good tents with Sibly stoves and were equipped for bad weather. But there were also several Southern outfits—so-called Greasy-Sack Outfits. They had no tents or stoves, just a chuck wagon, so the northern outfits took their men in so they could dry out and get warm.

One morning they were sitting around the tent drinking coffee. They had the sugar in a sawed-off coffee can and were passing it around, and when it came to one of the Southern hands, he said, no thanks, I don't like salt in my coffee. Dad said one morning they looked out and there were two Southern hands with their saddles on their shoulders sloshing down the road towards town. They hailed those boys and said, come on in, get warm and have some coffee. The boys replied, no thanks, mister, it was bad enough when this storm killed the cattle, but when it also killed our horses, we have had enough; we are on our way back to Texas.

Coming from the South, both the horses and the cattle were shed off, and they couldn't stand such a fierce storm. Dad said that when the storm finally quit you could walk for a mile under the rims around Billings and never step off a dead cow. They finally got the cattle sorted out, what was left, and moved to their range. This was in May but one of the worst spring storms ever.

After I moved to Augusta, I ran into an old hand, Alf Gregg. He said he was in that deal, but the herd he was with got moved out of Billings toward Roundup and turned their cattle loose in those breaks, and they made it through the storm okay.

Ray Krone
Augusta, Montana

DEATH IN THE YELLOWSTONE

One time we were swimming a herd across the Yellowstone at Miles City. The river was high and swift, and another cowhand and myself were working close together midstream with the cattle. A number of people were on the bank watching us. The young cowhand working with me was from Missouri. He was a little distance in front of me when his horse hit an air pocket, and all the folks on the bank began yelling. I'd seen him there ahead of me; I looked again, and he was gone. Then I hit the hole.

I was riding a good strong swimmer named Antelope. For those who have never known the thrill of riding a good swimming horse in surging water, they cannot fully understand how much I loved it. You see, the horse and rider are almost one, for the rider gives the horse confidence, and he swims well, but not all horses are good swimmers any more than people are.

When I hit the hole, Antelope went down. There was a big black steer right in front of him; I left Antelope in a hurry and grabbed the steer by the tail. This frightened the steer, and he swam to shore, taking me with him. As I looked back Antelope came up again and started swimming. When we hit the bank, I released the steer's tail and scrambled to safety.

We found the cowhand's body about a quarter mile downstream. He had been working to pay off a $400 mortgage on his parents' farm in Missouri. He had a roll of money on his person when we found him; the wagon boss sent the money to his parents, and all of us put in money for his burial and the shipment of his body to his people.

Bob Kennon
From the Pecos to the Powder
University of Oklahoma Press

WHEN DREAMS GO UP IN FLAMES

My father left Minnesota in 1961, at age seventeen, packing big dreams of being a real cowboy. He landed in Custer, Montana, and caught the eye of a local beet farmer's daughter, my mom, who was still in high school at the time.

Dad found his first cowboy job on the road between Custer and Melstone, on the Horace & Ethel White Ranch. Their place provided all he'd imagined: a bunkhouse, stout corrals, range horses, an old cowboy willing to teach him all he could absorb, and all of it right in the middle of the neighborless sea of grass that is that northside country.

Horace was an old hand, and he and Ethel had scraped, then survived, then prospered on their ranch. It was not too big but not too small, just the right place for Dad to learn how to handle cattle the old-fashioned way, the right way. When they gathered the rank young saddle stock from the pasture back of the house, it was time for Dad to make a hand.

He broke many young horses for the Whites. Though he doesn't talk much about those days, he treasures a handful of pictures taken then: him mounted on a gruella in the corral, him riding a sorrel outside the big White house. The horse's name is written on the back of each black-and-white snapshot in pencil.

That first summer Dad helped build a new barn on the White Place. Ethel was a fantastic cook and kept the whole crew well fed. She could create a feast from kitchen scraps, they say, and any company was call for a feast.

When Horace died, Ethel continued living in their prairie home, but she leased the land to the neighboring Grierson Ranch. Dad went to work for the big Grierson cow outfit and moved to a cow camp just a few miles north of the White Place.

Mom and Dad married in 1967 and settled in at their cow camp. Mom was a farm girl stranded out in the hills, and Ethel took her in. They shared recipes, played cards, checked on each other when the big snowstorms blew. When my sister and brother came along, Ethel loved them, too.

Like many cowboys and their wives do, Mom and Dad always held the dream of one day having a ranch of their own. People liked to help each other out back then, and Ethel loaned my folks the money to buy a bit of their own land. Though they continued to work for the Griersons, at least they could run a few cows.

Mom and Dad loved their cow camp and the work there, and their dream of a ranch was just that, a dream. A wonderful fantasy to escape to, a goal to subconsciously work toward. It was never something they planned to do next year, because they always felt they were right where they were meant to be. Yet the dream developed an epicenter of sorts: the White Place. Maybe because it held so much sentimental value, maybe because it was where Dad was living when he was young and green and falling in love with the land. Maybe because it always was proof that a small ranch could be a successful, happy place for a family. Their dream wasn't about lust. It more represented their faith in the goodness of people and the kindness of God and the truth that things will eventually come 'round right.

Even after Ethel moved to Forsyth to be near her daughter, Becky, the White Place continued to be a special place for my family. We visited Ethel in Forsyth often, and because the Griersons continued to lease her land, Dad rode through it regularly. For a few years ranch hands lived in the house seasonally. Then it was used only occasionally by passing hunters. Eventually, no one went inside the house except to explore, and it started to deteriorate.

In 1976 Dad broke his pelvis aboard a bronc. Healing was slow, and he was afraid he wouldn't be able to cowboy again. My family moved from the cow camp down to Custer to farm with my grandparents.

They felt so far from their dream in the fields of the Yellowstone Valley. They missed their cows and the freedom of the wind in the grass and the cow camp and their friends, the Griersons . . . and the White Place, too.

But they were not gone long. Two years later the Griersons offered Dad the foreman's job at their ranch. He took it, and my family moved to ranch headquarters. They were some thirty miles from the White Place, but they were back.

I was born not long after my folks returned to the ranch. Sometimes it seems like I was born carrying their dream, just like I have Dad's gray eyes and Mom's freckles. A place of our own. It was a wonderful thought that we all loved to think as I grew.

Though the White Place was crumbling, we still tried to use the working corrals there as much as possible. We always branded my folks' small herd there, and when we did I would explore the cool, musty darkness of the barn and the dank, creaking outhouse. I would pace along the sandrock walls built with Ethel's own hands and tiptoe along the dirt-filled cattle guard.

I would imagine the tall wheatgrass mown, horses in the horse pasture, and furniture and life filling the rooms of the house.

Time wore on, and so did we. The dream mellowed for my parents as they worked harder at their job and no longer thought of their own place so much as they did of one day not working so hard. They were content to let a dream be a dream. Oh, we all still loved the place—Mom and Dad, if not for the possibility it represented, then for its memories; me and my sister, if not for an inherent love for the land, then for the love of a dream.

Unfortunately, reality was more often the case. Eventually, we no longer even branded at the White Place. It was too much of a hassle to brand in corrals that could collapse at any moment.

On Wednesday, August 9, 2006, a wildfire started on the White Ranch, just south of the buildings. Before a crew arrived to fight the flames, the buildings and corrals had burned to the ground, and the fire went on to burn two thousand acres.

And our dream? Did it go up in smoke? My husband, Beau, who works with my dad on the ranch where I was raised, returned from fighting that fire at 2:30 in the morning. He quickly fell into a deep sleep, but I lay sleepless beside him, breathing in the sharp odor of burned grass and smoky pine trees carried in his hair and in the dust under his eyes.

I thought of how many people were hurt in the fire. First, of Becky White Heberle, who owns and cherishes her parents' ranch. Second, the ranch where Beau and Dad work. Replacement heifers were summering on that leased grass and will have to be moved.

But what about our family? Were we burned, too? The question rolled in my head like red smoke boiling out of a coulee as I lay there.

Not at all, I realized eventually. Because the White Place was not so much an actual place for us as the name for a dream—if not a present, then a past and perhaps a future.

Not at all, because we've already passed it on to the next generation. Should we fail, my son and nephew and niece will carry it for us.

No, our dream did not burn. Because a dream isn't something you can put under your arm and show to your neighbor. It is something you hold, way down deep in that place you go when you're thinking wonderful thoughts.

And that's why the flames couldn't touch it.

Tami Arvik Blake
Hysham, Montana

CHARLIE GANNON

The following story sounds like a dime novel except that it's true. I know I'm the only one left that knows both ends of this tale. The story was told to me by two old cowboys—Broady Saddler and Vic Pepion—and the ending by an early-day highway patrolman, Bud O'Brien.

This is the story of Charlie Gannon. The old Antler cowboy, Broady Saddler, was the first one to tell me about Charlie Gannon. Broady knew him from New Mexico, and he told me that in the 1920s Charlie owned a little ranch that a big outfit wanted to buy. Charlie wouldn't sell, so the outfit framed him on a cow-stealing charge, and he was sent to prison in New Mexico. His friends and neighbors were about to get him pardoned when him and another guy broke out of the pen and killed a guard during their getaway.

The scene now shifts to the Blackfeet Reservation in Montana. Vic Pepion, as a young man, hired out to punch cows for an outfit called the Portland Loan that was big on the reservation in the Browning-Cutbank area of Montana at the time. The Portland Loan place run a roundup wagon, and Charlie Gannon was the wagon boss.

Vic said Charlie was a good cowman and a good boss. He never slept in the bed tent with the crew but rolled his bed out away from everyone else by the edge of some brush. When anyone came to the wagon, he wanted to know right then who they were and what they wanted.

Vic said Charlie always went armed. He carried a .45 in a shoulder holster under his arm, and with his shirt over it, nobody could see it. In the north country there's lots of ponds and potholes, and in the fall these are full of flapper ducks that are not quite able to fly. Vic said the crew would be riding in to the wagon and Charlie would say, "A bunch of those flapper ducks would go good for supper." And he'd set there on his horse and shoot five or six of those flappers, and they'd take them to the wagon for the cook.

Bud O'Brien as a young man hired out to work for the Portland Loan at their ranch, not as a cowboy but as a ranch hand. Bud went on later to become an early Montana highway patrolman. His older brother, Bill, worked for me for years at our Augusta ranch.

Bud said it was late in the fall, and the roundup wagon and bed wagon had been pulled into the ranch and put under the shed for the

The wrangler holds the rope corral while Charlie Gannon, center, prepares to catch his horse for the next circle. The roundup wagon and tent are in the background. COURTESY OF RAY KRONE

winter, so all the cowboys that hadn't left were at the ranch. For some unknown reason the ranch had just hired a man that had once been a detective for the railroad. Charlie Gannon thought this man was after him, and he shot and killed him.

Bud said when this happened the whole crew gathered in the bunkhouse, and Charlie came in and told Bud and the rest of the crew, "I don't have a thing in the world against you boys, but don't any of you try to leave." He had his own quarters, and he went to his bunkhouse, took a bath, shaved and put on his best clothes, laid down on the bed, and shot himself.

I'm sure I'm the only one left that knows this story. Now you do, too.

Ray Krone
Augusta, Montana

THE BRASS BUTTONS FROM FORT KEOGH

As I've said before, Miles City cowboys and the soldiers stationed at Fort Keogh never got along together; in fact, they despised each other. At this fort were stationed both white and Negro troops, who upon more than one occasion came into Miles and fought some very bitter battles. As a matter of fact, fighting was expected from both groups.

One spring, just before the roundup started, we cowboys went into town to have one last fling before the long season's work began. We were going to make it a sort of farewell, as we knew we had a long, lonesome job ahead of us. There must have been forty or fifty of us gathered there and about the same number of white soldiers from the fort.

We were at one of the pleasure palaces run by a big woman called Mollie, and we had started to have a good time, singing, drinking, and dancing with the girls, most of whom had just gotten back to Miles City. They usually spent their winters in Chicago or some other place more lively than Miles. Lennie, a friend of mine from the 79 outfit, was up dancing with one of the girls, who was really very pretty. He'd been making a big hit with her all evening, and she was now wearing his best Stetson. They were really whooping it up.

One of the soldiers snatched the Stetson off the girl's head and proceeded to stomp on it. This was a signal for the fight to begin, and you can bet it turned out to be a knock-down, drag-out affair. Webb, the wagon boss for the CKs, always called his men "the CK Pups," and now he yelled for his boys to go after those brass-buttoned men from the fort. Believe me, those soldiers took an awful beating before they ran and hid under the freight wagons outside. The CKs ran right after them, with Webb cheering them on.

Ambulances from the fort had to come get those soldiers, but we only had a few black eyes and scratches to show for the fight. This cooled us off, however, and we lit out for the spring roundup, where there was plenty of real work for us.

I regret to say that my friend Lennie was later killed over the matter of a stolen beef at Gray Stud Springs, north of Jordan. It was a 79 yearling, and Len had just reported it to a Miles City sheriff and had then gone over to eat his dinner at the Miles City Hotel. As he was coming out, he was shot down by a fellow named Rolls, who was carrying a Winchester for this purpose.

Len was greatly loved by all who knew him, and a great crowd gathered to get Rolls out of jail for a lynching. The lawmen prevented this from taking place, but the killer got a life sentence and was taken to the state prison at Deer Lodge. Some time later, along with several other lifers, he made a break to escape and, using a sharpened case knife, killed the deputy warden, Robertson, and almost succeeded in getting Warden Connelly himself. The warden received a few bad cuts, but this Rolls, an Oklahoma half-breed, died there in prison.

Bob Kennon
From the Pecos to the Powder
University of Oklahoma Press

JOE HOLTZ

Joe Holtz had a sheep ranch just below the divide between the Yellowstone and Missouri Rivers, approximately fifteen miles east of Circle. He came to the area in the late 1880s and built up his band of sheep, corrals, and barns, etc., with a nice log house built from cottonwood trees found nearby. By 1916 Joe had several men working for him; one was Jim Ratter, a Texan who had ridden the open range for many years. He had worked for Joe a few months when the relationship between them became quite strained. Jim and Mrs. Holtz had become rather "friendly," and she had started divorce proceedings.

One day Jim was in Circle drinking and bragging that he was going to go out and shoot Joe Holtz. A young man who worked at the livery

Joe Holtz, 1916, who had to kill or be killed. COURTESY OF GEORGE A. MAHLSTEDT

stable heard him talking and, after finding Jim's gun in his saddlebag, took the bullets out of his gun and threw them in the bottom of the saddlebag. When Jim returned to the ranch, he rode to the corral where the other hired hands were, took his gun out of the saddlebag, and held it on the guys as he backed toward the house, telling them to stay put, as he was going to kill Joe.

Joe was in bed with the flu when Jim walked into the house and told the ladies in the kitchen to stay put. He went into the bedroom and pulled down on Joe with his revolver. *Click, click.* But his gun was empty. About that time Joe pulled a shotgun from under his pillow (as he had been expecting trouble) and said, "Well, Jim, I got to do it," and shot him twice, killing him instantly.

Joe Holtz ran for safety to this homestead shack of John Mahlstedt, uncle to author George A. Mahlstedt. COURTESY OF GEORGE A. MAHLSTEDT

Joe ran out and fled down the coulee after telling the hired help to see if Jim was dead. One of the hired hands was John Mahlstedt, who had a homestead about a mile away. Joe spent that night with John and was very frightened. Every time a curtain fluttered, he thought it was his wife coming to kill him. The next day John took him to Glendive, where he gave himself up. Joe claimed self-defense, and the jury returned a verdict of not guilty.

George A. Mahlstedt
Circle, Montana

THE COWBOY PREACHER

My dad was an excellent horseman, and by the time I was seven years old, I was breaking horses. We were raised on ranches on the Powder River in southeastern Montana, and Dad could bring the cow out of any horse. He'd start it, then turn it over to my brother Bob and me—and we'd ruin it! Dad would just cringe. But I kept at it, over and over, kept being trained until I started to improve. By the time I left home for the Navy, I'd ridden horses all over that country and worked for different ranchers. And when I wasn't riding, I was in a bar, drinking, partying, and betting lots of money on poker.

We weren't a churchgoing family. In fact, we were what you'd call "bar people." My mother was an alcoholic, two brothers were, and I guess if you go by the official stats, I was, too. But no one wants to call himself that.

I'd been raised with a little bit of prayer teaching though, through religious classes in summer school, and I knew enough about church to know I wasn't going to make Heaven if I died. That really bothered me, because deep inside, where no one ever saw, while dragging calves to the branding iron or when bottled up in the belly of a sub, I had a longing to know the Lord.

But I was proud. And that pride wouldn't allow me to ask or show any interest in the doings of God.

When I went home on leave, I met up with Sally, a girl I'd gone to school with while growing up. She was raised Catholic, and something quiet and solid drew me to her. By the time my leave was up, I knew she was the one I was going to marry. So in 1973 I left the Navy and went back to Powderville, taking up where I'd left off, cowboying, drinking, gambling—only this time I had a wife and kids to take care of.

A couple of years later, my boss was killed. I was breaking horses on a ranch that ran 150 head of mares. And I was riding some pretty rank horses. My boss had just quit and gone to work on another ranch. On a gentle horse—a fluke accident, just loping up a grass draw—the horse stumbled, run on his belly trying to get back up, couldn't, and so he rolled. Bob fell off, hitting his head on a rock. Three o'clock in the afternoon. At noon the next day, they pulled the plug—and he's off in eternity.

Now that bothered me. A few days later I came home after losing all kinds of money at the Bison Bar. I had a whole bunch of bad checks in town. I'm drunk, sick, and hung over, and I have to face Sally.

So I get a horseback, because the next best thing was to get out of the house and pretend like you want to work. And I headed across the flat, praying for Bob. I knew there was a Heaven, and there was a purgatory, and there was a hell, and I'm praying for Bob because I have no idea where he's at, but I'm making it an assumption that he's in purgatory, and I'm doing my level best to pray him from purgatory into Heaven.

I've got myself, I'm riding this horse and two dogs following me, when all of a sudden I hear this voice, and I mean it was *real*. And this voice said to me, "Well, where're *you* going?"

Now I know the Bible says that a dog can talk sometimes, but I know my dogs didn't say that. Nor did the horse I was riding. I knew who'd talked to me. It was God. And it was so real I answered out loud.

"I hope I go to Heaven. I'm praying I'll make purgatory, and I know I'm going to hell."

It was the first time in my life that I ever made that admission. And it scared the life out of me. I mean, everybody liked me. I was the life of the party at the bars. I didn't have an enemy on earth. So why would God want to send me to hell?

Right there I started asking. *God, let me know, please let me know, how can I get to Heaven?* For almost a year that cry was on my heart. Everywhere I went, everything I did, behind it all was that question.

By 1978 I'd had enough of bronc riding. I'd already handed in my resignation at the ranch when Sally hauled me off to a Bible study at a neighbor's place. A fellow by the name of Tom Figg was there, a team roper from Ekalaka who did a cowboy ministry. He simply told his story, read a couple of Scriptures, then looked out over that gathering in the living room and asked, "Is anybody sitting out there wanting to go to Heaven?"

I tell you what. I throwed my hand in the air so fast, then I looked around, and I'm the only one in the crowd with my hand up. And I'm with people I *know*. And my face turned bright red.

But that didn't matter. Because right there Tom Figg answered my question and showed me how to make Jesus my Lord. I was so grateful I turned to all my friends and said, "Hey! Come on into the bar and have a drink! I'm taking over the Hole in the Wall in ten days."

And you know what? One guy took me up on that. And that was Tom Figg.

Once a month he'd come in to Miles City, sit down at the end of the bar, and say, "Give me a Coke." Then he'd ask, "Larry, how's Jesus doing in your life?"

Now that is not a good question to ask a bartender. I'd go, "Ga-ga-ga-ga-a-a-a." Stammering and stuttering, because it was quite evident that Jesus was *not* doing well in my life. I made him a bartender, and that wasn't his choice of occupation.

Sally knew it, too. So we left the bar, and I went back to working on a ranch. About then Sally heard of a roping school Tom was holding in Ekalaka. She wanted to go, but I was helping the neighbors brand, so I said, "If you wait until the last night, I'll go with you."

A minister was there, and for three days he'd prayed there would be no rain so they could hold this school. That night he got up and said, "I'm asking for rain tonight." And there wasn't a cloud in the sky.

I was sitting in the back, trying to be hid, when another fellow looked up and saw me. "Larry!" he said. "What you doing here, you got saved."

"Yeah," I said, "but I don't feel like it."

This guy laughed and said, "What you need is the gift of the Holy Spirit."

Now, I didn't know what he was talking about, but I was never one to turn down a free gift, so I said, "Wait a minute, and I'll find Sally and we'll both get it." I rounded her up and *bam*! The Lord hit me and knocked me right to the ground. I stood up kinda reeling and *bam*! He hit me again. I struggled to my feet and *WHAM!*

This time I hit a woodpile so hard I knew my head was split open. I reached up to feel the blood, and there was no bump, no bleeding, it didn't even hurt. That's when I said, "Okay, God, I give up." And it just started to pour rain.

My life changed that minute. We drove up and down those gravel roads of eastern Montana hundreds of miles, going to cowboy church and talking to ministers. One night I had a dream. Thousands of people stood in the dark, rank and file, with me among them. Here and there one shone with a soft white light, but they were very few.

Out in front was God and Jesus. And they were calling names. Each time, a person stepped out, and I realized they were going to Heaven. Then they called mine. And I was *ecstatic*! Because I knew I was going to heaven. I took one step forward out of that line, and the minute my foot touched the ground, all my family and friends who stood behind me cried, "You *knew*! And you wouldn't tell us!" And my heart just crumbled.

I woke up and made a promise to God right there that I would do my level best to reach my family and friends. So Sally and I packed up our kids and moved to Tulsa, Oklahoma, where I went to Rhema Bible School.

After I graduated, we came back to Miles City, and I became a circuit preacher. Just like in the old days when this country was being settled, I worked a circle from Broadus to Jordan, breaking horses for ranchers by day and holding Bible studies and prayer meetings in their houses at night.

I knew these people. I could talk to them because I came out of their camp. I knew what it was like to have cigarette smoke blowed in your face and tobacco juice spit on each side of your boots. And if they wouldn't come to me, then, by golly, I'd go to them. Like God came to me, on the back of a horse, in the middle of nowhere, sick and hung over, to save me from going to hell.

Larry Phalen
Glendive, Montana

THE WAGON

The first day there, we rode in from the ranch,
Trailin' our horses, with our beds tied on a couple,
We rode about 15 miles, just to get there,
But it really wasn't all that much trouble.

It was in the later part of the spring,
And the weather was perfectly mellow,
We listened to the song birds sing,
I was a very appreciative fellow.

Could life be any better, for someone,
Lookin' to get away from it all,
To get himself a little "Peace of mind,"
In prairie grass, thick and tall?

We got there just about at sunset,
They were camped over on Bovey creek,
The Pryor mountains silhouetted in the background,
It looked like "cowboy paradise," so to speak.

We stopped on a hill, overlooking this scene,
Not a word passed between either man,
There was nothing that needed to be said,
This was surely part of God's plan.

It was some time before we finally rode in,
You know it was hard to break that spell,
The wrangle horse announced our coming,
So far things were going just swell.

Joe Charter
Billings, Montana